A HISTORY OF CHINA IN MAPS

Ancient Capitals and Cities

www.royalcollins.com

A HISTORY OF CHINA IN MAPS

Ancient Capitals and Cities

Zhang Xiaohong
Chief Editor: Ge Jianxiong

Books Beyond Boundaries
ROYAL COLLINS

A History of China in Maps: Ancient Capitals and Cities

Zhang Xiaohong
Chief Editor: Ge Jianxiong
Translated by Wang Su'e

First published in 2023 by Royal Collins Publishing Group Inc.
Groupe Publication Royal Collins Inc.
BKM Royalcollins Publishers Private Limited

Headquarters: 550-555 boul. René-Lévesque O Montréal (Québec) H2Z1B1 Canada
India office: 805 Hemkunt House, 8th Floor, Rajendra Place, New Delhi 110 008

ISBN: 978-1-4878-0935-5

To find out more about our publications, please visit www.royalcollins.com.

CONTENTS

Part II Ancient Capitals

Part III Cities

FOREWORD

The book series, *A History of China in Maps*, is comprised of four volumes: *Territories and Administrative Divisions, Ancient Capitals and Cities, Communications and Transportation*, and *Ethnic Migration*. Each volume tells one specific aspect of Chinese history with illustrated maps.

Many scholars have pointed out that the keys to understanding history are the five "Ws": what, when, where, who, and why. Any historical facts, regardless of who or what, and anything, be it spiritual or material, have to be connected with specific space. In other words, they have to take place either at a certain point, in a line, or on a surface of the earth. That's why the factor "where" is crucial to understanding history. Just as the late Professor Tan Qixiang said, "History is like a drama, and geography is its stage. Without a stage, there would be no drama at all."

Spatial factors have always played a significant role in history. They are not only important research contents but also indispensable elements to understanding history. Limited by time and energy, no one could be omnipresent; even if one could be there in person, one may not be able to master the entire range or features of the space. Therefore, maps are of vital importance. In ancient times, although limited by cartographic technologies and gadgets, scholars already recognized the significance of maps; when conducting historical research, they almost always had maps by their side.

Tu Jing (图经), a primitive form of chorography, combined records with illustrations, mostly in the form of maps. Some other historical classics were also attached to these maps, which later formed the historical atlas genre. As early as the third century, based on books such as *Zuo Zhuan* (左传), Jia Dan compiled an atlas of places for allied gatherings during the Spring and Autumn Period (770–256 BC) (春秋盟会图). Aside from this, Jia Dan also made the *Hai Nei Hua Yi Tu* (海内华夷图, *Map of Hua and National Minorities inside Seas*).

Based on this prototype, *Yu Ji Tu* (禹迹图, *Map of Yu's Sites*) was carved onto stone tablets in AD 1137. Such tablets have often been found in provincial schools, meaning they might have been used as teaching tools. In AD 1905, Yang Shoujing published *Shui Jing Zhu Tu* (水经注图, *Maps for Records of Rivers*). These ancient maps were printed in red and black ink with explanatory notes. It is a masterpiece of the historical atlas.

With the development of satellite remote sensing technology, information technology and the Internet, accurate images are now made possible by GPS and Google Maps. People tend to think that traditional maps have lost their charm and therefore should be replaced. However, this is not true. No matter how accurate they may be, Google Maps cannot replace traditional maps, nor their comprehensive, abstract, and specific geographic elements.

Modern maps are not sufficient to understand history. What we need are historical maps related to that era. As time goes by, the environment changes too. Features of physical and human geography in ancient times may differ from what we have today. Even if only minor changes have occurred in physical geography, features of human geography may have experienced profound change. Some elements may have disappeared completely, while some new elements have emerged. Historical maps have to be made according to the exact historical facts and corresponding geographic status.

In August 2010, a deadly mudslide took place in Zhouqu County, Gansu, China. While broadcasting the news, TV stations also presented maps on screen to inform the audience where exactly the catastrophe happened. The audience came to understand how far Zhouqu was from Lanzhou, the provincial capital of Gansu Province. Without a map, the audience would be unaware. The same goes for understanding history, which should be illustrated with maps. Otherwise, readers without such a background may find it hard to develop a spatial concept of historical events, even if they receive explanatory notes. This is because some geographic names no longer exist, while some topography has been altered considerably.

For example, in Cen Shen's poem, "A Song of Farewell to Field-Clerk Wu Going Home in White Snow," written in the Tang Dynasty, Cen saw Wu off in Luntai, and watched him disappear among the Tianshan Mountains. However, the modern Luntai is hundreds of miles away from the Tianshan Mountains. It only make sense when readers have learned that Luntai in the Tang was in fact located very close to Urumqi in Xinjiang Autonomous Region, and to the north of the Tianshan Mountains.

Another example is the city name of Nanjing. After the fall of the Northern Song Dynasty, Zhao Gou proclaimed himself as Emperor of the Southern Song in Nanjing. Later, under the increasing threat of Jin's armies from the North, he fled to Yangzhou and then crossed the Yangtze River. It might not be evident if the readers mix up Zhao Gou's Nanjing with the modern Nanjing, located to the south of Yangzhou. It would not make sense for Zhao to flee in the wrong direction! Nanjing in the Northern Song Dynasty was Shangqiu in today's Henan Province. From there, it went south and reached Yangzhou along the Bian Canal. Such a route is logical. A historical map would greatly benefit the readers in clarifying such cases.

Historical maps may also help bring about new research. For example, Professor Tan Qixiang once collected all the data he could of archaeological findings and cultural relics in the bordering areas of Hebei and Shandong provinces. Having marked them on maps, he discovered a region in the shape of a sea-shell, empty of any relics before the fourth century. And this region happened to be the lower reaches of the Yellow River. Based on further research on regional topography, Professor Tan was able to confirm the river had changed its course many times in that era, making it impossible for human inhabitation. This has never been recorded in any historical literature; only maps have provided a reliable means for research.

The four authors of *A History of China in Maps* have made breakthroughs in their work. Maps are not used for illustrations only, but as an essential part of the books—leading readers through comprehensive and accurate descriptions of history.

We have chosen four topics closely related to maps: Ancient Capitals and Cities, Territories and Administrative Divisions, Communications and

Transportation, and Ethnic Migration. Each book is full of ancient place names and other geographic elements. Without historical maps, one cannot fully understand history, no matter how many words have been written. If readers like our concept, it is possible that we will continue to write more books in future, illustrated with maps.

Here I would like to give credit to Jiangsu People's Publishing House. I am very grateful to have been chosen as the chief editor for this book series. I would like to specify what I have contributed: together with the writers and editors, I have determined the topics, style and requirements on the usage of maps. I have given feedback to the authors on their content and structure. And finally, I have written this foreword. Thank you!

GE JIANXIONG

INTRODUCTION

According to Chinese tradition, "5,000 years of Chinese civilization" started with the Three Sovereigns and Five Emperors Period. We might consider the Three Sovereigns and Five Emperors as representatives of the start of the Chinese community—the "kings of the country."[1]

In Chinese legend, Shennong said that "one would still fail to defend the city in spite of the high stone walls, wide moat filled with boiling water and millions of soldiers, if there were not enough grain."[2] Another legendary figure, Yellow Emperor, said, "build five cities and twelve buildings."[3] Gun, father of Yu the Great, was documented in the legend as building cities.[4] These records or legends actually point to one thing—cities were born with the formation of the Chinese community.

More importantly, these legends are indirectly confirmed by contemporary archaeological discoveries. Several city sites from the legendary period have been discovered, including sites along the middle reaches of the Yellow River Basin during the Longshan Culture era, sites along the Yangtze River Basin during the

---

1. See Lü Simian, *Pre-Qin Dynasty History*, chapters 6–7 (Shanghai: Shanghai Ancient Books Press, 1962).
2. *Book of Han · The Chronicles of Food, Silks Clothing, or Currency (Part One).*
3. *Book of Han · Suburban Worship Rite Records (Part Two).*
4. *Book of Origins · Inventors.*

Qujialing to Shijiahe Culture era, sites along the upper reaches of the Yangtze River Basin in the Baodun Culture Period, and stone sites in the Hetao area during the Tiger Mountain Culture Period. These are all city sites belonging to the era of the Three Sovereigns and Five Emperors.

In the early stages of human society, cities and states often united. A city was mostly a state, and most states were delimited by a city. These states or cities were scattered in all parts of China in various forms and sizes. Despite differences, states or cities were connected by either war, conflict, or trade. The Chinese community was eventually formed during this tangled process of dividing and integrating communication; cities were the materialized symbol of the formation of the Chinese community.[5]

During the Xia and Shang dynasties, the Chinese community developed steadily and formed its earliest capitals in the heartlands of the Luoyang area, Henan. Located in Zhengzhou, the Erlitou Site is considered the capital site of the Xia Dynasty; whilst the early capital of the Shang was set in Bozhou (today Yanshi) and later moved to Ao (Zhengzhou), and then Xiang City (along the Huan River in Anyang, Henan).

Archaeological excavation shows these cities were large in scale and magnificent. Besides these impressive capitals along the Yellow River Basin, several sites from the same period were also found along the Yangtze River Basin, which matched the scale and cultural relics of capitals found in Luoyang. The most typical site is the Sanxingdui ruins of the Kingdom of Shu. Panlong City in Huangpi, Hubei, also has a similar scale and shape to Sanxingdui.

The Western Zhou Dynasty, after the Xia and Shang dynasties, started an enfeoffment (granting land in exchange for a pledge of service) process to prevent rebellions after the Quest of Zhou by King Wu, particularly after quelling the Sanjian Rebellion by Duke Zhou. The first action these vassal kings achieved after the enfeoffment was to establish cities. Following the royal family's tradition of favoring big tribes in the Zhou, these vassal kings made great efforts to build big cities and extend the outer city (*Wai Guo*) and inner city (*Nei Cheng*) structures. Later, the Warring States Period further witnessed a peak in city building. We often see the records of "城" (city) in some places in *Zuo Zhuan*. The "city" here is a verb that means building walls and cities.

5. Qu Yingjie, *Ancient Cities* (Beijing: Cultural Relics Press, 2003), 4–5.

After eliminating the other six kingdoms, the State of Qin established the first centralized system of imperial power and changed the feudal land division system of the Zhou into a prefecture and county system. Although the Qin Dynasty only lasted two generations, its system was inherited by the Western Han. At the start of Han, Emperor Gaozu (Liu Bang) "ordered the counties and prefectures to build cities."[6] This led to a wave of urban construction confirmed by archaeological findings.

From the Hexi area conquered by Emperor Wu of Han in the west to the coastal areas in the east, from the Five Ridges in the south to the Great Wall in the north, archaeologists found ancient city sites from the Han Dynasty. Nevertheless, except for the capital—Chang'an—and the capitals of vassal states inherited from Western Zhou, most cities and counties were small in scale and could not compete with the major cities of later dynasties. Furthermore, even the capitals and bigger cities during this time lacked planning and were mostly built out of location convenience. Even Chang'an was just a residential area crammed with palaces and official buildings, whose city walls were not built until many years later. Chang'an was called "City of Dipper" (斗城) for the southern part of the city was in the shape of the Southern Dipper, and the northern part the Big Dipper. In fact, this was just a forced result without the concept as exaggeratively described in later generations.

However, since the campaign launched by Emperor Wu of Han to "oust all other schools of learning; only Confucianism should be allowed," Confucianism became the dominant ideology of the ruling class, leading to a fundamental change in the physical construction of capital cities. Although the Western and Eastern Han dynasties failed to accomplish the Confucian rites system thoroughly in their capital planning and construction, the concept was popularized so much that later dynasties attempted to enact this too. Therefore, whether it was the Jiankang of the Six Dynasties or the Yedu, the capital of Cao Wei, they all tried to reflect the Confucian ritual system in city construction and concretize the national ideology.

However, the pinnacle of applying Confucian rites to city construction was embodied by the Northern Wei Regime, established by the Xianbei, a minority ethnic group originating from northeast China. Luoyang, the capital they established, was considered the best representative of building principles, as

6. *Book of Han · Records of Emperor Gaozu.*

described in the *Rites of Zhou · Record of Trades,* and clearly inspired Yuwen Kai, who established Daxing—the capital of the Sui. This will be elaborated on in future chapters.

The Tang Dynasty, the heyday of Chinese feudal society, built magnificent Chang'an and Luoyang. Their neatly planned residential *fang*s and majestic palace cities became a model for neighboring states, such as Japan, Bohai, and Nanzhao, to imitate. In fact, Chang'an during the Tang era was actually another typical example of applying Confucian rites to capital city planning: it took over the planning and design concepts from Luoyang of Northern Wei, and had a profound influence on the following generations of capital city planning, especially Dadu (Beijing today), capital of Yuan Dynasty, underpinning the influence of Chang'an in Tang Dynasty.

Besides the national capital, other cities also made considerable progress in this period. Yangzhou and Yizhou (Chengdu today) in the Yangtze River Basin "were considered the most prosperous and luxurious cities of China" with their large urban scale and bustling economic life. These were signs of an economic shift in South China, indicating the importance of the economy in city development.

The dynasties of Song, Liao, Jin, and Yuan are the significant phase in the history of China's city development. In terms of city planning, the Yuan capital of Dadu was a perfect embodiment of Confucian rites as described in the *Rites of Zhou.* Simultaneously, the development of the local economy across China gave rise to many local cities, which competed with the capitals both in terms of scale and influence, thus entering a transitional stage from the Tang to the Ming and Qing dynasties.

Described by the Western Sinologist as the "late imperial stages," the Ming and Qing dynasties witnessed a new type of urban development. Although there was little innovation in city planning, the prosperity of local cities allowed them to assume a crucial position in the Chinese economy. Urban economic development was arguably the key economic factor of the era. Due to the increased presence of Western Powers at the end of this period, several cities along the coast (near the Yangtze River Basin) emerged and grew. This uprooted the old patterns of Chinese cities and became what scholars called a "a new style of lace embroidered to an old robe."

PART I

LEGENDARY TIMES AND ARCHEOLOGICAL FINDINGS

CHAPTER ONE

CITIES AND MARKETS: THE ORIGIN OF EARLY CHINESE CITIES

The city is an inevitable outcome of social and economic development. In other words, the city is a natural result of social and economic development reaching a certain stage. This is historical materialism, which was first proposed by Karl Marx in the 19th century.

Specific to the era of the emergence of Chinese cities, it is currently a controversial issue in academia. One opinion holds that cities first appeared during the Longshan Culture (circa 2500–2000 BC), due to ancient city relics discovered by archaeologists. The *cheng* (settlement) is the prototype of these early cities.[1] A second opinion argues that Chinese cities appeared during the third division of labor during the "Primitive Society," evolving directly from the market—the predecessor of cities.[2] A third opinion holds that the earliest Chinese cities were village settlements with enclosures. The cities with real scale appeared in the Western Zhou period and late Spring and Autumn Period. They made extensive development until the Warring States Period.[3]

In fact, the real differences among these three contradictory opinions lie in the difference in the definition ascribed to a "city" (this translates as two characters

1. Du Yu, "Origin and Development of Chinese Cities," *Chinese History Research*, no. 1 (1983).
2. Fu Chonglan, *History of China's Canal Cities* (Chengdu: Sichuan People's Press, 1985), 8–11.
3. Zheng Changgan, "An Overview of the Rise and Development of Ancient Chinese Cities," *Teaching and Research*, no. 2 (1962).

pronounced *cheng-shi* [城市]; *cheng* [城] means settlement, and *shi* [市] means market). Therefore, we must clarify the term city (*cheng-shi*) to accurately determine the emergence of the first Chinese cities.

Generally, a city is conceptually opposed to a village or idyllic settlement. The Chinese dictionary, *Cihai,* defines "city" as a small, narrow region where a large number of the non-first industry population congregate—an area where residents engage mostly in the second and third industries; it is also the social, economic, cultural, and political center of the surrounding area. Friedrich Ratzel, an early German geographer and ethnographer, pointed out in *Human Geography* that a city is a densely-populated area of human beings who live in their habitation permanently, which also serves as a transport hub.

Clearly, the *Cihai* definition emphasizes the economic functions and forms of the city, while Ratzel's definition is more flexible. He recognizes that areas inhabited by dense populations could be considered cities even if they perform less political and other functions. Reviewing these aforementioned opinions, the first argues that an area with walls enclosed should be considered a city, consistent with Ratzel's point of view. The second opinion emphasizes the economic function of cities—namely the commodity trading function consistent with the definition of city in *Cihai.* The third opinion is not essentially different from the second, but postpones the formation of cities in China to the Spring and Autumn and Warring States periods; when city development matured with both the building of city walls and the development of market functions—two conditions for the real appearance of Chinese cities.

Next, we investigate the history of Chinese urban evolution through ancient Chinese documents and archeological findings of city sites. Due to endless fighting, early humans needed to establish effective defense systems to preserve their strength. Consequently, city walls were built in residential areas. These were recorded in early Chinese classics, such as *A Biography of Yellow Emperor, Book of Origins, Huainanzi* (a philosophical work written by Liu An and his followers), and *A History of Wu and Yue,* which introduces Gun, the first man who builds cities walls in China history and states "cities were built to protect the monarch, and the outer walls were built to protect its people."

Archeological investigations indicate China's long history of building cities can be traced to the Yangshao and Longshan Culture periods when city sites were discovered (around 2500 BC, before the Xia Dynasty). Of course, due to the more advanced cultural development of the Central Plains area, more than forty prehistoric sites were distributed in the Yellow River Basin.[4] However, during this period cities were only defense projects as described in *Mozi · Seven Ills*: "*Cheng* is used to defend oneself." Clearly and crucially, they still did not possess the two elements or functions of later cities—concentration of residents and fixed markets.

Fig. 1-1: Chengziya Site during the Prehistoric period, Zhangqiu, Shandong

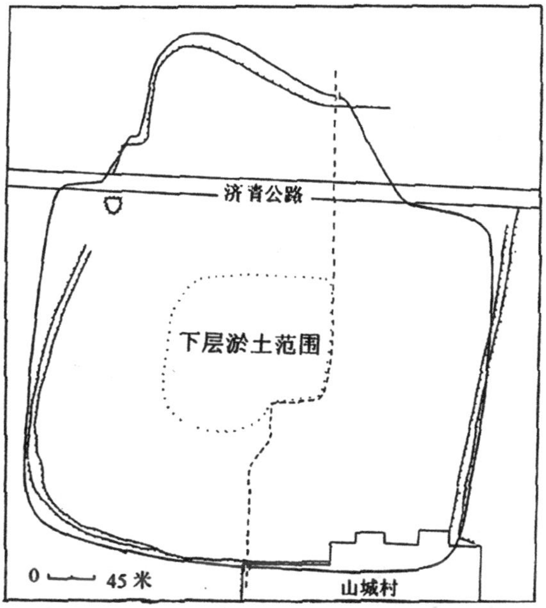

The main elements of later cities, such as commodity trading and large markets did not have a direct relationship with cities in China at the very beginning. *Book of Origins · Inventors* recorded the Zhurong started the market during Zhuanxu's time. Yan Shigu, a scholar of the Tang Dynasty, made notes about this: "There was no market in ancient times, and because people gathered in the morning to withdraw water from the well, goods were sold around the well. This is the so-called *shi* [市, market] *jing* [井, well]" (*Shijing* has been used to refer to urban life in Chinese). This is the early market—only a bartering site.

Mostly people conducted trading around the wells without a designated space. This might be similar to a farmer's market or rural bazaar today and had little

4. Qu Yingjie, *Ancient Cities* (Beijing: Cultural Relics Press, 2003), 11.

relationship to a *cheng*, or city. Hence, some scholars argued these markets lacked the basic forms of later cities and could not be considered as city predecessors. Consequently, it would be somewhat unsatisfactory to claim cities originated from these late primitive societies. Although there were *cheng* and *shi*, the former was for residents and the latter was for trading; they were independent.

Still, even adhering to the strict definition of city in *Cihai*, Chinese cities emerged no later than the Western Zhou Dynasty. There was neither literature nor archaeological evidence to show whether *shi* (market) was established in the capitals of the Xia and Shang dynasties. Thus, in the *Book of Changes*, written during the Warring States Period, the following is explicitly stated:

> After the death of Baoxishi, Shenrongshi inherited and designated chan in the capital. He set up the market in the daytime. He told his people to gather the commodities and trade with each other. So each could get their own place which is called Shihe.

Shihe is a hexagram in the *Book of Changes*, meaning to provide things needed. This literature shows that the evidence of a city in Chinese history lies in the phrase "chan in the country." Chan means the market, and country means the capital. It is the first time these two terms appear together. More importantly, this paragraph stressed the economic function of the capital: to assemble the people and collect goods from the world. Another example from the literature was provided by the *Rites of Zhou*, which is believed to be written during Western Zhou. This book mentioned *Sishi* (which means market administration), suggesting that the establishment and management of the market had become part of the government's administrative functions. Moreover, the responsibilities of this function have been clarified, such as the management of fair trading, pricing, lawsuits, security, and business fraud. In this period, the market in the capital was already a fixed place, which opened and closed on time and traded regularly. According to the *Rites of Zhou*:

> The popular market starts trading at noon, and it is dominated by the common people. The morning market starts trading in the morning, mainly merchants. The evening market began to trade at night, mainly individual street dealers.

From such examples it can be inferred that cities in Western Zhou were not always so different from later cities, in both function and physical structure. This supports the third opinion stated above—that cities truly emerged during this period.

Still, it should be noted no "*cheng shi*" (together means "city" in Chinese) is mentioned in the literature for the Western Zhou Dynasty, in spite of cities emerging during that period. The earliest document that combines *cheng* and *shi* is a poem entitled, "Settled down in Fangzhong" in the *Book of Songs · Folklore of Yong*, which described Wei Wengong "started to build cities and establish palaces" after his migration to Chuqiu during the Spring and Autumn Period. Still here, *cheng* and *shi* had separate, different meanings from what we later would mean when we use the word *cheng-shi* (city). In the *Strategies of the Warring States*, there are such terms as *cheng-shi-yi*. For instance, in a chapter of the book, *Strategies of Zhao*, Zhao once conceded fifty seven *cheng-shi-yi* and offered them to Qi. Qi sent General Tian Dan (Duke Anping) as the commander to protect Zhao. During the same period, the State of Han promised to offer 17 of its *cheng-shi-yi* to the king of Zhao, when it asked Zhao for help to prevent the attack of the Qin State.[5] This shows the term *cheng-shi-yi* was popular around the Warring States Period. Hu Sanxing, a famous scholar during the Song and Yuan dynasties, made a particular note in his annotation about this: "If a *yi* is mentioned with *cheng shi*, then it means this is a big *yi* (means city or settlement)." Here, the *cheng-shi* refers to both the *cheng* (settlement) and the *shi* (market).

The term "city" with the same concept as we talk about today appears in *Hanfeizi*: "Even if the minister's salary is large, he cannot abuse his own power by virtue of the city." But this has come to the late Warring States Period.

1. Attracting People of the Country

Although there is no agreed opinion on when exactly Chinese cities were formed, this does not prevent us from exploring the basic characteristics of early cities from ancient excavations. Modern archaeology usually classifies the period before the Xia (around 2000 BC) as prehistory. The excavation of the city site during

5. *History of Mirror · Fifty-Third Year of King Nan of the Eastern Zhou Dynasty.*

this period began as early as the early 1930s.

After nearly eighty years of research from archaeologists more than 50 sites in this period have been found.[6] One of the most famous is the Chengziya Site of the Longshan Culture Period. The site is located along the Wuyuan River, Longshan, Shandong. In the winter of 1930, the Central Research Institute of China and the Shandong provincial government organized the Shandong Archaeology Research Institute to conduct its first excavation, supervised by Li Ji. Among the participants was the famous scholar Dong Zuobin.

In October 1931, another famous archaeologist, Liang Siyong, supervised the second excavation. Based on these two excavations, *Chengziya: Longshan Black Pottery Culture Sites of Licheng County, Shandong Province* was published in 1934 in Nanjing, and was co-authored by Fu Sinian, Li Ji, Dong Zuobin, and others. In this book's appendix, Dong Zuobin named the early culture, in which shiny black egg pottery was unearthed, the Longshan Culture. Consequently, this black pottery became one of the characteristics of Longshan Culture. In the third chapter of the book, *The Legacy of Architecture*, the characteristics of Longshan were described for the first time.

During the 1980s, the same institute once again explored and excavated the Chengziya Site, which produced a more accurate understanding of Longshan. In the 1930s report, the ancient city of Chengziya was described as about 450 meters long and about 390 meters wide, with the remaining walls' height between 2 and 3 meters, while the city wall base was about 10.6 meters wide. The archaeologists measured the entire city again during the 1980s. It was determined the city was 455 meters wide and 540 meters at its longest distance, with a total area of about 200,000 square meters. The wall's ruins were buried 2.5 to 5 meters below the ground's surface and had a width of 8–13 meters. However, the city was irregular, with its northern part being crooked, the middle part curved outwards, and the remaining three walls straight. The walls were built both by accumulation of earth and molded buildings with rounded corners—known as the tableland style. The walls were steep outside and had a slope inside. In addition, the walls on the south and north were connected with passages. Under the northern convex, there was a large-scale construction base site.

6. Qu Yingjie, *Ancient Cities* (Beijing: Cultural Relics Press, 2003), 11.

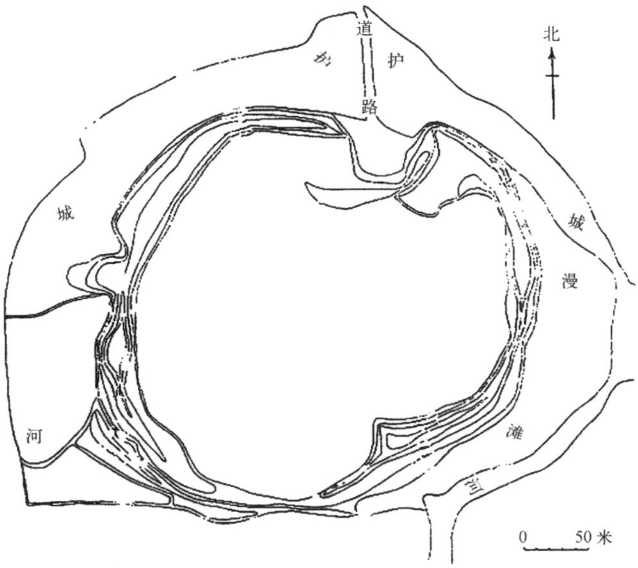

Fig. 1-2: Chengtoushan Site, Li County, Hunan during the Prehistoric period[7]

According to the many investigations, scholars found the construction of the Chengziya walls started during the early Longshan Culture Period (about 2600 BC) and lasted until the Xia. Part of the site was even used during the Spring and Autumn Period, clearly showing its continuous use by early humans. Many city sites around this period were also found along the Yangtze River Basin, another region of Han Chinese origin. One typical example is the Chengtoushan Site in northwest Li County, Hunan. Located along the northwestern bank of Dongting Lake with the Dan River to its south, the site is connected with the Jianghan Plain. Protruding from the ground, relics are still seen today.

During the winter of 1991, Shan Xianjin and his team from Hunan Archaeology Institute conducted trial digging at the site. Later, He Jiejun and others joined and made eight excavations, acquiring valuable information.

A survey showed the walls of Chengtoushan were 5–6 meters higher above the ground outside the city. The site plan shows an almost regular circle, very different from those in the Yellow River Basin. The outer diameter of this site is about 325 meters, and the diameter of the inner circle is around 314–324 meters, with a total area of about 80,000 square meters. A gate was on the east, south, and

7. Qu Yingjie, *Ancient Cities* (Beijing: Cultural Relics Press, 2003), 29.

north sides of the city, respectively, and a gravel road was found under the gate on the east side. However, the north seems different. It seems the north part is the lowest point with a round dam which had a diameter of about 30 meters. The dam connected with the moat through the north gate, which was considered a water gate. The moat around the city site was as deep as 4 meters and as wide as 30–50 meters. This was unsurpassable for people at that time. In addition, part of the moat was excavated by man, and natural rivers were also taken advantage of.

A stretch of stylobate made by rammed earth was found in the center of the Chengtoushan Site, and some houses were built on a one-meter high stylobate. These houses might belong to people with higher social rank. While in the east and southwest parts of the city, the foundations of many houses were also found. Notably, in the living area of the southwest houses, archaeologists found a road about two meters in width, paved with burnt soil. Even more surprising is that there are also drainage ditches on both sides of the road. A pottery workshop was also discovered as well as multiple pottery kilns, many ditches for earth, and numerous water storage puddles and mud puddles along with working sheds. This belongs to the Daxi Culture Pottery Workshop area. In the northwest of the city, large grave areas with about five hundred graves were found too. There was also an altar along the inner side of the eastern city walls. This altar is roughly an irregular oval; the north-south diameter is about 16 meters, and east-west diameter is about 15 meters, covering an area of more than 200 square meters.

In addition, shallow round pits, urn burials, and tombs were found. Outside the altar, dirt pits were used for animal skeletons as well as pottery and boulder findings. These were related to sacrificial activities. Archeologists believed the altar was built during Phase One of the Daxi Culture (that is, no later than 6,000 years ago) and continued until late Phase Two—about 5,800 years from today. Thus, we conclude that Chengtoushan is the earliest city known in China to date.[8]

In fact, the characteristics of ancient Chinese cities or early states are largely known from these multiple excavation sites. Many states (cities) fought one another and coexisted during the Three Sovereigns and Five Emperors Period, leading eventually to the formation of the Chinese community.

---

8. See Hunan Relics and Archaeological Research Institute and County Li Hunan Cultural Relics Administration Office, "Chengtoushan Qujialing Cultural Relics Survey and Trial Excavation," *Cultural Relics*, no. 12 (1993); Hunan Relics and Archaeological Research Institute, "Chengtoushan City Site, County Li Annual Excavation Brief," *Cultural Relics*, no. 6 (1999).

2. Building *Guo* to Protect its People

The primary function of early cities was defense, rather than trade or housing.

In 1975, an archaeological team from Henan excavated the Yangcheng Site of Eastern Zhou. The site is located in the west of Gaocheng Town, southeast of Dengfeng, Henan Province, and was divided into two parts. According to expert judgment, the eastern part was built earlier but was destroyed by floods. Its western walls were utilized as the eastern walls of the newly-built west city. From the excavation, the walls are seen clearly, although only the base groove and the rammed earth of the earthen walls remain.

Of these, about 65 meters of the eastern wall and about 30 meters of the southern wall survive. In the corner of the southwest walls, where the surviving walls intersect, the inner walls showed a concave arc, while the outside showed a convex arc shape of 2 meters. Most notably, the west city used the east city's west wall as its east wall. A 9.5-meter gap exists between the east end of its southern wall and the southwest end of the eastern city. This is assumed to be the gate facilities of the west city. Its southern wall was 82.4 meters high, its western wall 92 meters, and its northern wall 29 meters in the western end. The southwest and northwest corners of the city were similar in terms of the arrangement with the southwest of the east city. The total city area is 10,000 square meters.

Fig. 1-3: Plan of Wangchenggang Site, Dengfeng, Henan[9]

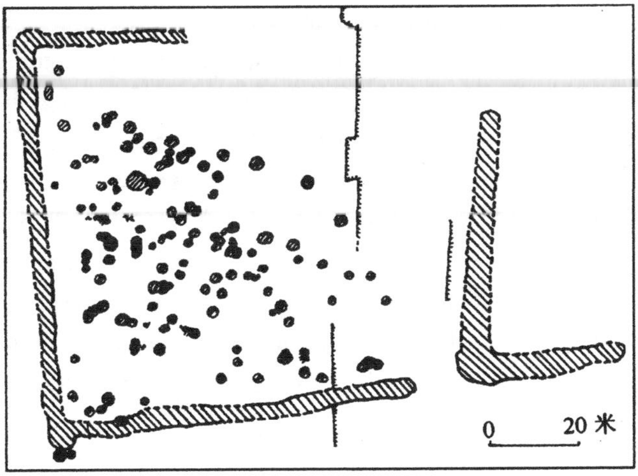

9. Qu Yingjie, *Ancient Cities* (Beijing: Cultural Relics Press, 2003), 13.

From these findings, it was very common to use walls or ditches as the first line of defense—not only in Yangcheng City in East Zhou, but also in other prehistoric sites. We also found many city sites on the east and west banks of the Yellow River in the Hetao area outside the Great Wall, such as the city site of Saizita, the city site of Zhaizishang, the city site of Maluta, and the city site of Houchengzui. It should be noted most of these sites, either grouped or adjacent, were deliberately built on hills or cliffs, or along riverbanks. This could infer their primary purpose was to fortify defense.[10] From later descriptions of ancient China, cities still retain this important function even long after the Western Zhou Period.

During the early Zhou Dynasty, the country's land was divided, and many ruling and defense settlements were developed. This made Zhou's rule deep with the old tribes. As mentioned in *Master Lü's Spring and Autumn Annals*, the Zhou empowered over 400 vassals and conquered around 800 tribes. This large number of vassal kings were surrounded by other tribes. Therefore, immediately after arrival in the new territory, the vassal kings built castles and protected themselves with strong walls and wide, deep ditches. At the same time, the kings took strict precautions against the conquered people. On the one hand, they "occupied the local people's settlement and lived in their houses,"[11] and on the other hand, they constructed high walls and deep ditches to separate themselves. The Ji nobility spent most of their time within the city and rarely went outside its walls. A feudal settlement, established as such, would consist of military fortresses with the purpose of protection and defense.

During the Eastern Zhou era, with economic and political power strengthened, society became divided, and the vassal kings began to rise and declare power over their counterparts. Between these vassal kings, "the strong country bullied the weak country, and the country with a large population annexed the country with a small population," so they "competed for the city through war, and the city was full of people who died in the war."[12] As a result, the winning sides annexed the losing sides. Because of the constant wars, the vassal kings had to expand the old city or build a new city and build a strong and large-scale city wall according to their own political and military needs, whether for attack

10. Qu Yingjie, *Ancient Cities* (Beijing: Cultural Relics Press, 2003), 23.
11. *Book of Han · Admonishment.*
12. *Mozi · Li Lou* (Part One).

or epidemic prevention. Therefore, the defensive function of the city was more prominent. There are many such examples recorded in various documents of the Spring and Autumn Period and the Warring States Period.

> *Discourses of the States · Duke Huan of Qi* ordered the construction of several fortresses, such as Kuizi, Yan, Fuxia, and Lingfuqiu, to defend against the invasion and plunder of the neighboring vassal states by Rong and Di people. He also ordered the construction of several passes, such as Wulu, Zhongmou, Gaiyu, and Muqiu, to defend the important areas of the Xia and show his authority to the states in the Central Plains.
>
> When the Di people in the north attacked the Xing state, Duke Huan of Qi built a castle in Yiyi and let the Xing state move there, so that the people of the Xing state could take refuge. The Di people attacked the Wei state, and the people of Wei were forced to flee to Caoyi as a refuge. Duke Huan of Qi built a castle in Chuqiu for them to rebuild their homes.
>
> *Commentary by Guliang*: Zhongsun Jie met with Xun Ying of Jin, Gao Zhi of Qi, Hua Ding of Song, Shi Shuyi of Wei, Gongsun Duan of Zheng, the representatives of Cao, Ju, Zhu, Teng, Xue, and Xiaozhu to rebuild Qi City. In ancient times, the emperor divided lands among the nobles, and the lands given to the nobles were enough to accommodate the population under the rule. The population given to the nobles was also enough for the whole city to defend itself. The State of Qi was in danger and could not defend itself, so the officials from the various states came to the State of Qi one after another to rebuild the city.

Other similar events were kept in the record during the Spring and Autumn Period and the Warring States Period. It fully shows that until the Spring and Autumn Period, both the expansion of old cities and the construction of new cities were for defense. In this subject, our ancestors have thorough understandings and unique insights. According to the *Commentary of Zuo*, When Ji Kang wanted to conquer the Zhu state, he gathered his ministers to discuss the matter. Zifu Jingbo said, "The people are protected by the city, and the city is protected by virtue." A similar quote can be found in the *Commentary by Guliang*, "cities are built to protect their people." We can list several examples to support this kind of view:

> *Mozi*: Food is the treasure of the state, the weapon is the claw of the state, and the city is used to defend itself. These three things are important tools of the state.
>
> *Guanzi*: The land's security lies in the city, the security of the city lies in the army, the security of the army lies in the people, and the security of the people lies in food. Therefore, if we do not engage in development and construction and continue to expand the land, then the city will not be strong.

The evidence above shows that in the early days of Chinese history, the most significant function of cities is defense. Likewise, the city is also the center for the monarch to rule the periphery lands. The defense function was incorporated in later cities and continued until the end of the Chinese empires.

3. Merchandise Gathering Center

As mentioned previously, early urban defense functions were very important, yet the early cities were destined to become regional centers of economic activity because of the large congregation of people. This is supported by findings from archeological research of these sites.

In 1979, Cao Guicen, from the Henan Institute of Cultural Relics, presided over the excavation of the Pingliangtai ruins in Huaiyang, Henan. In this city, not only high-profile construction remains but also ground construction of houses. More importantly, three pottery kilns and a large quantity of copper pieces were uncovered too. Built before 2500 BC, this city belonged to an oil workshop style of the Longshan Culture—a very important city of handicrafts.

Explored from 1991 to 1993 by archaeologists from Shandong University, relics of kilns and wells were also found in Dinggong City. At the Shijiahe City Site in Tianmen, Hubei, the Department of Archaeology of Peking University and the Hubei Archaeology Institute have excavated many times. A large number of birds, dogs, chickens, sheep, elephants, and turtles, along with figures kneeling and holding fish pottery, were unearthed at the Dengjiawan Site. Probably, it was a worksite specializing in ceramic products. Several cicada-shaped ornaments, dragon-shaped rings, phoenix-shaped rings, jade, and human head figures—all kinds of delicate jade items—were found as well as semi-finished products and raw stones at the Luojiabailing Site to the southeast.[13] These did not show how advanced the city's economy was but indicated that these economic activities would be an important component of city life, even in prehistoric cities.

Fig. 1-4: Plan of the Prehistoric Shijiahe Site, Tianmen, Hubei[14]

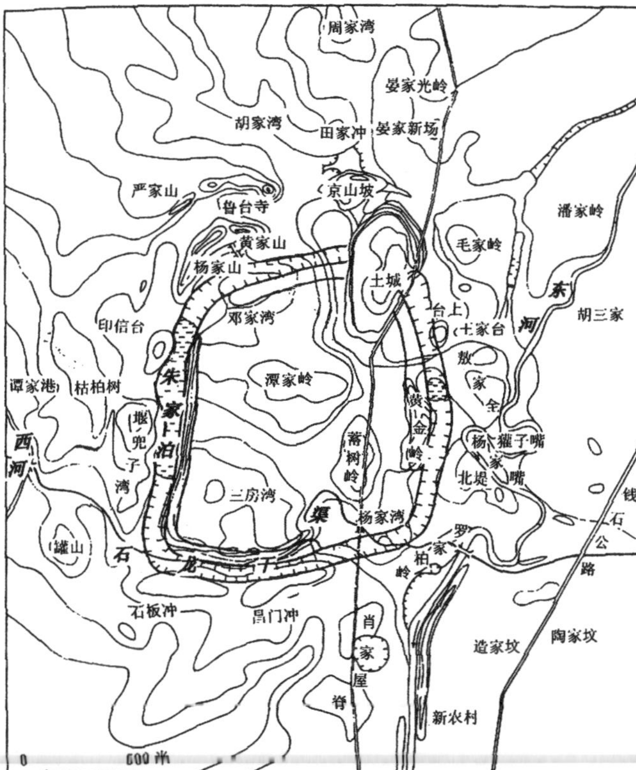

In view of this, earlier cities in China were developed for political and military purposes. Still, some established cities happened to be located along with a traffic hub, river port, or were rich in produce. Therefore, the industries and businesses of these cities would develop gradually because of the transport convenience, hence, became economic capitals.

For instance, Luoyang could conduct trading in the east with the Qi and Lu states and in the south with the Liang and Chu states because of its central

13. Qu Yingjie, *Ancient Cities* (Beijing: Cultural Relics Press, 2003), 11.

14. Ibid., 26.

location,[15] outshining the Jianghuai regions in the east with its proximity to a major river, and enjoying the benefits of Xiaoshan and Mianchi in the west which are difficult terrains.[16] Therefore, when businesses developed, the customs of Luoyang became "profits-oriented and properties were considered as more important, the rich were respected, the poor were considered the lower class, and people were happy to be business people." Undoubtedly, this phenomenon was the outcome of a strong economic function. Still, it should be noted this occurred only in the Spring and Autumn and Warring States periods when urban development had matured in China.

---

15. *Records of the Grand Historian · Annals of Zhou.*

16. "Superior Prefecture of Henan," in *Dushi Fangyu Jiyao* (*Essence of Historical Geography or Essentials of Geography for Reading History*), vol. 48.

CHAPTER TWO

CAPITALS AND *YI*S: THE CAPITALS OF THE XIA, SHANG, AND ZHOU DYNASTIES

As often mentioned in ancient Chinese documents, *Yi* is the hieroglyphic representation of land and people and refers to all settlements in general. Sometimes, markets were located in these settlements; thus, they were called settlements with markets. From the definition of city, these settlements with markets were the real urban residential settlements. As recorded in the *Strategies of the Warring States,* when Su Qin lobbied King Min of Qi, he said: "all these settlements, including those small ones around the capital, should have altars and markets. All of them should definitely serve Your Majesty." Here, he referred to the settlements with markets.

Another Chinese character related to city—*du*—is used specifically to refer to settlements with ancestral temples. The ancient Chinese believed in ancestor worship: there were family temples for individual families and imperial ancestor temples for the state, a settlement place for its monarchy. Therefore, the character *du* referred to the power center. This meaning was further extended and became the word *guo-du* (state capital).

However, early state capitals, like early history, were very obscure. These state capitals were not located in solely one place and, therefore, perplexed historians. Since the beginning of the 20th century, archaeologists continue to work on the capitals of the Xia and Shang dynasties, particularly on the Ruins of Yin and the Erlitou Site, eventually making and recording preliminary findings.

1. Capital of the Xia Dynasty: The Erlitou Site

Excavation of the Ruins of Yin at the end of the 1920s encouraged Chinese archaeologists. They attempted to find the "Ruins of Xia" of the legendary Xia Dynasty. However, these efforts were interrupted by war and other matters. In 1959, Xu Xusheng, from the Archaeology Institute of China Science Academy, resumed the investigation in Dengfeng, Yu County, Gong County, Yanshi, and other places in Henan, finally discovering the now famous Erlitou and Dongxiafeng sites.

The Erlitou Site is located along the south bank of the Luo River, about 10 kilometers southwest of Yanshi. The entire site is about 2,000 meters long and 1,500 meters wide. There are four higher plots, with the largest located in the middle, covering an area of about 120,000 square meters. On this raised area, archaeologists detected the base of dozens of palaces, covering an area of about 80,000 square meters. Around this area, archaeologists also found some ordinary house bases and tomb burial items, bronze, bone workshops, pottery kilns, etc. These buildings ranged from 1900 to 1400 BC.

Archaeologists focused on excavating "Palace One" and "Palace Two," which were even larger than the former. The plane of the palace base is square, with an area of 10,000 square meters. The plane center hall is rectangular, about 30 meters long, 11 meters wide, facing south—possibly a four-slope roof building. In front of the hall is a courtyard surrounded by corridors with a gate on the south. At the same time, archaeologists also conducted excavations on the base of Palace Two located northeast of Palace One. Palace Two is larger than Palace One and roughly a rectangular north-south extension—about 58 meters wide and 72 meters long. The center plane of this palace area is also rectangular, roughly the same with the center hall scale of Palace One—about 32 meters long and 12 meters wide, and a courtyard in front of the palace. But the difference is a large tomb from the same period as the building behind it. In addition, Palace Two has rammed walls for the west, east, and north sides, and on the south there is a grand gate with halls attached to it. The two palaces were constructed between 1700 and 1600 BC, according to archaeologists who concluded the palaces belong to Phase III of the Erlitou Culture.

Judging from the location, time period, and scale of the Erlitou Site, Chinese archeologists and historians once concluded it was the capital Bo of Tang—the founder of the Shang Dynasty. Later, they considered this site was actually the earlier Xia, that is, the capital of Zhenxun during the Jie era of Xia.[1] However, *Yi Zhou Shu (Lost Book of Zhou)* mentioned that "building palaces would lead to the downfall of the state. In the old days, the Youluo Family constantly upgraded its palaces and expanded its pools. These constant renovations made its people have no time to rest and farm. Consequently, a famine came, and King Cheng launched wars against the Youluo Family and the family perished."

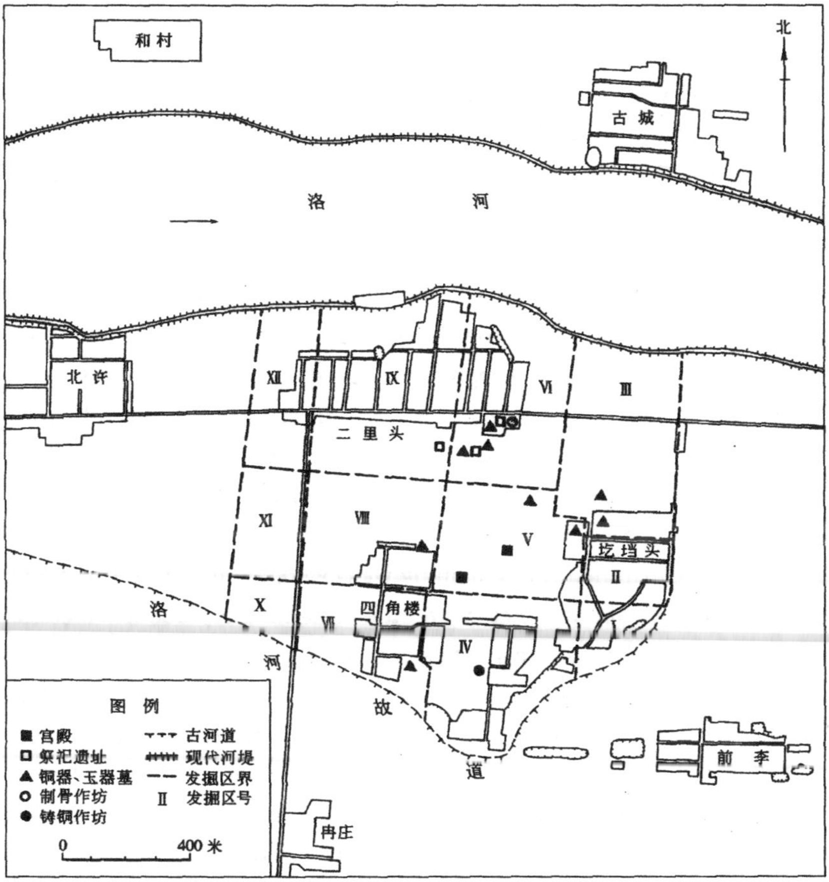

Fig. 2-1: Plan of Xia in Erlitou, Yanshi, Henan[2]

1. Luoyang Archaeological Excavation Team, Science Academy of China, "Excavation Brief on Erlitou Ruins, Yansh, Henan," *Archaeology*, no. 5 (1965); Zhao Zhiquan, "Is Erlitou Site the capital of the late Xia Dynasty?" *Chinese Archaeology*, no. 2 (1987).
2. *Chinese Archaeology, Xia and Shang Volume* (Beijing: China Social Science Press, 2003), 62.

Archaeologist Qu Yingjie speculated that the Erlitou Site was the capital of the Youluo Family, attacked by King Cheng who established the Shang. The Youluo Family was just an affiliated vassal of Xia.[3] Whether this site was the capital of Xia or the capital of an affiliated state remains undecided. Yet, the fact that no walls were found at the site has perplexed archaeologists and historians, since it obviously differed from the early Chinese capitals and cities known to us.

Therefore, from the autumn of 1974 to the winter of 1979, the Archaeology Institute continued its excavation efforts of the Ruins of Xia. Meng Fanren and others excavated the area that would later be called the Dongxiafeng Site. The site totals an area of 250,000 square meters divided into four areas of East, Middle, West (Southern bank), and North (Northern bank). In general, the appearance is similar to Erlitou Culture. Archaeologists defined it as the Dongxiafeng type. This type belongs to the age of about from 1900 BC to 1600 BC, which is precisely the era of the legendary Xia Dynasty.

In the center of the Dongxiafeng Site, a city was discovered by archaeologists. Although the northern part of the site was destroyed by floods and even the remaining part was covered, a rough silhouette of the city can still be seen. The remaining eastern wall was about 52 meters, the remaining west wall was about 140 meters, and the southern wall was about 440 meters, but some of the middle parts were curved. Therefore, the average distance between the eastern and western walls was about 370 meters. In the southwest corner of the southern wall, archaeologists determined the remaining walls were about 1.2–1.8 meters high, with a foundation of about 8 meters and the remaining top about 7 meters. The external side was almost vertical, while the internal side of the wall had slopes. Therefore, the intersection of the walls was trapezium. There were rammed slopes and ditches on both sides of the walls. The ditches were 5.5 meters wide on the top, 4 meters at the bottom, and about 7 meters deep. These walls were built upon the fourth level of an unidentified time period and the fifth level of the Miaodigou Period II Culture. The slopes had cultural relics from the Upper Erligang Culture accumulation of the Shang Dynasty. In the southern part of the eastern wall, archaeologists also explored and determined this part of the remaining wall was about 1 meter high with a bottom width of 7.8 meters and 6.7 meters on the top. Ditches were outside the walls. This section of walls was built upon the

3. Qu Yingjie, *Ancient Cities* (Beijing: Cultural Relics Press, 2003), 35.

second level of the Miaodigou Period II Culture. The slopes to protect the walls were covered by the Upper Erligang Culture. Additionally, southwest of the city there were also round-shape-based construction clusters, ash pits wells, burial grounds, etc.

The excavators concluded that Dongxiafeng was built during Phase V of the Dongxiafeng Site. In terms of time, this should be well into the early Shang Dynasty.

The excavators concluded that the Dongxiafeng was built approximately 3,500 years ago—well into the early Shang era. However, some archaeologists and historians argue the possibility that the city was built before the Xia based on the whole site and the overlapping walls.[4]

Although we are still uncertain about the exact location of the capital of Xia, we are positive large-scale cities emerged at this time based on the archaeological findings from this period.

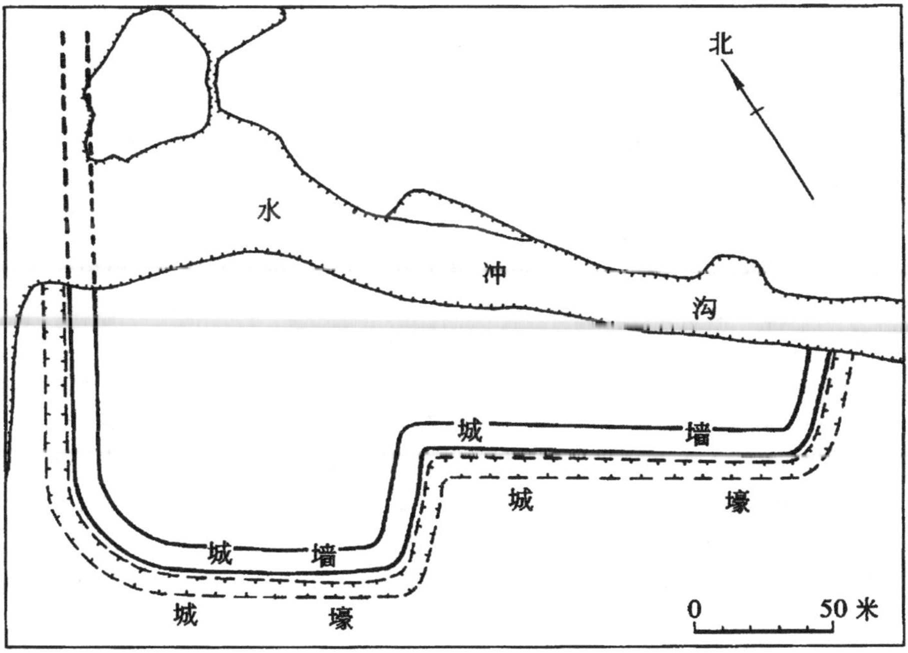

Fig. 2-2: Plan of the Dongxiafeng Site[5]

4. Qu Yingjie, *Ancient Cities* (Beijing: Cultural Relics Press, 2003), 35–36.
5. *Chinese Archaeology, Xia and Shang Volume* (Beijing: China Social Science Press, 2003), 235.

2. Capital Relocation to Yin by Pangeng and Discovery of Ruins of Yin

The Shang, presumably an eastern tribe, built their capital in Bo after Tang declared himself king. Shang moved its capital to Ao in Zhongding's era and to Xiang in Hedanjia's era. By Pangeng's time, it was said the capital had moved seven times. However, from the archaeology finds, most of these moves could not be bound to specified locations. The exact location of the Shang capital and the reasons why it could not be fixed remained a mystery of early Chinese history. What we can do is explore the possible locations of the Shang capital, particularly during Pangeng's time from Shang's city sites. The first sentence of the *Book of Documents · Pangeng* is about moving the capital: Pangeng planned the fifth migration and chose Yin as the capital. The people were sighing and complaining to each other, so he composed three articles of *Pangeng* to educate his people.

Pangeng's move to Yin was a major event in the history of China's early capitals. Before this move, especially from the Tang to Zhongding, the capital was established in Bo, which some scholars believe is today's Shangcheng of Zhengzhou. However, after Zhongding, the princes and dukes struggled for power, causing chaos and instability. As a result, the capital was moved several times.

After this major move, the nation was revitalized and society stabilized. The capital remained unchanged until the downfall of the Shang by its last King, Zhou (纣). Therefore, Yin plays a very important role in the history of the Shang. That is why Yin-Shang or Yin is used to refer to the Shang today. Now, the question is where exactly is Yin located?

Both archaeological studies and discoveries in the past several decades have unearthed oracle bone scripts proving the Ruins of Yin at Anyang were the capital of Shang between Pangeng and its last king. The discovery of the Ruins of Yin is an important yet circuitous event. In fact, the capital was found by research and the discovery of oracle bone scripts. During the late Qing Dynasty, village farmers in Xiaotun, a village in Anyang, Henan, often dug shell sheets with inscriptions in their farming fields. At first, local farmers considered this ominous; inscribed tortoise shells were discarded along the roadside. Later, these shells were collected by Chinese herbal medicine shops as a medical ingredient for keel medicine.

In AD 1899, Wang Yirong, Chancellor of the Imperial Academy, suffered from malaria. He found the keel had indistinct carved symbols in the preparation of herbal medicine. Wang was well versed in epigraphy, particularly bronze inscriptions. These carved symbols aroused his interest, and he collected many shells for research. Wang finally concluded the carved symbols on the shells were the lost Shang Dynasty tortoise oracle bones. Since then, oracle bones have become the first-hand materials for the studies of Shang history.

The discovery attracted scholars to Xiaotun Village, Anyang. In 1928, an archaeology team began excavations in search of scientific evidence. However, this first effort was halted in 1937 with the outbreak of war with Japan. During this period, fifteen major excavation works were conducted and more than fifty rammed earth platforms were discovered in the palace area. Many bronzes, jade wares, and stone inscriptions were found among over 20,000 pieces of lettered tortoise shells. In the royal burial ground area, ten major tombs with tomb paths and more than 1,000 smaller tombs were also discovered. After the founding of the People's Republic of China in 1949, large-scale excavations were conducted; the Ruins of Yin gradually revealed itself to the world, and the mystery over the capital of Shang unraveled.

Viewing the Chinese topographic map reveals a zonal distribution of plain areas in the topographic transition from the second level to the third. This is the plain alluvial east of the Taihang Mountain Range. Ruins of Yin were in the middle and southern part of this alluvial with a total area of 30 square kilometers: approximately 6 kilometers from east to west and 5 kilometers from south to north. The land is fertile, and the terrain is rocky and dangerous. It is so-called "Mount Mengmen on the left, Zhang River and Fu River on the right, facing the Yellow River in the front and the mountains on the back."

The Ruins of Yin were divided into three parts based on archaeological excavation importance—key areas, general areas, and peripheral areas (see Fig. 2-3). It has been almost eighty years since excavations began here. Unfortunately, no walls have been found so far; thus, the exact plane shape of the Ruins of Yin cannot be identified. We can only infer the rough function quarters—a residential site is located along both sides of the Huan River, mostly along the southern side of the river. Along the north side of the river, ruins were discovered in Dasikong Village, south of Wuguan, and south of Houjiazhuang villages. Xiaotun Village and Garden Village belong to the palace district. The Huan River runs on the west and north sides of the palace district. Moreover, moats were built on the west and south sides. The moats and rivers formed a closed defensive loop. The constructions suggest that this is the key area of the Shang capital defense system. Archaeologists found more than 50 ruins of palace buildings in the northeast of Xiaotun Village. Among these palaces, the buildings are the ruins of a copper mill, jade workshop, bone workshop, and pottery workshop. These workshops were clearly designed to serve the nobles of the district.

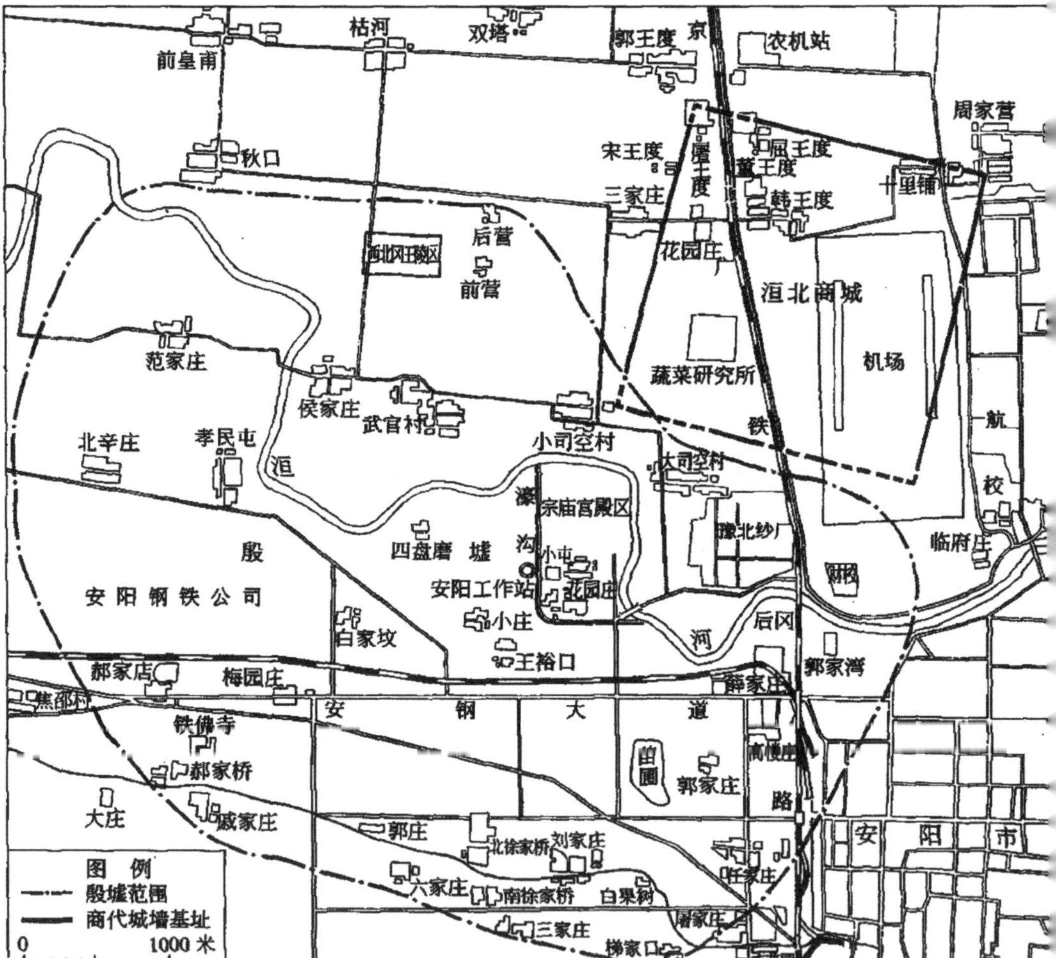

Fig. 2-3: Plan of the Ruins of Yin, Xiaotun Village, Henan[6]

6. *Chinese Archaeology, Xia and Shang Volume* (Beijing: China Social Science Press, 2003), 285.

3. King Wu's War with Zhou (纣) and the Establishment of Two Capitals: Feng and Hao

The last King of Shang, Zhou (纣), a degenerate devoid of principles, was replaced by the Zhou (周) tribe, which became the new leader in the Central Plains of China. According to historical records, Western Zhou had been thriving in Guanzhong (a historical region corresponding to the lower valley of the Wei in today's Shaanxi) for many generations. Western Zhou moved from Qishan in the west to Feng along the bank of the Wei during King Wen's era. King Wen's son built Haojing, and henceforth there were two capitals of Western Zhou. As to the building process of these two capitals, records are found in the *Book of Songs · Major Court Hymns*:

> King Wen was bestowed the power by Heaven. He launched wars and started the capital city in Feng. King Wu was a great oracle reader and built the capital in Haojing. Following Heaven's oracle, King Wu built the capital.

According to *Records of the Grand Historian · Annals of Zhou*, the Zhou tribe originated in the present areas of Shaanxi and Gansu. Legends foretold their eldest ancestor was called Qi, a child of Youtaishi, Jiang Yuan. Qi was awarded the title of agricultural division officer and obtained his land in Tai—today's Wugongxi, Shaanxi. Qi's courtesy name is Hou Ji. We are more familiar with his courtesy name. After his death, Qi's descendants inherited his title for many generations until Buku, who lived during the period of Xia's decline.

Buku escaped and ran to those northern minority groups. Shortly after, however, his grandson, Gongliu, settled with his people in Bin in the west of today's Xunyi County, Shaanxi. Gongliu developed agriculture and soon turned Bin into a rich agricultural area where "travelers would carry money with them and those who settled down would have an abundant surplus."[7]

Nine generations after Gongliu, Gugong Danfu moved the center from the Jing River, where northern minorities lived together, to the Zhouyuan area in the south of Qishan, Guanzhong Plain. The cultural relics of Zhouyuan were rich with archaeological finds, which included five periods—Yangshao, Longshan,

7. "Annals of Zhou," in *Records of the Grand Historian*, vol. 4.

Late Shang, Western Zhou, and Eastern Zhou.[8] Here, we see Zhouyuan developed before Gugong Danfu. Yet it was not until Gugong Danfu's era that the Zhou tribe finally settled to reclaim lands, constructed palaces, and built Qiyi—the first capital of the Zhou Dynasty.

According to archaeological excavations, the scope of Qiyi was roughly centered in today's Hejia Village in Shaanxi. It reached Qiyangbao in the north and Kangjiazhuang Village to the south, and was located about seven kilometers northwest of Famen Temple, Fufeng County.[9] This matches the records of Du Yu from the Jin Dynasty in the *Annotation on Zuo's Commentaries*, "The city of Zhou is located in the northwest of Meiyang County," and the records in the *Sequel to the "Book of Han"*—"There is a Meiyang County in the city of Zhou, and Zhou Plain in the south."

Zhou people have lived and managed their households for an extended period of time, and their power has continued to expand. In the later years of Shang King Wuyi, Gugongdanfu's son Jili entered the court. Wuyi gave him land, jade, horses, etc. With the Shang King's help, Ji Li marched his army to the west, conquered the Rong tribe, and captured twelve of their leaders. When it came to Wending's era, Ji Li further expanded his territory by launching wars against minorities, such as the Yurong Shihu, and Yitu, expanding Zhou's territory east of the Yellow River. Although Ji Li was awarded *Mushi* (head of the feudal lords) by King Wending, Ji Li's power caused envy and hatred—finally Ji Li was killed by the King. When his son, Ji Chang, inherited the throne, he increased tributes to the bigger state, Shang. He was awarded the title, "Xi Bo," after he offered the lands along the west bank of Luo River to King Zhou (纣).

Although Ji Chang resided in the relatively remote Guanzhong area, he tried his best to recruit talent from around the country. Chang was committed to the development of the economy. Finally, his state rose to become the most powerful in the west. During this same time, the Shang King was living a degenerate life and his people were resentful.

According to the *Book of History*, "the King of Shang was living an existence too comfortable to know the difficulties of its farmers or the difficulties of the

8. Chen Quanfang, "An Exploration on Qiyi, the Early Capital of Zhou," *Cutural Relics*, no. 10 (1979).

9. Xu Xitai, "Gains from the Archaeological Work in Zhouyuan," *Archaeology and Cultural Relics*, no. 5–6 (1998).

commoners. He only lived a luxurious life." Therefore, many of his dependent states betrayed Shang and turned to Zhou instead. When Zhou developed sufficient power, it became natural that people believed "King Wen was destined to be the future king."[10] The bronze artifacts made by Zhou included inscriptions showing, "King Wen was ordered by God to be king."[11] Thus, it may have been nothing more than a justification for him to wage a series of wars.

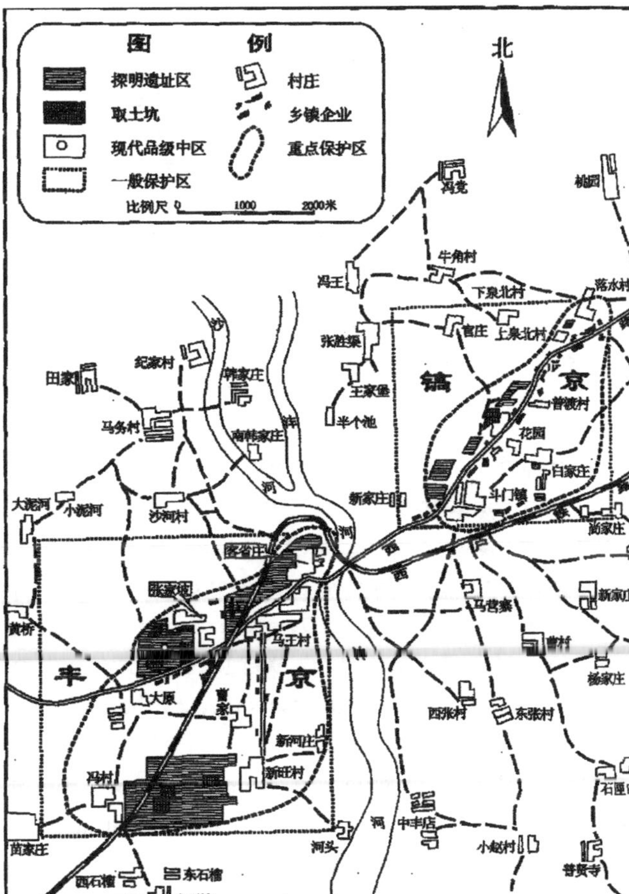

Fig. 2-4: Site of Feng, Western Zhou[12] today

10. Dong Zhongshu, *Chunqiu Fanlu · Jiaoji (Season Changes and Ancestor Worshpping).*
11. Archaeology Institute, Chinese Academy of Social Sciences, *Report of West Feng Excavation* (Beijing: Cultural Relics Press, 1962).
12. Zhu Shiguang, ed., *Ancient Capital Xi'an: Historical Change and Development of Xi'an* (Xi'an: Xi'an Press, 2003), 116.

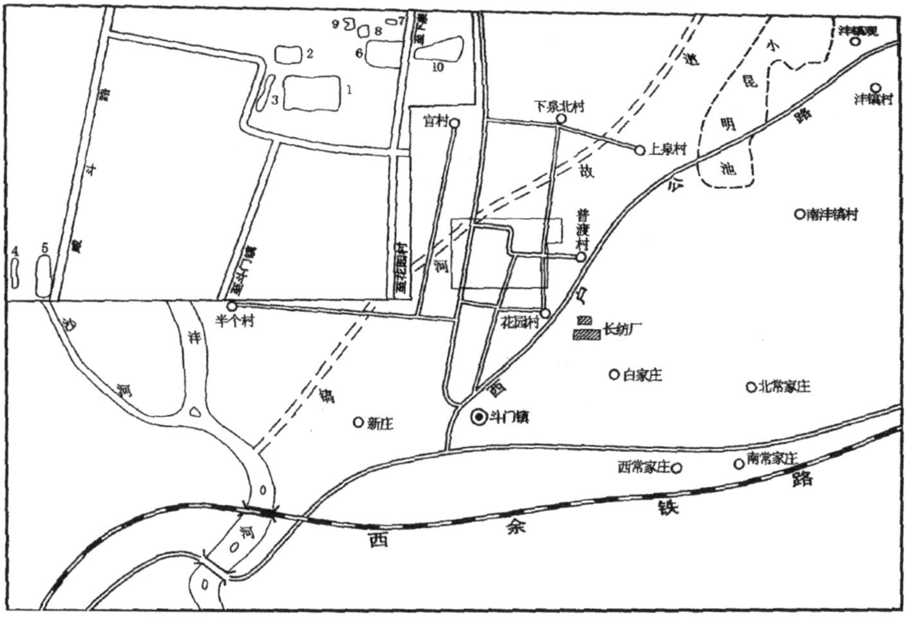

Fig. 2-5: Site of Hao, Western Zhou[13] today

Two capitals, Feng and Hao, were built during these wars. "Xi Bo was destined by God to conquer the minorities ... and next year he would conquer Chonghouhu and make Feng into a city."[14] King Wen established the capital in Feng for two reasons: first, to shorten his distance to the Shang people in preparation for the destruction of the Shang Dynasty; second because Feng had superior national conditions. As a branch of the Wei River, Feng was a tributary basin with open terrain. Archaeological finds also suggest it had a long history of human habitation since the Neolithic period.

During the era of King Wu (King Wen's son), the Zhou people continued to expand their sphere of influence and launched attacks against the Shang by taking advantage of their own wars with people from the east. To improve his chances of conquering the Shang, King Wu moved his capital from west of the Feng River to Haojing, located near Hao Pond, east of Feng River. The two capital moves were

13. Zhu Shiguang, ed., *Ancient Capital Xi'an: Historical Change and Development of Xi'an* (Xi'an: Xi'an Press, 2003), 119.

14. "Annals of Zhou," in *Records of the Grand Historian*, vol. 4.

considered to be significant events of the time, leading to the building of capitals near Guanzhong, which became a national political center in the era following King Wu's conquest.

Fig. 2-6: Plan of the large palace No. 5, Haojing, Western Zhou[15]

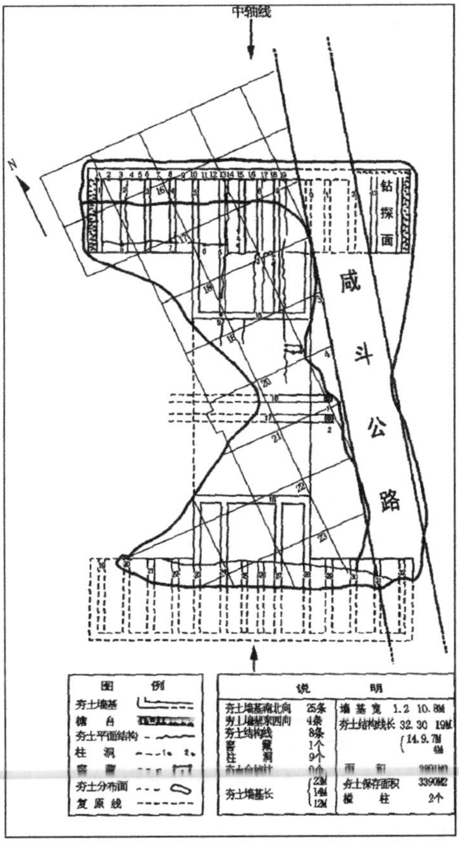

At the end of the Western Zhou Dynasty, the Feng capital and Hao capital were destroyed, and the city sites were buried. Therefore, when historians talk about the city of Feng and Hao in the Han and Tang dynasties, they can only roughly point out their locations. Fengyi is near Feng River, located in the southwest of Chang'an or east of Huxian City, or it was situated in the west of Chang'an in the Tang Dynasty; Hao is located in the east of Fengshui and near the Hao River,

15. Zhu Shiguang, ed., *Ancient Capital Xi'an: Historical Change and Development of Xi'an* (Xi'an: Xi'an Press, 2003), 122.

also known as Kunming Pond. Because Feng city and Hao city have significant meanings in Chinese history, in the 1930s, Academia Sinica organized two archaeological investigation missions in the area. After liberation, the Institute of Archaeology of the Chinese Academy of Sciences and its successor, the Chinese Academy of Social Sciences Institute of Archaeology, Shaanxi Institute of Archaeology, and Xi'an Institute of Cultural Relics Protection and Archaeology have all sent investigation teams into this area. They gradually revealed Feng and Hao city's shapes, exact locations, and inner-city designs. In particular, the excavation of the No. 5 palace ruin outlined the essential characteristics of the interior layout of Haojing.

Ancient Chinese cities were symbols of the state and royal power, with the city layout centered on the king's palace. The craftsman's management of the country as described in *Record of Trades* was to put the palace at the center of everything. Therefore, the palace area represented by Palace foundation No. 5 is almost certainly the center of Haojing. And it is located in the north of Haojing, which may suggest that since then, the location of the palace in the north of the city has become a significant feature of the capital structure. In addition, according to the *Book of Songs* and *Mozi*, there are not only large-scale palace buildings in Feng and Hao but also spirit studios, spirit bower, spirit parks, and other places for nobles' activities.

There is another pertinent question—what is the relationship between Feng and Hao? In fact, these two cities were often mentioned together like twins. That is, after King Wu moved to Hao, he would continue to return to Feng whenever there were major events as the imperial ancestor temple was in Feng. However, most of the political and residential activities were concentrated in Haojing.

4. The Construction of Chengzhou, Zhou's Eastern Capital

After the conquest of Shang, King Wu of Zhou set up the Three Guardian system and returned west. However, Zhou's dominance was not fully realized, and Shang's influence was strong. King Wu was aware "the nation was not fully settled." However, two years later, he died of disease and King Cheng was too young to assume power, so Wu's brother Ji Dan, or the Duke of Zhou, stood as regent. His two brothers, Guanshu and Caishu, suspected that the Duke of Zhou was trying to usurp the throne, so they started a campaign called "Qi Shang," aiming to lure Wu Geng (the survivor of the Shang Dynasty) to rebel against Zhou. After a series of events, the situation in the Western Zhou was unstable, especially when there was a series of issues with the legitimacy of the domination of the previous Shang's land.

The Duke of Zhou then began another large-scale crusade, which took three years and completely eradicated the influence of Yin-Shang in the east, and consolidated the ruling of Western Zhou in the west. Subsequently, the Duke of Zhou issued two important decrees: first, dividing the relatives and sending them to different lands to strengthen Zhou's ruling. Second, constructing Zhou's Eastern Capital of Chengzhou.

The second decree was actually thought up by King Wu after his conquest of Shang. King Wu even chose a rough location personally: "From Luo River all the way to Yi River, it is flat and free of obstacles. This was the place where the Xia Dynasty settled. I once looked south to Santu Mountain, north to Taihang Mountain, and when I looked back from my shoulders, I saw the Yellow River; this place is also not far away from our ancestral land." The Riot of the Three Guardians further convinced the Duke of Zhou that it would be difficult for Feng and Hao to pacify the east with their locations in the west. Therefore, a new ruling station should be established in the original center of Yin-Shang. With this, the Duke started building the Eastern capital. This event was described in the *Table of Contents (Book of Han)*: "The Duke of Zhao managed the court in Haojing. The Duke of Zhou went to Luoyang to build the Eastern Capital. He sent the envoy to report to the court, pray to the God and write the *Luohao*." It is the incident that was told. The construction of Luo City began during King Wu's time and was completed while the Duke of Zhou worked as regent to the young King Cheng. As noted in *Records of the Grand Historian*, "King Cheng was living in Fengyi, he sent the Duke of Zhou to measure the Luo City again, in order to follow the will of the late King Wu of Zhou. The Duke of Zhou also augured and checked the terrain repeatedly. Finally, the construction was successful, and he placed the tripods there. He said, "This is the center of the world, and the journey of tribute is the same from all directions."

The new capital built along the Luo River was described in the *Book of Yizhou*: "The city had a circumference of one thousand and seven hundred and two *zhang* (*zhang* is a unit of length in China). The outer city had a circumference of about seventy *li*. In the south, it was next to the Luo River, and in the north, it nestled near the Mountain Xia. This would be a great capital." There were many ritual buildings constructed within the city, such as the Five Palaces, religious temples, ancestor temples, Kao Palace, and the King's Palace. After completion, it became the Eastern Capital of Zhou.

With the completion of the Eastern Capital, the Duke of Zhou believed the territory would be protected and King Wu's last words would be realized so he could return the power to King Cheng. Therefore, during his seventh year as regent, he declared in Luoyi personally that power was transferred to King Cheng. Since then, Feng, Hao, and Luoyi became the ruling centers of the Zhou Dynasty at the same time.

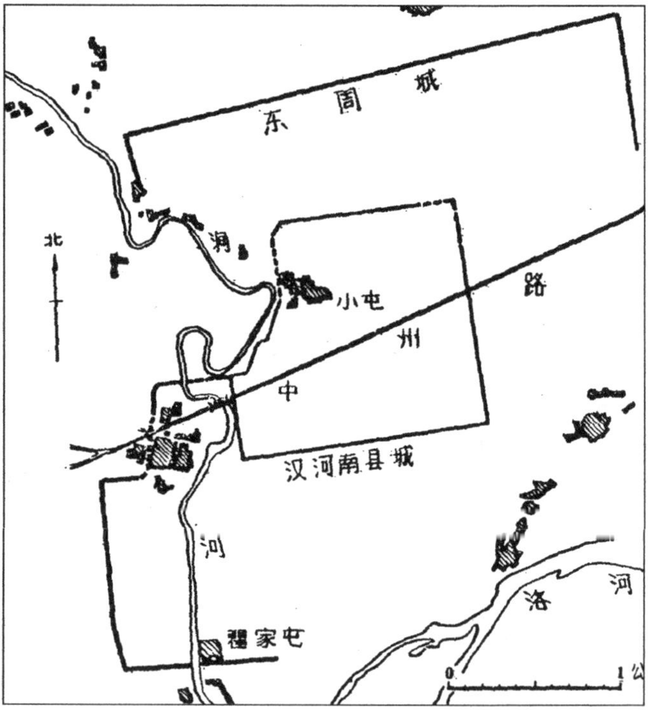

Fig. 2-7: Plan of Luoyang, the Eastern Zhou's capital (Chengzhou)[16]

16. Zhang Yuhuan, *The History of Chinese Cities* (Tianjin: Baihua Literature and Art Publishing House, 2003), 12.

PART II

ANCIENT CAPITALS

CHAPTER THREE

JING AND *SHI*: ESTABLISHMENT OF NATIONAL CAPITALS AND THEIR SHIFTS

When a dynasty was established, the first thing it usually considered was the location or position of its capital. From a macro perspective, this location should be the most advantageous, while from a micro-perspective, the physical environment is key.

In ancient China, the character *Jing* (京) meant large areas of highland full of sunshine, and the character *Shi* (师) refers to a military station. These two characters often combine (since the military would often be stationed in highlands). Sometimes, the capital is also referred to as Jingshi (京师) because capitals, in general, are heavily guarded. In ancient times, the most important consideration in choosing a capital was usually its suitability as a defense or fortress; all other considerations were secondary.

1. Capital Location Decisions

After several wars between the Chu and Han states, Liu Bang, the Han King, established the Western Han Dynasty following a significant victory with key support from his advisors. Although he established his sovereignty by force, he could not govern the country by force. Thus, it was imperative to establish an administrative center as soon as possible.

The generals and soldiers who had assisted Liu were mostly Shandong (of the Qin and Han dynasties) natives who lived east of the Yao Mountains. They wished to return home with pride and dignity. Therefore, Luoyang—in the center of the country—became a natural first choice for many soldiers. This place is not only in the center of the country but also close to their hometown Fengpei. Unexpectedly, Liu Bang was somewhat hesitant to choose Luoyang as his capital, in spite of its convenient location for transport, and support from generals and soldiers. Why? Because he was concerned first and foremost with military security. The Han Dynasty was just established, and the country was not stable yet. There were vassal kings with different family names in the east and the barbarian Xiongnu tribe in the west.

In fact, ancient people have long been aware of the geographical situation in the construction of the capital. According to the *Commentary of Zuo*, "The national events of a country are military security and temple ceremony." It means only military forces can secure the country, and it is equally important to religious events. As noted in the *Book of Changes*, "Ancient rulers set up barriers to protect their countries." Therefore, in terms of selecting capital locations, the nearby shape of mountains and valleys has all been considered.

Therefore, just when Liu Bang hesitated, Lou Jing, one of Liu's advisors, cleverly proposed to Liu Bang. After learning that Liu Bang wanted to set the capital in Luoyang, Lou Jing went to visit Liu Bang. At the beginning of the Han Dynasty, it was relatively easy for ministers to see the emperor.

When Lou Jing met Liu Bang, he asked: "Your Majesty wants to set the capital in Luoyang. Is it to compare the country's longevity with the Zhou Dynasty?"

"Yes!" Liu Bang answered well.

Lou Jing went on to say, "But Your Majesty's method of acquiring the country is different from that of the Zhou Dynasty."

"Why?" Liu Bang was puzzled.

Lou Jing went on to analyze that after more than ten generations of people in the Zhou Dynasty accumulated virtue and good deeds, they had laid a good foundation for the rule, and the country had a long-term fortune. And His Majesty gained the world by relying on more than seventy big and forty small battles. The people were killed and injured countless times in the war, and the bodies of fathers and children were exposed in the wild; the cries were heard one after another; the people who had been traumatized by the war had not recovered.

Under such circumstances, it was not advisable for Liu Bang to compare the prosperity of the country with the Zhou Dynasty. Liu Bang agrees with Lou Jing's analysis. Then, where is the best choice if not setting the capital in Luoyang? Lou Jing's following answer is Guanzhong (a region corresponding to the modern-day Wei River lower valley in Shaanxi).

Lou Jing expanded on the advantages of this site. He said, "The State of Qin was surrounded by mountains and rivers, and there are also strong stations around. Even in an emergency, one million soldiers would not be sufficient (to breach it). In addition, because it was the capital of Qin, it had developed with fertile soil. For this reason, it is called heaven's land of plenty."[1]

Because of the location of the Guanzhong area, Lou Jing suggested making it the capital. As early as the Warring States Period, Su Qin had viewed Qin as a country with four fortresses. Zhang Shoujie from Tang Dynasty explained the geography in detail: "To the east are the Yellow River, Hangu, Pujin, Longmen, Hehe, and other passes; to the south are Nanshan, Wuguan, and Yaoshan; to the west are Dalong Mountain and Longshan Pass, Dazheng, Wulan, and other passes, and to the north is the Yellow River south pass, so it is called the country of four fortresses." Yellow River south pass refers to the Great Wall built by King Zhaoxiang of Qin in the Warring States Period. This Great Wall starts from Min County of Gansu Province, through northern Shaanxi, and reaches the Inner Mongolia Zhungeer banner. It is located south of the Yellow River north branch, so-called the Yellow River south pass. It was precise because of the situation in Guanzhong that Lou Jing submitted such a proposal. He further used the example of wrestling to persuade Liu Bang:

> The Qin's area was surrounded by mountains and rivers plus the four strong shields around. Even in a critical situation, millions of soldiers can still be gathered to prepare for a battle. Depending on the terrain of Qin and the fertile land, this is an area with dangerous terrain and abundant natural resources, truly a blessed land. If Your Majesty enters the Hangu Pass and builds the capital there, Qin can still guard their original territories even if there is trouble in Shandong. There is no guarantee for victory in a fight without grabbing him by the throat but hitting him on the back. If your Majesty

1. "A Biography of Liu Jing," in *Records of the Grand Historian*, vol. 99.

enters the Hanggu pass and establishes a capital there, you will control the original areas of Qin. That is to take the world by the throat and hit him on the back.

Here, Lou Jing discussed the geographic situation of Guanzhong. Financially, the area would be self-sufficient after many years of development and become fertile. In terms of military defense, Guanzhong has four strong shields surrounding it.

Great minds think alike. Zhang Liang, the master of strategy who had assisted Liu Bang in his conquest, shared Lou Jing's view. He even used similar words to persuade Liu, and mentioned the mountains to the southwest and north of Guanzhong, which could help prevent outside harassment. There were also major rivers for transportation and trade. In critical moments, the Emperor's army could ride down the river to pacify dukes. Indeed, these arguments impressed Liu Bang. Very soon, he ordered the people to move westward and establish the capital there.

Both Lou Jing and Zhang Liang agreed that placing the capital in Guanzhong would make it possible to control the entire country. Even if Shandong were lost due to insurgency, the monarchy could still be secure. Consequently, it would be better to build the capital around Xi'an rather than Luoyang.

Judging from the history of the Western Han, this prediction was correct. Soon after the Western Han was established, some dukes from different families started rioting against Liu Bang. There were the Wu and Chu riots, and another seven states against Emperor Jing—Liu Bang's grandson. The rebels boisterous, at the beginning, were completely pacified by the government several months later.

Therefore, although the Qin and Han dynasties were faced with different adversaries, both were faced with a threat from the east. The Qin State needed to deal with potential risks of the old nobilities in the six states in the east, while Han needed to deal with the separatist forces among the feudal princes in the east. This also applied to the transition period from the Qin to the Han. When Xiang Yu overthrew the Qin State, strategist Han Sheng also made similar suggestions to Xiang Yu as Lou Jing did to Liu Bang. Unfortunately, Xiang Yu was short-sighted and insisted on building his capital in Pengcheng, a place close to his hometown. Consequently, he was defeated by Liu Bang, who initiated his conquest from Hanzhong.

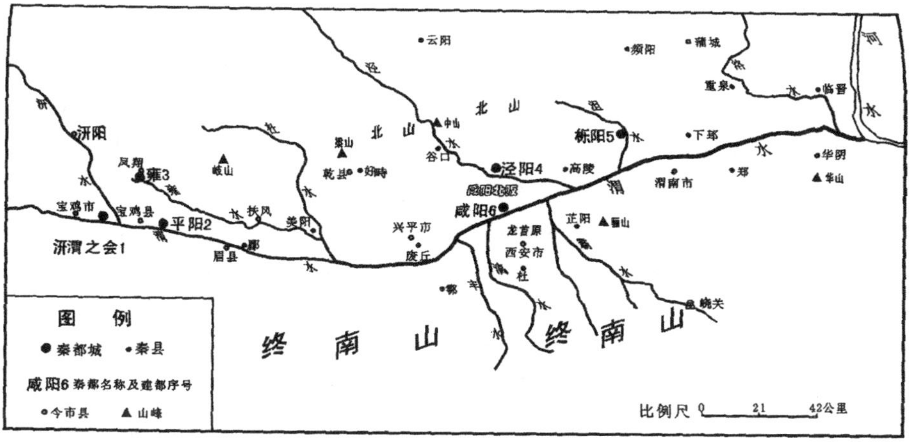

Fig. 3-1: A map of Guanzhong in the Qin and Han dynasties[2]

Lou and Zhang's argument on the capital focused on internal control by Guanzhong, when, in fact, the strongest enemies faced by the Qin and Western Han dynasties were the Xiongnu—a minority in northwest China. Establishing the capital in Guanzhong would be beneficial for defense against the Xiongnu. During the Qin era, Qin, with its capital advantage, reclaimed the Hetao area and occupied the areas in the southern part of the Yellow River to build the New Guanzhong. This was a blow to the Xiongnu.

The Han Dynasty was not powerful at first, so it dealt with Xiongnu harassment by intermarriage. However, since Emperor Wu, the country became more powerful and defeated the Xiongnu overwhelmingly in the northwest with Guanzhong as its base. The Han not only established five counties west of the Yellow River beyond the original Qin territory boundaries, but it also further extended its territory to the west. Most of the modern-day Xinjiang became part of its territory. Under such circumstances, Chang'an was not as far west, but was almost at the center of the nation in comparison to the past.

The debate and hesitation about where to set up the capital not only happened at the beginning of the Han—it was a dilemma for many later dynasties. At the beginning of the Tang, Turkic forces in the north were so powerful they often came to harass them near the Wei River. Some of Tang's senior generals and strategists

2. Li Huifu, *Urban Layout and the Geographical Foundation of Ancient Capital Xi'an* (Beijing: People's Publishing House), 3.

had no confidence in the security of Chang'an and suggested moving the capital. This suggestion was accepted by Emperor Gaozu of Tang, who intended to move the capital to the south of Nan Mountain. During this time, his son, Li Shimin, Prince of Qin was against the suggestion. Therefore, this idea was abandoned. Shimin could stand against the suggestion by the majority, partly because of the confidence in Tang's strength and partly by considering the geographic advantages of Guanzhong. Besides, only an active defense could help consolidate the borders and bring long-term stability of the country.

A similar situation also occurred in the early years of the Ming Dynasty. Zhu Di, Prince of Yan, was clear that the northern Mongolians were the main threat to the empire's national security based on his experience of living in the north as well as war experiences with the Mongolians. Therefore, after Zhu Di gained the upper hand in the fight for the throne with Emperor Jianwen, he moved the capital to Beijing for two reasons.

First, if he stayed in Nanjing, he would be restricted by the old imperial forces; more importantly, he could not control the situation along with the northern border defense. Second, if the capital were close to the enemy, he could remain alert and guard against possible threats. These examples point to the most important question in the establishment of capital—what factors should be considered when choosing a capital in ancient China?

From a political-geography perspective, there are several principles to consider. The first is a geographic location in relation to the entire territory. The second is the geographic environment of the location, including the natural environment and cultural foundations. In fact, the first factor can be subdivided into two sub-points: choose the geographic center of the whole country or a location advantageous to control the interior and exterior; whether this place is close to the origin of the ruling group.

The simplest, most common way of thinking would locate a country's political center in the geographic center, in order to facilitate effective administration. The *Master Lü's Spring and Autumn Annals*, written in the late Warring States Period noted: "the kings from ancient times would choose the center of their territory and establish their state." Here, state refers to the capital.

There are many similar descriptions in other books. For instance, *Xunzi* said: "If the king would like to get close to his territory at the four borders, staying in the center is the best choice. Therefore, the kings would stay in the center. This is a rite requirement." This statement was refined to illustrate the importance of being in the center of the world according to the regulations of the rites. Besides, *Guanzi*, another book, also said, "The king should stay in the center, and this should show us the importance of the strength of the sky and earth. The inside would be called the city, and the outside could be called settlements."

Thus, the idea of taking the geographic center as the capital could be described as the simplest. From the perspective of the history of capital construction in China, before the Tang Dynasty, the capitals were built in the Yellow River Basin due to the unification of political and economic centers. From a macro perspective, the center of the world is in the Three Rivers area. Academically, this is the core of political geography. From this view, the center would be located in the Three Rivers area. Where is this? Sima Qian once made a note on it: "In previous days, most of the Tang people were from east of the river, the Yin-Shang people lived within reach of the rivers, and the Zhou People lived in the southern part. Therefore, the Three Rivers area crossed each group and was an ideal location for the royal family."[3] Presently, this refers to an area of southeast Shanxi and northwest Henan. More specifically, the center of the world refers to Luoyang—located within the Three Rivers area. Many dynasties, including the Western Zhou and the Tang planned or established their capital here, based on its central location, to apply the philosophy of governing the world from the center of the world.

Even if the territorial center is the ideal location for the capital, it may not be the most appropriate or realistic position. Sometimes, military and economic factors played a more important role in deciding the location. For the peace and stability of the dynasty, it is necessary to control internal hostile forces on the one hand and resist external aggression on the other hand. In the balance of these two forces, the choice of capital location may deviate from the geographic center. Before the Tang, Guanzhong, where Xi'an was located with its advantageous higher ground, would command areas in the east with ease. As noted in the *Commentary of Salt and Iron*, "So that the vassal states had to submit respectfully to the State of Qin in the west." Just as Lou Jing's argument of the geographical strength of the four fortresses in the previous text, Guanzhong can defend itself and stay independent even if it fails to control the east. Luoyang, however, did not have this advantage despite its central location. If rebellions rose from other

3. *Records of the Grand Historian · Biographies of Merchants.*

palaces, it was difficult to maintain power. In terms of external defense, the dynasties up to the Tang were most threatened from the northwest, such as the Xiongnu in the Western Han and the Turks in the Sui and Tang dynasties. In such circumstances, it would be favorable to set up the capital in the front of anti-external forces to better defend the throne. Since the Song Dynasty, most of the external threats came from the north or northeast so the capital's location then moved and changed places accordingly.

Another factor contradictory with the geographical center principle is the location of the ruler's political base. There is a specific term in ancient China to describe it: *Dragon Rising Place*, which literally means the place where the future Emperor began his conquest. In Chinese history, the ruling class attempted to choose its capital near its political base; this is an important factor. Liu Bang once thought of building the capital in Luoyang because of its proximity to his hometown, Fengpei. This was also the hometown of many of his generals and soldiers. The most prominent is the relationship between the Guanlong Group in the Northern Dynasties and the Sui and Tang dynasties and building the capital in Guanzhong.

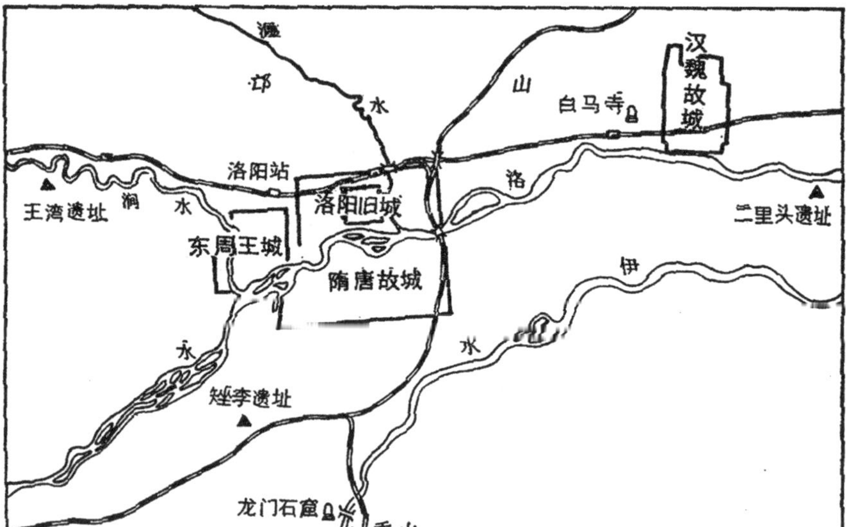

Fig. 3-2: A map of Luoyang[4]

4. Chen Qiaoyi, *China's Six Ancient Capitals* (Beijing: China Youth Press, 1983), 126.

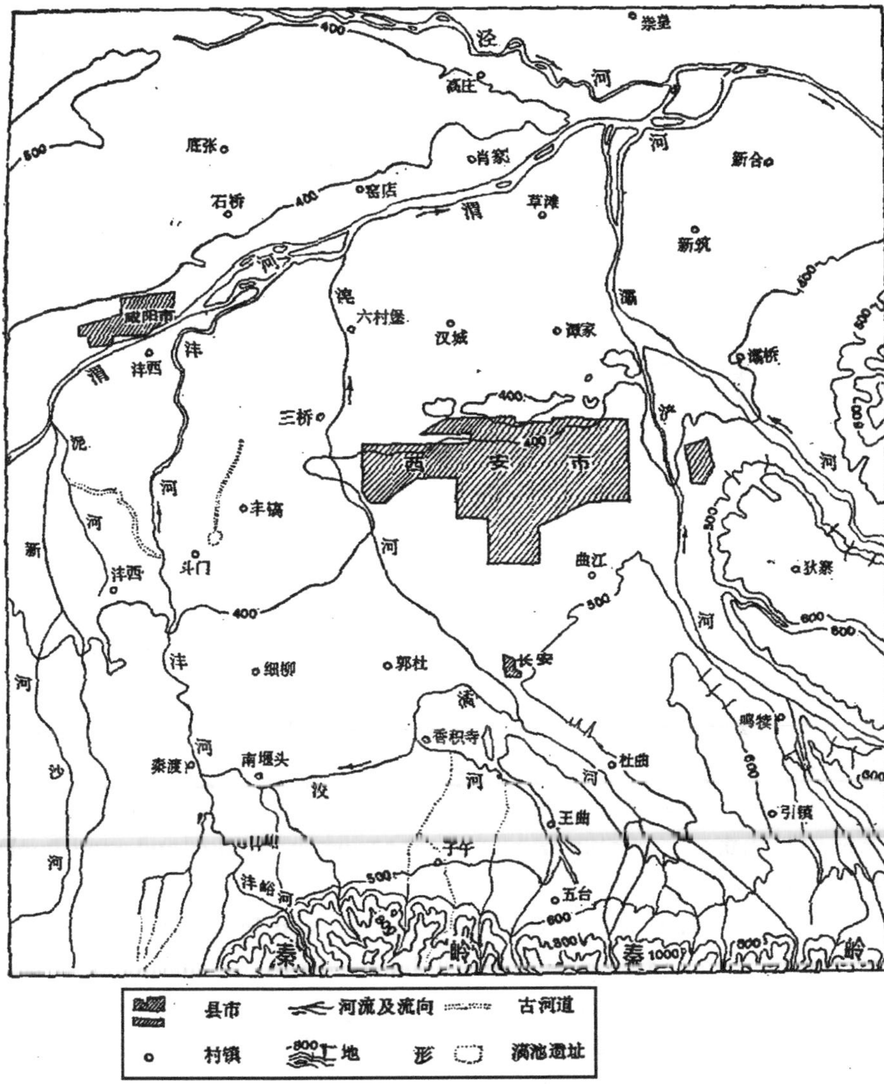

Fig. 3-3: A sketch map of Chang'an during the Sui and Tang dynasties[5]

5. Chen Qiaoyi, *China's Six Ancient Capitals* (Beijing: China Youth Press, 1983), 72.

The regulations and rites of Western Wei and Northern Zhou greatly influenced Sui and Tang. Sui and Tang inherited their capitals, Chang'an, from previous dynasties. In fact, Northern Zhou and even Sui and Tang formed their capitals in Chang'an and had a very close relationship with the Guanlong Group (a local clan that was very influential and which these dynasties had to depend on).

Yuwen Tai, the man behind the Western Wei regime, was once a follower of Heba Yue who conducted the conquest in Guanlong and received support of major influences from the Guanlong Group. Later, Yuwen Tai was defeated around Mang Mountain near Luoyang by Gao Huan, the actual controller of the Northern Wei. The former then expanded his power by recruiting people from the Guanlong Group, which later became the cornerstone of his power base. Later, when Northern Zhou overtook the Western Wei, they still had to rely on the Guanlong Group.

After Northern Zhou came to the Sui and the early Tang. These dynasties used the Guanlong Group as a pillar in their regime as well. However, the Western Wei and Northern Zhou were confined in a small area west of Hangu Pass with no choice but to have Chang'an as their capital and depend on the powerful Guanlong group. The situation changed dramatically after Yang Jian (first Emperor of Sui) overtook the Northern Zhou. At the time, the Northern Qi was destroyed, and the Chen withdrew to the south of the Yangtze. Still, Sui followed Wei and Zhou, remaining in Chang'an mainly to take advantage the Guanlong Group. Even during the early years of Tang, the situation changed little. Mr. Shi Nianhai, a famous history and geography expert, studied and wrote books on the Guanlong Group.[6]

This was not only the case with Zhou, Qin, Sui, and Tang, but also later with the Liao, Jin, Yuan, and Qing dynasties, all clinging to their original political bases. Even Zhu Wen of the Later Liang, Zhu Yuanzhang, and his son Zhu Di all acted in this way. Later, the national government of Nanjing during the Republic of China (1912–1949) also established their capitals in their political base. The saying, "I would rather only drink the water of Nanjing than to eat the fish of Wuchang," was coined by the Eastern Wu, whose political power remained in eastern China.

6. See Shi Nianhai, "The Geographical Factors in the Establishment of the Ancient Capital of China," in *Studies on Ancient Capital of China*, vol. 2 (Hangzhou: Zhejiang People's Press, 1986).

However, the political base has two sides. On the one hand, it might guarantee lasting stability of the dynasty; on the other hand, it might hinder the reform of those in power. Therefore, sometimes moving the capital became a means to shun the interference force. For instance, Xiaogong of Qin moved Qin's capital from Yueyang to Xianyang in an attempt to remove interference from the nobles opposed to reform. Emperor Xiaowen of the Northern Wei regime also moved the capital from Datong to Luoyang for the obvious purpose of reducing assimilation resistance with the Han.

Besides this, economics and geography were also important. Although it was common practice in Chinese history to deploy grain and other supplies from all over the country to meet the needs of the capital, the capital should be capable of meeting basic grain demands to avoid any disturbance, i.e., it should be partially self-reliant.

For instance, after the An-Shi Rebellion, the lifeblood of the Tang Dynasty depended on the supply of grain from the Southern Yangtze. During Emperor Dezong's reign, the grain supply once failed to arrive in the capital on time, so the royal guards began to plot against the Emperor. Fortunately, the grain arrived at last. Allegedly Emperor Dezong and his son hugged each other in tears and shouted: "We are saved finally!" Because of this, it was a reasonable demand to have a plan in place for growing grain near the capital.

Lou Jing emphasized how Guanzhong was like heaven on earth with a land of plenty. He took into consideration the proximity of agriculture to the capital. In the story of Emperor Dezong, the importance of transportation is underlined. After all, when a city with a large population is the political center of a country, it is inevitable that even with rich land surrounding it, it cannot provide sustainable supply in the long term. Therefore, the capital must be a transport hub as well as other things. Another important reason for this is not economic but political: convenient transportation can help control the entire country. This factor was mainly reflected in choosing Kaifeng as the capital of the Northern Song Dynasty.

At the beginning of the Northern Song Dynasty, Taizu, Zhao Kuangyin took Kaifeng as the political center but later decided not to use Kaifeng as its capital. In AD 976 (the ninth year of the Kaibao era), Zhao Kuangyin visited Luoyang and intended to make it the capital. However, his brother Zhang Guangyi and his ministers strongly objected. Zhang Kuangyin compromised by suggesting Chang'an for the capital.

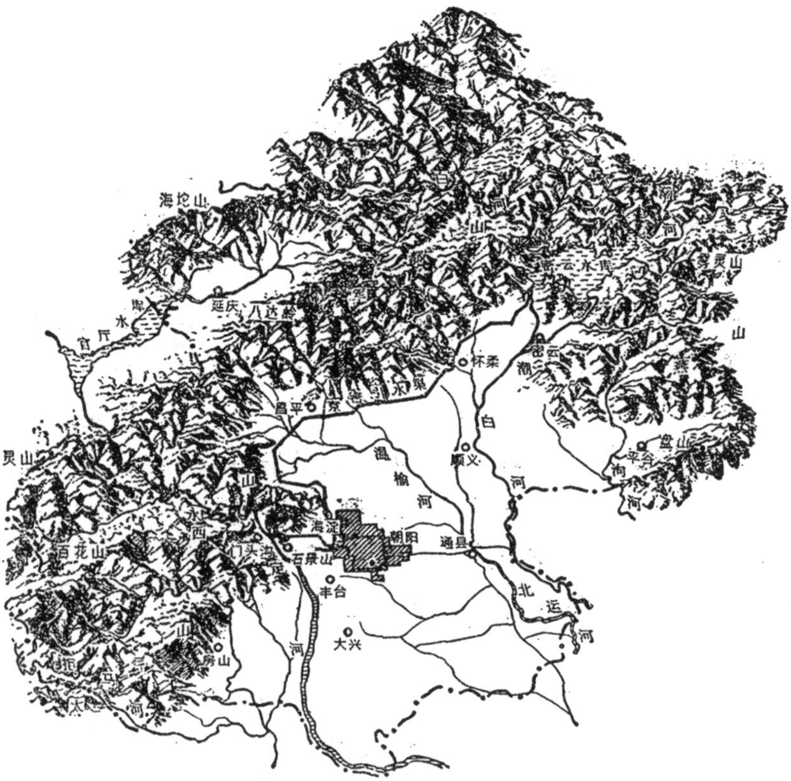

Fig. 3-4: A topographic map of Beijing[7]

Kuangyin stated that he wished to reduce the number of redundant soldiers by taking advantage of Chang'an's location; this also followed Zhou and Han traditions to bring peace to the country. However, this suggestion was also strongly opposed by the others, including his brother, who considered Kaifeng the optimum choice. They argued that despite Kaifeng being prone to attack from all directions, this could be remedied by a large number of troops. More importantly, Kaifeng was connected with the Yangtze and Huai Rivers through canals.

Of course, this choice was costly. Kaifeng of the Northern Song was the most heavily guarded among all dynasties. In spite of this, it could not withstand attack from the northern Jin cavalry, which led to the dynasty's demise.

7. Chen Qiaoyi, *Six Ancient Chinese Capitals* (Beijing: China Youth Press, 1983), 19.

2. Chang'an and Luoyang

Because of the several principles discussed above, ancient and medieval dynasties mostly chose Xi'an, Luoyang, Beijing, Nanjing, or Kaifeng as their political and administrative center. There are other options, but the five cities above are the long-lasting capital cities in 3,000 years of Chinese history. Xi'an, Luoyang, and Beijing were arguably the most important, whilst Kaifeng holds the shortest time as capital in Chinese history. Thus, some scholars argued Kaifeng was only a transitional ancient capital of China.[8]

From another perspective, these five cities could be divided into two groups: Xi'an, Luoyang, and Kaifeng on the horizontal axis, and Nanjing and Beijing on the vertical axis. The first group was mostly capitals during China's early history while the second group was capitals of later Chinese history. More explicitly, the shift of capitals was not as some scholars have argued—from Xi'an to Luoyang, from Luoyang to Kaifeng, from Kaifeng to Nanjing, and eventually Beijing. In reality, the situation is more complicated. There are often two capitals of equal importance that coexist in the same dynasty. For example, there were Xi'an and Luoyang during the 2,000 years from the Western Zhou Dynasty to the Tang Dynasty. Likewise, Luoyang and Kaifeng are in the same position from the end of the Tang Dynasty to the Northern Song Dynasty. Finally, during the 800 years from the Jin Dynasty to the present day, it is Beijing and Nanjing.

Xi'an as a capital began in the Zhou Dynasty. The Zhou tribe continually moved its political center from west of Guanzhong to the east, settling down at Feng during the reign of King Wen. However, Zhou was only a vassal state of the Shang Dynasty. Later, King Wu of Zhou moved the political center from Feng to Hao across the river. Soon, King Wu launched attacks against Zhou, the last King of Shang.

He overthrew the Shang and ruled the Central Plains. As King of a much bigger territory, King Wu probably thought Hao was too far west and would be difficult to govern. Luoyang, located in the center, would be better suited for controlling the East. Therefore, King Wu favored Luoyang. The *Book of Yizhou*

---

8. See Zhou Zhenhe, "East-West Oscillation and South-North Rotation: The Political-Geographic Factors in the Location of the Five Capitals in Chinese History," *Journal of East China Normal University (Social Science Edition)*, no. 1 (2009).

(A history of pre-Qin times) recorded the story of the king's intentions to build a capital in the Yiluo area. However, the construction of Luo was not completed until the Duke of Zhou was serving as Regent to King Cheng. The *Book of Yizhou* recorded the Duke's description of the building of Luoyi. The *Book of Zhou* recorded the Duke's description of Luoyi. He said, "On the morning of Yimao Day, I arrived in Luoyang. First, I augured in the Li River area, which is located the north of the Yellow River, and then the east of Jian River and west of Chan River. Among these areas, only Luoyang showed auspicious signs. I also augured at the east of Chan River, only Luoyang augur well. Therefore, I invite you to discuss more of the matter and present you the augury." He was very cautious when choosing the Luoyang, and in order to receive the divine right to rule through the city, he did not stop to ask for signs from heaven.

When Luoyi was complete, it became a co-capital with Haojing. Luoyi consisted of two sections: one was the king's city, the other was Chengzhou, implying it was a substitute for the capital. The original Zhou capitals (also called Zongzhou), Haojing, and Luoyi (also called Chengzhou) coexisted for a long time because of their respective advantages and disadvantages. Zongzhou was in Guanzhong with favorable geographical conditions and sufficient supplies of grain. The second is that Zongzhou is surrounded by fortresses, with barriers to rely on, which helps to resist the invasion of Rong and other minorities from the northwest.

More importantly, this was the home of Zhou's influence, the origin of its culture and the guarantee of political royalty. Despite all its merits, Feng and Hao had one fatal flaw—it was located too far west and was thus difficult to conduct administrative orders. Therefore, when it came to Eastern Zhou, the power of the throne declined and its ability to manipulate the situation both inside and outside of the country weakened. As a result, they had to move the capital east to gain further control and defy rebellions.

With its location in the center, Luoyang's merits included administrative convenience and the ability to collect taxes and payments from the whole country, as well as being a balanced transport hub for business exchange. Its demerits, as part of the Central Plains, were a vulnerability from attack in all directions—particularly the Xiaocheng Plains where Yiluo was located. In later times, the so-called holds the essential pass Chenggao in the east, with Mount Xiao and Mount Mian in the west, facing the Yi River and Luo River, back against the Yellow River. These were the excuses of those who advocated establishing Luoyang as the capital. When it comes to war, as Zhang Liang said, "Although there are fortresses, they are small in scale, only a few hundred *li*, the fields are thin, and the enemy can surround them on all sides. So Luoyang is not a good capital to defend." Compared with Guanzhong, where Fenghao's were located, Luoyang was far less secure from the outside to resist the enemy or from the inside to control the rebellion. If one must compare, arguably Feng and Hao still held the slight upper hand as a capital.

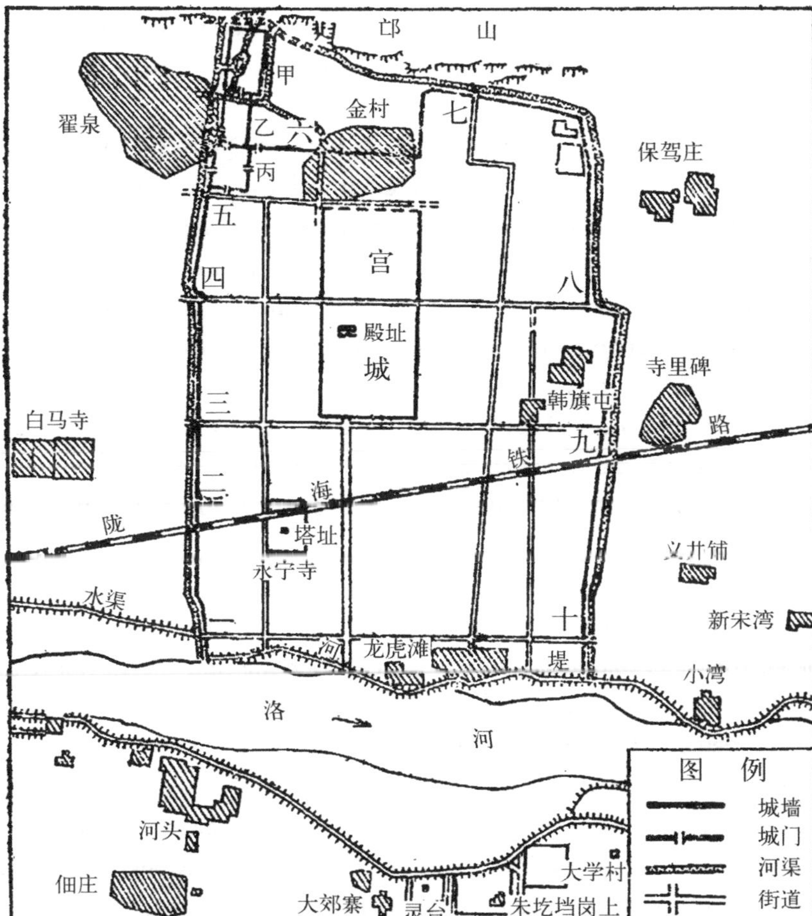

Fig. 3-5: A topographic map around Luoyang[9]

9. Chen Qiaoyi, *Six Ancient Chinese Capitals* (Beijing: China Youth Press, 1983), 140.

Similar to the Zhou people, the Qin also migrated from western China. The Qin moved their capital from west of Long Mountain to Yong, then to Yueyang, and finally Xianyang to the north of Wei River. The Qin state defeated the other six states with Xianyang as its base, which became its capital after unification.

After the Qin Dynasty was replaced by the Han, Liu Bang and his people came from the east, which differed from the Zhou and Qin people. This explains the story at the beginning of this chapter—where to establish the capital. In fact, because Liu Bang came from the east, he preferred Luoyang, the center of the country and close to his hometown, Fengpei. That was why he stayed in Luoyang for three or four months, but later, following the suggestions of Lou Jing and Zhang Liang, he realized that if he wanted to stabilize his throne, he had to go west to Chang'an.

Here a short analysis of the political situation of Qin and Han shows how people like Lou and Zhang were far-sighted. It was also admirable that Liu Bang listened to advice. Both Qin and Western Han faced the same strong enemy in the north—the Xiongnu. Building the capital in Guanzhong would be advantageous in fighting against powerful enemies. In fact, Qin reclaimed the Hetao area occupied by the Xiongnu for many years and developed this reclaimed area into a new part of Qin territory.

At the beginning of the Han Dynasty, the country's military strength was not strong enough. It could only use marriage alliance to deal with Xiongnu. After the reign of Emperor Wu, the state's military force grew more powerful. With the Guanzhong as its military base, Emperor Wu attacked Xiongnu in the northwest and achieved a landslide. The Han Dynasty not only took the five counties west of the Yellow River but also developed westwards and governed most of today's Xinjiang. The Han expanded its territory far beyond the Qin. These achievements could not have been attained if the capital had been established in Luoyang. By this time, Chang'an in Guanzhong did not look in the far, remote western corner but was almost the center of the national territory.

History often repeats itself: hundreds of years later, Tang Taizong also copied the story of Emperor Wu, who fought against the Xiongnu. The scenes were similar as well as the results—the territory border of Tang expanded to the Palmer Plateau just like before. In these times, if the Western Han, Sui, and Tang established their capitals in Luoyang, they could not claim land so far west due to the threat from the Xiongnu and the Turks.

Therefore, ambitious dynasties built their capitals in Chang'an, and those who were more content with their present state chose their capitals in Luoyang. This almost became a rule in early Chinese history. For instance, Eastern Han, which was far less powerful than Western Han, built its capital in Luoyang for preservation purposes. The following Western Jin Dynasty was even weaker than Eastern Han. Therefore, Luoyang was a natural choice. The period of the Wei State was before the Eastern Han Dynasty and after the Western Jin Dynasty, and its territory was only half of theirs. It is natural to choose Luoyang as its capital.

However, the situation changed. After the Sixteen States Period, the Northern Wei chose Luoyang as the capital, not for self-protection but to expand to the south. Thus, Luoyang had a significant advantage over Chang'an, which could not be used as a base. Only the Western Wei and Northern Zhou dynasties, which occupied western China, used Chang'an as their capital after the country's split. The Eastern Wei and the Northern Qi gave up Luoyang for Yecheng since these powers were influenced or even set up by the Xianbei Minorities. These regimes were either in charge by Han Chinese converted to Xianbei culture or sinicized Xianbei people. It was natural for them to build the capital city closer to the original Xianbei tribe. However, this period was concise, and the impact was limited.

Later, when the Sui rose to power on the foundation of the Northern Zhou, it would only be natural to inherit the capital of the Northern Zhou as its own. The Tang followed the Sui, continuing the tradition by adopting the capital and copying Sui regulations. Thus, many efforts were saved and proven highly productive. Still, there were some changes happening when compared with the Western and Eastern Han.

In the Sui and Tang dynasties, China's economic and cultural center was still in the Yellow River Basin, but it had lost its absolute advantage. Because of the Eastern Jin and Southern Dynasties' endeavors, the Yangtze River Basin became more prosperous. Jiangnan area has become an important pawn in balancing the whole of China. Therefore, although the Sui Dynasty built its capital in the Guanzhong area and carefully constructed a magnificent Daxing City, it still regarded Luoyang as important, apparently because Luoyang had easier control over the Yangtze River Basin. The same is true of the Tang Dynasty. Therefore, the Sui and Tang dynasties are different from the Qin and Han dynasties. Luoyang is as important as Chang'an and even has a little advantage.

Emperor Yang of Sui spent most of his time in Luoyang. Emperor Gaozong of Tang moved to Luoyang completely and renamed it the Eastern Capital. After his wife, Wu Zetian, declared herself the monarch, Luoyang became the official capital and Chang'an became an alternative capital. Later, the Li family regained power and changed the capital to Chang'an. Still, Luoyang was a favorite destination. Xuanzong sojourned there five times during the first part of his reign.

Clearly, by then, Chang'an could not compensate for its location in the country with its geographical advantage. This all indicates the implicit decline of Chang'an as a capital. Sure enough, by the end of the Tang Dynasty, Zhaozong was forced by Zhu Wen to move the capital to Luoyang. Hence, Chang'an lost its position as a capital for good. The only exception was when it served transitorily as the provisional/western capital of Later Tang (AD 923–936).

After the Northern Song Dynasty, Chang'an bid farewell to its position as the capital forever, even for its symbolic value. In the early Ming Dynasty, When Zhu Yuanzhang established the capital, Hu Ziqi, the imperial censor, thought that "Guanzhong was the most powerful place in the world because of the advantages of several rivers and mountains." Zhu Yuanzhang also thought so and appointed Zhu Biao, the Crown Prince, to inspect Shaanxi, which seemed to have the intention of establishing the capital. However, there were no follow-up moves after Zhu Biao returned to Nanjing. It seems that Zhu Yuanzhang's establishment of the capital of Guanzhong was only a temporary idea.

The last time Chang'an radiated briefly was during the Chinese National Government Period. After the January 28 Incident in 1932, the national government moved from Nanjing to Luoyang. Given the fact that Nanjing was on the front line, it would be difficult to preserve the status of the capital once the Sino-Japanese War broke out. Therefore, the Kuomintang held the Second Plenary Session of the Fourth Central Committee in Luoyang in March 1932. They decided to use Luoyang as the war capital and at the same time set up an alternative capital of Xi'an, naming it Xijing (western capital). The Kuomintang delegated Zhang Ji et al. to form the Xijing Preparatory Committee, which existed for about thirteen years (March 1932 to June 1945). Eventually, when the War of Resistance against Japanese Aggression was in full swing, Chongqing, instead of Xi'an, was chosen as the alternative capital.

3. The Central Hub of China: Kaifeng

For about 2,000 years, from Western Zhou to the Tang, the reason why the capital of China largely alternated between Luoyang and Chang'an is that from the recorded history until the mid-Tang Dynasty, China's cultural and economic center of gravity has always been in the Yellow River Basin. Compared to other places, the areas of Luoyang and Chang'an have a rich cultural heritage since they had a long history of serving as political centers and alternative capitals. They have accumulated years of imperial rules, regulations, and dress codes; other places could not rival this. However, in the late Tang era, the situation changed significantly as the cultural and economic center shifted to the south. This made it very difficult for Chang'an to remain as capital.

Therefore, before the mid-Tang Dynasty, unless for some special reasons, a unified dynasty's capital was only chosen between Chang'an and Luoyang. However, the situation changed after the mid-Tang Dynasty, with the southward relocation of the culture and economy center. Especially with the southward shifting of the economic center, it is hard to call Chang'an as capital; the example of Dezong of Tang mentioned above could explain this situation in detail. Not only Chang'an, because of the wealth in the Jiangnan area, Luoyang was also no longer the center of the country. Therefore, the status of the eastern city of Kaifeng has gradually increased. During the late Tang Dynasty, Kaifeng officially became its political center. However, this capital transition did not occur from Chang'an directly to Kaifeng, but had Luoyang in between as a kind of buffer. During this time, the Military Commissioner of the Xuanwu Branch, Zhu Wen, the actual controller of Tang's power at the time, forced Emperor Zhaozong to move the capital to Luoyang. Then, when Later Liang usurped Tang's power, he openly declared Kaifeng as his capital.

We assume that Later Liang choosing Kaifeng as its capital is a typical example of using one's own base as the capital. However, the real reason was the economic advantages of Kaifeng—it could channel riches into southern China through the canals. Still, because Luoyang was the capital for so many generations, Zhu Wen was determined to build the capital in Kaifeng and only chose Luoyang instead two years later. This was the first shift between these two capitals during the Five Dynasties Period. The Later Tang, who conquered Later Liang, moved back to Luoyang. However, Later Jin moved back to Kaifeng two years later, which continued as the capital until the Song Dynasty was destroyed.

In fact, when the Northern Song built its capital in Kaifeng, it had become an important economic center due to its advanced water transportation system. After the An-Shi Rebellion, northern China became the focus of a power struggle, and the economy of the middle and lower reaches of the Yellow River Basin was severely damaged. Many people migrated southwards and promoted economic development there. Kaifeng was fully developed because of its location at the center of the Grand Canal. In the Five Dynasties Period, Kaifeng became a large city in the north of China. It was recorded as "Controlling the Bian River, connecting Huai–Si River in the south, and Wei River in the north, a communication hub between ships and vehicles."[10] Therefore, it was inevitable that there was a shift in the political center of gravity from Chang'an and Luoyang to Kaifeng. The disadvantage of Kaifeng was its openness. Hence, it was difficult to defend. For this reason, Luoyang has always been an alternative capital.

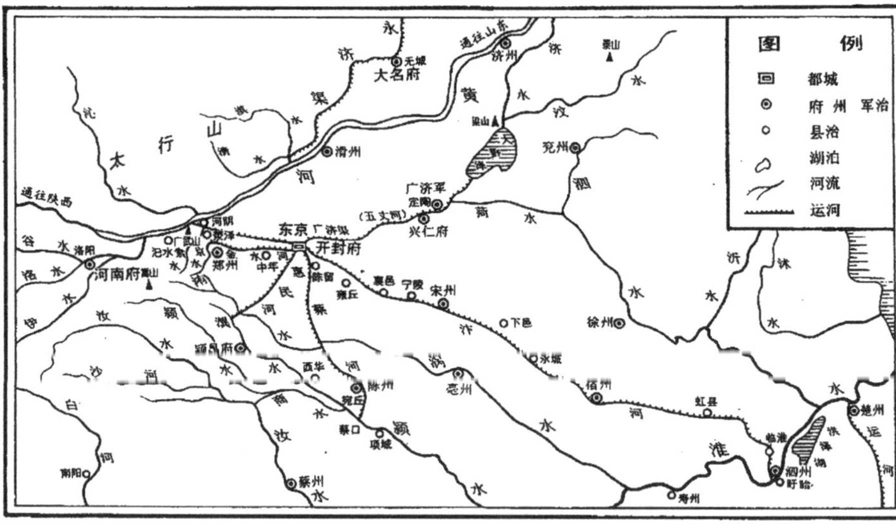

Fig. 3-6: A map of rivers around the Eastern Capital in the Northern Song[11]

10. *History as a Mirror*, vol. 274, quotes of Shi Jingtang, in March, the first year of Tiancheng, Mingzong's reign of the Later Tang Dynasty. Annotated by Hu Sanxing.
11. Zou Yilin, *An Outline of Chinese Historical Geography* (Shanghai: Shanghai Education Press, 2005), 340.

In AD 1214, after the Song Dynasty, Kaifeng was again selected as the capital. Then the Nüzhen (Jurchens) moved their capital to Nanjing and Kaifeng to avoid Mongol oppression. This lasted until AD 1233 (the second year of the Tianxing era), when Emperor Aizong of Jin fled and Nanjing fell. Since then, Kaifeng's position as capital or alternative capital has been vanquished. It was briefly used as the northern capital in the early Ming era, but otherwise remained a less important city.

If there was any possibility for Kaifeng to become a capital, it was at the beginning of Ming when Emperor Zhu Yuanzhang located his capital in Nanjing. Zhu Yuanzhang also ordered Kaifeng to be the northern capital. He admired the Song system so much that he copied it almost exactly—for instance, the three provincial offices: (1) Military Commissions, (2) Administration Commissions and Surveillance Commissions copied the Tax Transport Bureau, and (3) Stabilization Fund Bureau and Judicial Bureau. He even thought of building the capital in Kaifeng; however, by this time, the city's waterways had filled with silt. Thus, it lost its traffic advantage and could not become the national capital. Regardless, Kaifeng's title as the northern capital lasted for about ten years.

4. South-North Rotation

The building of capitals in the Yangtze River Basin really started in the Southern dynasties era. During the dividing period of the Wei, Jin, and Southern and Northern Dynasties, the focus of capital construction began to shift from Chang'an to Luoyang. It can be regarded as the beginning of the deviation of the capital from the east–west axis. For Northern dynasties, there was a chance to build the capital in Chang'an. However, for the Southern regimes, they could only build their capitals along the Yangtze. Different from the Yellow River Basin, it was difficult to determine a suitable location for the capital. Only one city had the right geographical location and economic factors—Nanjing.

Located in the Yangtze delta, Nanjing's agriculture was highly developed and economically prosperous, as well as occupying an extremely favorable location. From a military perspective, it faced the Yangtze River and was built upon a series of ridges. Zhuge Liang, a famous strategist during the Three Kingdoms Period, praised Nanjing profusely as an ideal for imperial residency. He said, "In

Jinling, the Zhong Mountain is like a dragon and crouches in the southeast, and the Stone Mountain is like a tiger in the western riverside. The terrain has the atmosphere of an emperor." Thus, since the end of Eastern Han, Nanjing was considered the optimum capital, even if the emperor could only control half the country.

At the end of Eastern Han, Sun Quan renamed Nanjing (then called Moling) as Jianye, and took it as the capital of Wu. It had been sixty years since the Eastern Wu Kingdom established its capital at Nanjing, except for the two brief relocations of the capital to Wuchang, which is today's Hubei Echeng. This was longer than the Ming Dynasty and Nanjing national governments. After the Youngjia Uprising, the Jin family established the Eastern Jin by changing Jianye to Jiankang. After that, Nanjing continued to be the capital of the Southern Dynasties (Song, Qi, Liang, and Chen). The six dynasties of Sun Wu, Eastern Jin, Song, Qi, Liang, and Chen, with Nanjing as their capital, ruled half of the regions south of the Huai River for 330 years. Historically, it is known as "the ancient capital of six dynasties," referring to this period in China.

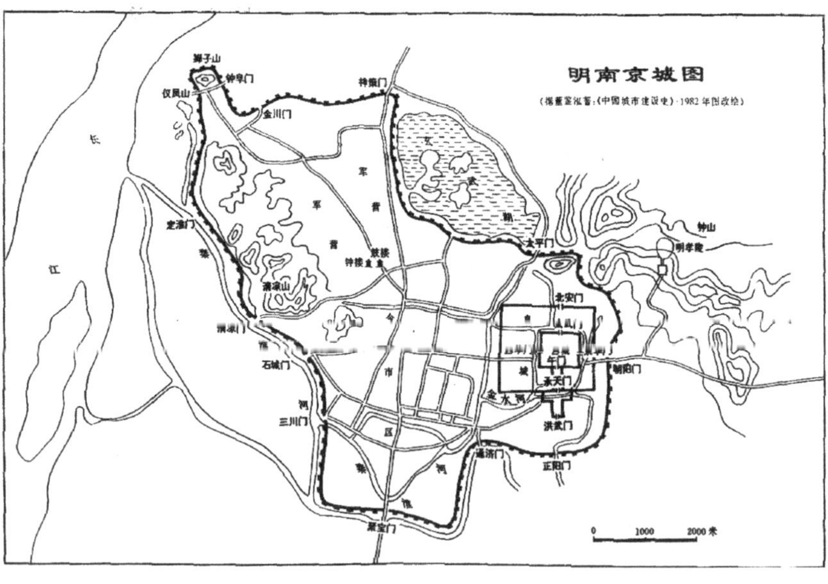

Fig. 3-7: A map of Nanjing[12]

12. Ma Zhenglin, *Historical Geography of Chinese Cities* (Jinan: Shandong Education Press, 1999), 231.

However, after the Southern and Northern Dynasties, Nanjing's status as a political center and capital declined. During the period when the Southern Song Dynasty conflicted with the Jin State, Nanjing should have been chosen as the capital based on the practice of the previous dynasties, but Emperor Gaozong of Song did not have the ambition to restore the Song Dynasty. He preferred to hide in Hangzhou, where he could have the Yangtze River and the Qiantang River as two defense lines. Therefore, the next time Nanjing was chosen as the capital is the Ming Dynasty and the Republic of China, these are the rare examples in Chinese history that the leader conquered the country from south to north, but the regimes both have only lasted for a concise period of time. In both cases, as power shifted north, Nanjing was replaced by Beijing.

Beijing might appear the obvious choice as the capital today, yet it has been on the margins of the Central Plains in China's long history. For centuries, Beijing was only the capital of a prefecture. Its crowning glory was a brief tenure as capital of the Yan State in the Western Zhou Dynasty. Although Yan was one of the seven major states during the Warring States Period, it was a weak state in northern China.

Early Beijing was rarely noticed because it was located far to the north of the Chinese civilization's core. Even none split dynasties that occupied half of the country never chose it as capital. However, with a political shift towards northern China, Beijing's status grew from a side city to a political center, eventually becoming the official capital.

After the mid-Tang Dynasty, minorities who threatened the Central Plains dynasties, and even entered the plains as the ruling class, came from northeast China. For example, the Khitans: they expanded their military forces gradually into the Central Plains, causing great threat to the regime—whether a separatist regime or a unified dynasty.

During the Five Dynasties Period, Shi Jingtang of Later Jin was forced to cede 16 prefectures to the Khitans, which enabled the tribe to extend their borders to the middle of today's Hebei. It placed part of its political function in Youzhou—today's Beijing. In the year AD 938, the Kihtans changed their regime into Liao and changed Youzhou into Youdufu, the southern capital. Later, Youdufu was renamed Xijinfu and functioned as the alternative capital. Since this was once the territory of Yan in the Warring States, it was sometimes called Yanjing. Today, Liao is paralleled as one of the Central Plains dynasties with the Northern

Song and the Western Xia dynasties. Beijing, as an influential capital, began its alternative capital status during the Liao Dynasty.

At the beginning of the 12th century, the Jurchens, a subgroup of Liao, rose to power and destroyed the Liao regime, and twelve years later, the Northern Song Dynasty. Then, the Jurchens established the Jin Dynasty across northern China. The southern border of Jin extended to the Qinling Mountains and Huai River, far beyond the borders of the Liao regime. Still, it had its base in the northeast. Imitating the Liao system, Jin used the southern capital of Liao as its capital and changed its name officially to Yanjing.

Apparently, it's due to the concern that the southern territory would be too distant to govern. In AD 1153, to strengthen control over the Central Plains, Jin moved its capital from Huiningfu (today Acheng, Heilongjiang) to Yanjing and renamed it Zhongdu (Middle Capital) Daxingfu. This was the first time that Beijing had become a capital.

At the beginning of the 13th century, the Mongols rose to power in the northern prairie and conquered China by storm. Soon after they obliterated Jin, Kublai Khan moved the capital from Kaipingfu on the Mongolian Plateau to Jin's Zhongdu. They also changed its name to Dadu (Big Capital). Since then, Beijing has been the capital of half of the country. Although there was a brief change to Nanjing, this was for a relatively short period.

The Jin and Yuan dynasties were faced with similar situations. They needed to conquer the Central Plain regimes in the south, as well as take care of their own base. Thus, Beijing was ideal for the capital. The small area of Beijing Plain is located in the northernmost part of the Northern China Plain. It goes down from the north and passes through the foothills of the Taihang Mountains to reach the core area of the Central Plains. Further up north, it enters the Mongolian grasslands through the mountain passes of the Yan Mountains and then to the northeast, where the border road enters from the Bohai Gulf to the Songliao Plain. The situation that the Mongolian Plateau and the Northeastern Regions were brought under the control of the Central Plains after the Jin and Yuan dynasties make Beijing became the best choice for building a capital city. This was explicitly pointed out by a Jin-man named Liang Xiang, who said: "Yandu (Beijing) is located in a strategic position, with mountains to the north and the Central Plains to the south. It is like sitting in a high hall and looking down into the yard. It will be very easy to defend with passes, such as Juyong, Gubei, and

Songting around, and a flow of steep ridges extends thousands of miles from east to west." This is a favorable geographic position.

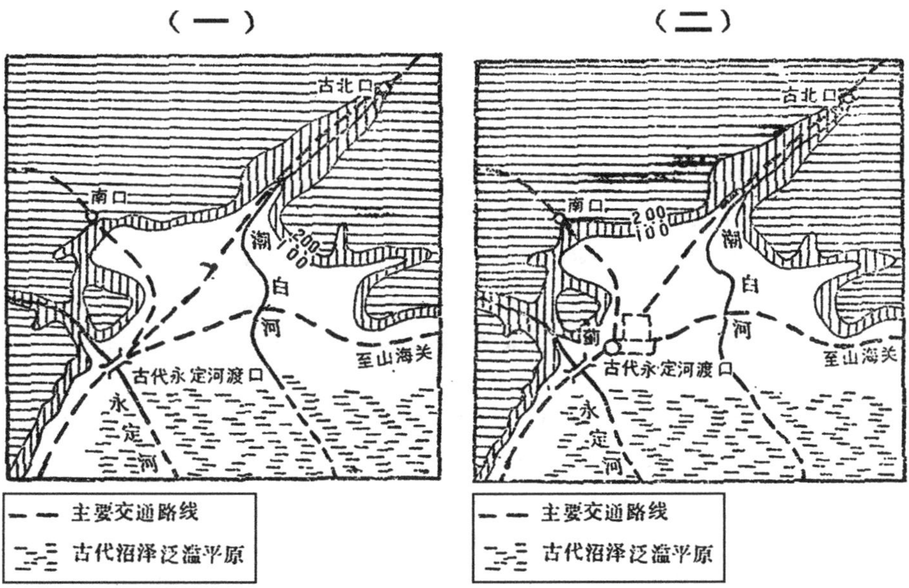

Fig. 3-8: A geographical map of Beijing[13]

When the Qing began their reign of China, they continued the stance of the Jin and Yuan. Starting in northeast China, it seemed there was no better place for a capital than Beijing. In fact, a multi-ethnic empire was established during the Qing Dynasty, covering almost all the Mongol tribes in the north, the Junggars, the Muslim regions in the northwest, and Tibet in the southwest. Hence, the geographical location of Beijing was not considered too far north. Besides, for nearly 700 years Beijing has served either as an alternative capital or capital.

Later, the Beiyang government of China and the People's Republic of China after 1949 both acknowledged the importance of the city. It can be said that only Xi'an/Chang'an can compete with Beijing. The difference between these two cities lies in the fact that Xi'an is in the west and reigns east, while Beijing is in the north and reigns south. Of course, this is also determined by the political structure in Chinese history.

13. Chen Qiaoyi, *Six Ancient Chinese Capitals* (Beijing: China Youth Press, 1983), 180.

Before the Tang, the eastern regions of the Taihang Mountain Range, namely, the lower reaches of the Yellow River Basin, had political and economic forces to compete with Guanxi. The political structure during this time was a confrontation between east and west China. After the Song, the political structure changed dramatically, and the real divide was between the north and south, which suited Beijing instead of Chang'an. When choosing the capital city, the political structure is one of the most critical factors in Chinese history and a deep-rooted traditional view. This factor sometimes outweighs the importance of the economic center and the belief that the capital should be the center of the world. Xi'an and Beijing are the two most outstanding capitals throughout history.

Moreover, for the northern minorities to build the capital in Beijing, their motives are highly practical. For example, after the Yuan Dynasty was defeated by the Ming Dynasty and retreated to the north, the Northern Yuan Dynasty still existed for a long time. The Mongolian Yuan's successor, Tartar Wala, also posed a significant threat to the security of the Ming Dynasty.

Similar to the relationship of Chang'an and Luoyang, Beijing and Nanjing coexisted and developed with one another. A typical example was during the Ming—Zhu Yuanzhang became Emperor in AD 1368 and established the capital in Nanjing. Unfortunately, this situation did not last long. His son, Zhu Di (later Emperor Yongle), seized the throne from his nephew. And he had completely different ideas from his father—he planned to move the capital to Beijing for several reasons.

First, Beijing was his base. Second, according to tradition, his throne was usurped and was not a natural inheritance. Therefore, by avoiding Nanjing, the capital his father established, he avoided problems associated with it. However, the most important factor was probably because the main enemy of the Ming were the forces that fled to Mongolia. With the capital in Beijing, it would be easier to fight these enemies. This last factor could be proven by Zhu Di's experiences. He expedited warriors six times to Mongolia from Beijing. Therefore, the establishment of the capital of Beijing played a positive role in strengthening the border defense of the Ming Dynasty.

Still, because his father decided on Nanjing as the capital, Emperor Yongle could not change it immediately. Thus, the first step was to change Beiping to Beijing and raise its status to the alternative capital in AD 1403 (the first year of Emperor Yongle's reign). Later, the Emperor made three tours to Beijing—during the seventh, eleventh, and fifteenth year of his reign. After the third tour, he never returned to Nanjing. Gradually, the functions of the capital moved. In AD 1421, he formally moved the capital to Beijing and renamed it Jingshi.

However, Emperor Yongle's descendants thought differently and wanted to return to Nanjing. As a result, there was an oscillation between the two cities during the Ming era. After the death of Emperor Yongle, Emperor Renzong made Beijing the alternative capital in AD 1425 and intended to return to Nanjing, but after his early death, this plan was dropped.

The plan to move south was not fulfilled by later emperors, such as Xuande and Zhengtong. In AD 1441, the "provisional" was officially dropped from Beijing, and it finally became the full capital. In total, this drawn-out process took around seventy years. The oscillation not only showed the complexity of external factors when deciding the location but also reflected the internal mental state of the emperors who had the right to decide. Emperor Yongle naturally wanted to move the capital to Beijing, but it was delayed for 19 years, during which he spent nearly half of his time in Beijing to handle state affairs or use Beijing as a base to conduct personal expeditions. But when he left Nanjing, his crown prince Hongxi was in Nanjing to supervise the country; and Hongxi was generous and kind, and he also had considerable affection for his grandfather Zhu Yuanzhang's capital in Nanjing, so he wanted to move back to Nanjing. Just because he had only been emperor for one year, it was too short to complete this task. When it came to his crown prince Xuande Emperor, he thought differently. Although he planned to move the capital as his father planned, as the grandson of Emperor Yongle, he was by his side during his grandfather's expedition to Mongolia. He was aware that the defeated Mongolian army could still pose a threat. Therefore he was not in high spirits regarding moving back to Nanjing. After decades of operation, Beijing was indeed better than Nanjing as a national capital in many aspects. After these numerous oscillations, the capital of the Ming Dynasty was finally chosen as Beijing. Still, Nanjing as the previous capital had a higher status than most alternative capitals. It included six major ministries like Beijing, which was unprecedented in other dynasties. Of course, this is a tribute paid to the system of their ancestors.

During the Republic of China (1912–1949), the political foundation of the Beiyang Government was in northern China. Thus, Beijing was an obvious choice for the capital. However, when the government was established by the

Kuomintang, its political foundation was in Jiangsu and Zhejiang provinces. The actual control areas did not reach the scope of the Qing Dynasty; therefore, it was natural to choose Nanjing. Another important reason why Nanjing was chosen as the capital of the early Ming Dynasty and the Republic of China was that the unification of both was completed from the south to the north. In the Yuan and Qing dynasties, the situation was just the opposite. Therefore, the capital, the military headquarters, plays a significant role in selecting the city's location.

British geographer, V. Cornish, studied the geographical conditions of China's capitals in great detail and noted three main requirements: the first is a natural storehouse—the capital is rich enough in resources and abundant food to satisfy demands. The second is logistics—if it's located at the intersections of major trade routes, transport will be more convenient. The third is fortification—how easy it is to defend.[14] These three points are vital for capital.

Xi'an fits the requirements of these three conditions: though it is not in the center of the country, which could be inconvenient to the national administration—yet, Xi'an is located at the crossroads, reaching beyond the Long Mountains in the west, to Bashu in the south, the Central Plains in the east, and Mongolia in the north. It is very convenient and can compensate for the defect that it is not in the geometric center.

Luoyang only met one of these conditions—logistics; therefore, as a capital, it is inferior to Xi'an. Additionally, both Xi'an and Luoyang are appropriate capitals of dynasties built by the Han in the Central Plains, with the political and economic center located in the Yellow River Basin reaches. When the economic center shifted to the Yangtze region while the political center moved to the north, the capital was split between the south and north. For this reason, Beijing and Nanjing were more important. Between economic and political factors, political factors were understandably considered more vital, indicating Beijing's prevalence over Nanjing.

However, there was one very important factor that Cornish did not mention: the so-called geographical circumstances of Chinese tradition—the political and geographical features of sitting condescendingly in the east and overseeing the west, or sitting high in the north and managing down in the south. One is momentum, and the other is the terrain. When applied to politics, this geographical

14. V. Cornish, *The Great Capital* (London, 1923).

feature becomes a political, geographical factor. This is extremely important in positioning China's capital, which can also be said to be a feature of Chinese culture and human geography.

Gu Zuyu, in *A Concise Record of Geographic History of China,* pointed out that "Shuntianfu (today's Beijing) was not only surrounded by steep mountains but also flowing rivers. Sitting on the ridge of the country, Shuntianfu had the entire country firmly under its control. It was like a heavenly gift." A capital needs "such kinds of affirmations." When talking about Shaanxi, i.e., Guanzhong, Gu Zuyu said: "They were on the upper reaches of the country and in control of the country's fate. If Shaanxi decided to rise and start small, it would grow big. The weak would become strong. Even if it could not become the number one capital in the country, Shaanxi would still create a huge uproar ... Shaanxi to China is like the head to a person. If the head is under attack, then the person will surely die. If the person stays alive, then the person's trouble must not be a real one." Therefore, for the ancient capitals of China, Xi'an is superior to Luoyang in theory, and Beijing is superior to Nanjing. By this concept, Xi'an and Beijing are China's two most suitable capitals.

CHAPTER FOUR

DU AND *JING*: CAPITALS AND ALTERNATIVE CAPITALS

A capital's location choice is very important for any dynasty. Hence, political, economic, cultural, and transport factors were considered critically when choosing this. However, in reality, not all requirements can be met, and there are always some anomalies. Even the best choices, such as Xi'an/Chang'an and Beijing, have been proven by history to have some drawbacks. For instance, Xi'an was established in far western China most of the time, while Beijing was nearer the northern borders.

To compensate for these problems, Emperors would choose another, more appropriate location as an alternative capital. Sometimes, one alternative capital would not suffice and multiple alternative capitals were set up. In fact, capitals could be located in the center, north, south, east, and west—this was called the Five Capitals System.

1. The Eastern and Western Capitals

In Chinese history, it was not uncommon for capitals and alternative capitals to coexist. Among them, the most famous are Zongzhou and Chengzhou of the Western Zhou Dynasty. The Zhou continually moved their political center from the west of Guanzhong to the east in order to expand their territory. King Wen and his son, King Wu, established Feng and Hao after they destroyed the most important vassal state of the Shang. The *Book of Songs* recorded this event: "Under the orders of King Wen, who has the momentum of martial arts and conquered the Chong state and built Fengyi City, which is beautiful. King Wen is a great king! ... Augur my king for good fortune, picked a good place Gaojing as capital, rely on fortune turtle to set project, King Wu's achievement surely worth praising, King Wu is a great King." King Wu moved the capital further east to show his determination to conquer the Shang people. Judging from historical documents, in general, Feng and Hao were one city, although they were divided by the Feng River. After the establishment of the Zhou regime, Feng and Hao served as a single capital called Zongzhou.

After the Zhou eradicated the Shang, it quickly expanded to the vast east—the lower reaches of the Yellow River Basin. This expansion necessitated the creation of bases eastwards. Luoyang, located in the center, now became the first choice for King Wu. After Luoyi (Luoyang) was completed, it coexisted with Zongzhou, which functioned as an alternative capital. However, Chengzhou was always the base for the Zhou people to subdue the hostile forces in the East.

Zongzhou's political and economic factors were good. However, its geographical position in the western corner of China made it inconvenient for ruling eastern parts of the country; a more central position was necessary and Luoyi was directly in the center. Yet, Luoyi was difficult to defend since it was open in all directions. Therefore, it could only serve as an auxiliary location.

Although we have mentioned that more aggressive dynasties would choose Chang'an as their capital, while those more conservative would select Luoyang, even strong dynasties would use Luoyang as the alternative capital if the dynasty's focus was on the east, despite establishing their capital in Chang'an. This is common during early Chinese history.

From the Sui to the mid-Tang era, Chinese economic and cultural centers were still located in the Yellow River Basin but had lost absolute dominance. Population growth promoted sustained economic prosperity and it became an important region for generating tax income for the central government. Therefore, even the Sui and Tang dynasties, which based their capitals in Chang'an, valued Luoyang greatly. Emperor Yang of the Sui Dynasty often lived in Luoyang. Emperor Gaozong of the Tang Dynasty moved to Luoyang, known as the Eastern Capital, forming the system of two capitals. After Wu Zetian proclaimed herself as emperor, in order to prevent the interference from the Li family of the Tang Dynasty, she moved the capital to Luoyang and changed Chang'an the original capital, into an alternative capital.

Today, the capital of China is called Beijing (literally the northern capital) because it was the product of the dual-capital system. Emperor Taizu of Ming positioned the capital in Yingtian and renamed it Jingshi. However, his son, Zhu Di, moved the capital to the north, and the original capital was renamed Nanjing (literally the south capital). Later, Emperor Renzong moved the capital back to Nanjing and changed Beijing into the provisional capital. During the reigns of Emperor Xuande and Zhengtong, the plan failed. Finally, in AD 1441 (the sixth year of the Zhengtong era), Beijing officially declared the capital of the Ming Dynasty. However, the dual-capital system began in the first year of Yongle. In addition, compared with the dual-capital system of other dynasties, Nanjing, as the remaining capital, had a higher position than the general deputy capital and even had six ministries like Beijing. This situation has never occurred in the previous dynasties.

2. The Five Capitals System

The Liao Dynasty was established by the Khitan tribe in northeast China. Emperor Taizu (original name Yelü Abaoji, 耶律阿保机) of Liao, started building a city in Linhuang in AD 918 and named it the imperial capital. In AD 928 (the third year of Tianxian), Emperor Taizong promoted Dongpingjun as his southern capital. Then, in AD 938, Shi Jingtang, Emperor of the Later Jin Dynasty, presented the Sixteen Prefectures of Yan and Yun to Emperor Taizong of Liao, Yelü Deguang. And sent his envoys to present the honorific title to the Khitan. In accordance with the Han rites system, Yelü Deguang sat on the throne of the imperial palace and received the ceremony at Chengtian Gate.

He changed his era's name to Huitong and the imperial capital to Shangjing (supreme capital). Emperor Taizong promoted Youzhou to Youdufu as the southern capital, and changed Dongpingjun, the southern capital, to the eastern capital Liaoyangfu; thus, forming the one-capital-two-alternative-capital system.

Emperor Shengzong changed Youdufu to Xijinfu, and in AD 1007, added the central capital, Dadingfu. Emperor Xingzong established Yunzhou as the western capital, Datongfu. Together, these were called the "Five Capitals."[1] This system was not formed suddenly but was influenced by the capital system of the Central Plains from the Tang, the Five Dynasties, and the Northern Song, including influence from the Bohai State. It also had a direct impact on the Jurchen capital system.

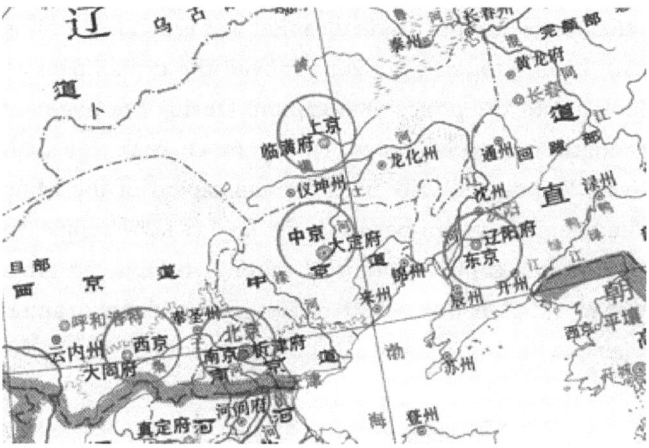

Fig. 4-1: Location map of the Five Capitals in the Liao Dynasty[2]

Among the Five Capitals of Liao, Shangjing was established by the earliest Khitan people and remained the political center of Liao. The Shangjing ruins were located south of today's Lindong Town, Balin Zuoqi, and Inner Mongolia. About 14 kilometers in circumference, it is consistent with the 27 *li* (500 meters per *li*) description mentioned in various historical documents. From these, we can ascertain that it was the administrative location of the central government and the living quarters of the Khitan aristocrats.

When an envoy from the Song Dynasty—Xue Ying—visited Liao, he recorded the imperial city contained two palaces, Zhaode and Xuande, and yurts facing east.[3] It was clear the Khitans still lived in yurts; facing east is also a Khitan tradition. The Han section of the city could be considered an outer settlement, where Han people and residents from other ethnic groups lived. Judging from this, it seemed that the Shangjing of Liao retained the original customs of the Khitans.

1. See Yang Kuan, *Studies on Ancient Chinese Capital System History* (Shanghai: Shanghai People's Press, 2003), 442.
2. Adapted from Tan Qixiang, *Chinese Historical Atlas*, vol. 6 (Beijing: SinoMaps Press, 1987), 3–4.
3. Quoted in *History of Liao · Geographical Annals.*

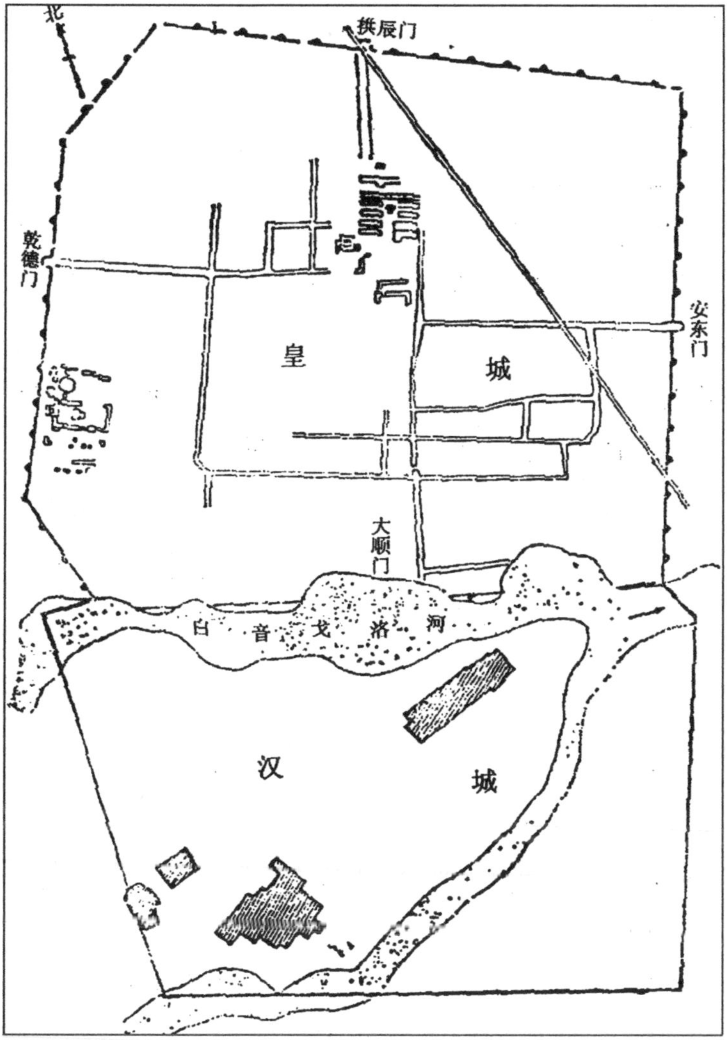

Fig. 4-2: Plan of Shangjing of Liao[4]

With the Khitans growing in power, Liao Taizu conquered Bohai State in AD 926, took its territory, established the eastern Dan State, and declared the crown prince as king. However, when Emperor Taizu died that year, his younger son (Liao Taizong) took the throne, and the crown prince had to flee. In AD 928,

4. Yang Kuan, *Studies on Ancient Chinese Capital System History* (Shanghai: Shanghai People's Press, 2003), 444.

Emperor Liao Taizong moved the inhabitants of Longquanfu to east Pingjun and elevated it to the southern capital. In AD 938, the southern capital was changed to Liaoyangfu.

The eastern capital, Liaoyangfu, was located near the present Liaoyang. From the records of *History of Liao · Geographical Annals*, we know the city structure was similar to Shangjing's—it both coexisted with Khitan and Han towns, respectively, in a dual-city system. Within Khitan, there were portraits on the palace walls of the crown prince who abdicated the throne. This is very different from other ordinary cities. Yet judging from the markets, which would gather in the morning and disperse in the evening in the Han part of the city, its urban development was still at an early stage.

At the beginning of the Five Dynasties, Youzhou belonged to Later Tang. Because Liao Taizong helped Shi Jingtang, the Military Commissioner of Later Tang, to rebel, Shi offered the Sixteen Prefectures of Yan and Yun as a reward to the Khitans; hence, elevating Youzhou to Youzhoufu as the southern capital. Later, during Emperor Liao Shengzong's reign, the southern capital was changed to Xijinfu. However, because it was once Yan territory, it was also called Yanjing.

Since Nanjing, the capital of the Liao Dynasty was the previous capital of the Central Plains, it was obviously more prosperous than Shangdu and Eastern Capital, which were located in the north of Yan Mountains.[5] The scale of the city was also larger, about 26 or 27 *li* around. Most of the imperial cities in the southwest adopt the architectural design of Youzhou in the Tang Dynasty. The city is divided into 26 squares, each with a gate marked with the square's name, most still using their old names from the Tang Dynasty. It was a thriving place: The *History of Liao · A Biography of Emperor Shengzong* said in AD 1025, "that night, the streets were lit as day, and both nobles and commoners were on the street, enjoying themselves. Even the Emperor disguised himself to join in such a celebration of great harvest."

Built in AD 1007 during Emperor Liao Shengzong's reign, the central capital, Dadingfu, was located in today's Damingcheng Laohahe, Inner Mongolia. It was said that when Emperor Liao Shengzong passed the Laoha River near the Nine Head Mountains, he saw clouds resembling a city with buildings. Thus, he decided

5. Yang Kuan, *Studies on Ancient Chinese Capital System History* (Shanghai: Shanghai People's Press, 2003), 446.

to build a capital here. Craftsmen were recruited to construct a heaven-given capital with all the settlements, palaces, pavilions, offices, markets, and verandas.

History of Liao · Geographical Annals recorded that there were the portrait palaces of Emperor Jingzong and Empress Suntian, acting as the imperial ancestor worship temples. Also, Datongyi was built as the reception place to meet with Song envoys, Chaotian Hall, and a Guest Residence to meet with western Xia envoys. The entire structure was modeled on the eastern capital of the Northern Song and had three components—the outer city, the imperial city, and the palace city. The central capital was very prominent, even within these Five Capitals.

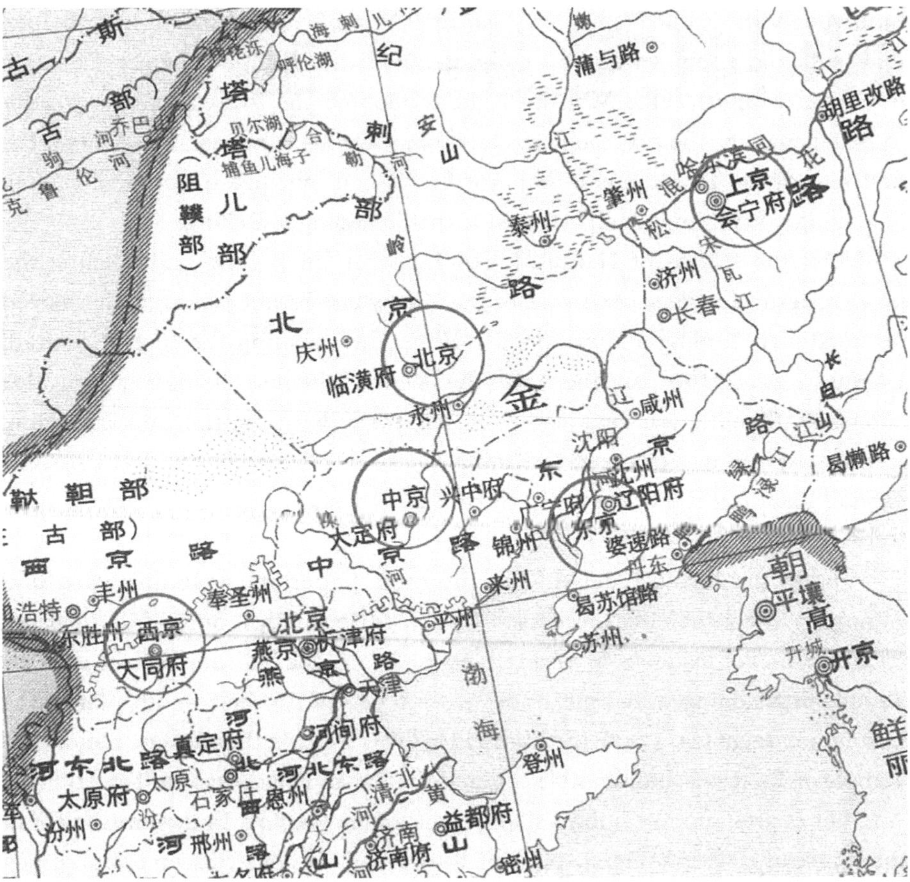

Fig. 4-3: Plan of the Five Capitals in Jin[6]

6. Adapted from Tan Qixiang, *Chinese Historical Atlas*, vol. 6 (Beijing: Atlas Press, 1987), 44–45.

Located in today's Datong in Shanxi, Datongfu, the western capital of Liao, was also the last capital among the five established by the dynasty. In AD 1044, during Emperor Liao Xingzong's reign, Yunzhou was elevated to Datongfu, the western capital. The city's design was the simplest among the five and added very little to its base. Still, it had temples with stone or bronze statues of emperors to be worshipped. These statues distinguished Yunzhou from other city capitals.

After rising from the Ashi and Lalin River areas in today's Heilongjiang, the Wanyan tribe of the Jurchen Dynasty established its capital south of Acheng County, located southeast of Harbin. When the country was first established, there were no outer city walls, and the names of the scattered buildings were the Emperor's Villa, Prime Minister's Villa, and Crown Prince's Villa.[7] It was obvious that tents and temples were still constructed as they had been before. Emperor Jin Taizu (original name Wanyan Aguda) adopted the five-capital city system to better manage the previous Liao territory after his conquest. In AD 1138, the first year of the Tianjuan era, Emperor Jin Xizong renamed his original capital, Shangjing, to Huiningfu and changed Liao's Shangjing to Beijing.

Later, the Prince of Hailing killed Emperor Jin Xizong and became the new Emperor. In the second year of the Zhenyuan Period (AD 1152), he moved his capital to Yanjing and renamed it Zhongdu (meaning the central capital), Daxingfu to further expand into the Central Plains. Shangjing was also abolished, Bianjing was renamed as Nanjing (southern capital), and Zhongjing (central capital) was changed to Beijing. These three, together with the eastern capital, Liaoyangfu and the western capital, Datongfu from the previous Liao, were collectively called the Five Capitals.

Among the Five Capitals of Jin, the most important were Shangjing and Zhongdu. The remaining three used Liao's previous cities, only adding palaces and temples. For instance, in AD 1114, Jiahui Palace, the Bedroom Palace, and the Temple of Xiaoning were built in the eastern capital. In the seventh year of the Huangtong reign (AD 1147), the Yurong Hall was built. In the western capital, the Temple of Taizu was built in AD 1125, and the Baoan Palace was built in AD 1165. Another reconstruction is the Kaifeng Mansion in Nanjing. In the fourth year of the Prince of Hailing's reign (AD 1159), he ordered the construction of the ruined

7. "The System of Yanjing," in *Chronicles of the Great Jin State*, vol. 33.

palace. It is also like Dading Mansion in Beijing. After modern archaeological excavations and investigations, it is known that the Jin Dynasty only built a small castle in the imperial city, which was superimposed on the original palace site of the Liao Dynasty. Each side of the castle was about 180 meters in length, and the gate faced to the east. It is probably where the prominent offices of the Jin Dynasty were located.

Yet, Shangjing and Zhongdu were built on a large scale, and their previous designs were completely changed. Although Aguda established the capital in Shangjing, there was no innovation in urban construction, and still applied the original tribal tent system. Emperor Jin Taizong built the new city of Shangjing and renamed it Huipingzhou in AD 1124. A decade later, more new palaces and ritual buildings were constructed in Shangjing, such as the Hall of Qianyuan, and Qingyuan Palace. And then, he built the Imperial Ancestral Temple, Altar of Grain, so that the name of palaces and religious sites could match. The current remains of the city show it had two connecting cities from south to north. Also, it had mountains to the west and the Ashi River to the east. It's like a curved ruler. The northern city is 1,828 meters long from north to south and 1,553 meters wide from east to west, while the southern city is 1,528 meters long from north to south and 2,148 meters wide from east to west. The existing city wall is about three meters thick and four to five meters high. Outside the city, there is a round-shaped Mamian (rectangular pier for military defense) and a square-shaped turret in the corner.

There are circular defense platforms built outside the city and square watch towers on the corners. There are nine unsymmetrical gaps around the city walls, which may have been gated. Wengcheng, a kind of structure to strengthen the gates' defense, was also built outside these gates. Northwest of the southern city, where the palaces were built, was high and flat. The palaces' main gate faced south in the southern city. The entire southern city had the nature of an imperial district with some palaces, Buddha temples, and Confucius temples inside. The northern city was probably for regular people, with the Ashi River flowing from southwest to northeast—the waterway of Shangjing. Along the banks were business and handicrafts districts. Metallurgical sites and pottery kiln ruins were also discovered.

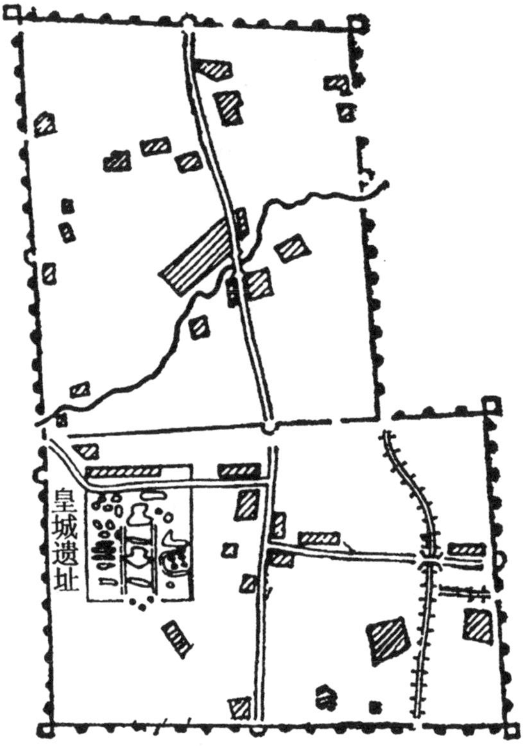

Fig. 4-4: Plan of Shangjing (the Supreme Capital), Huiningfu Site in the Jin[8]

Emperor Jin Xizong adopted the ritual system of the Central Plains. For instance, he personally participated in worship at the Confucius temple and awarded himself the title, Yanshenggong. In AD 1125, Emperor Song Huizong sent Xu Kangzong to Shangjing to offer congratulations on Emperor Jin Taizong's ascendance to the throne.

Xu Kangzong's book, *Travel Notes in His Majesty's Order in the Yisi Year of the Xuanhe Era,*[9] recorded in specific detail what he saw of the capital. Xu Kangzong discovered the palaces of Shangjing already imitated the style of the Central Plains, but because it was limited by scale and planning, it could not imitate successfully. Although the city scale is similar to Bianjing, it can only get 20% to 30% from the architectural point of view.[10]

---

8. Yang Kuan, *Studies on Ancient Chinese Capital System History* (Shanghai: Shanghai People's Press, 2003), 458.
9. *A Chronicle of Three Northern Song Emperors,* vol. 20.
10. *History of the Jin Dynasty,* vol. 12.

Shangjing of Jin was deserted after King Hailing won the throne and moved the capital to Yanjing. In the second year of his reign (AD 1157), King Hailing also ordered the original Shangjing palace, ancestral temple, noble mansion, and Chuqing Temple to be flattened and turned into farmlands. In AD 1173, Emperor Jin Shizong ordered the restoration of Shangjing; however, its previous glory was never restored.

Fig. 4-5: Plan of Zhongdu (the Central Capital)[11]

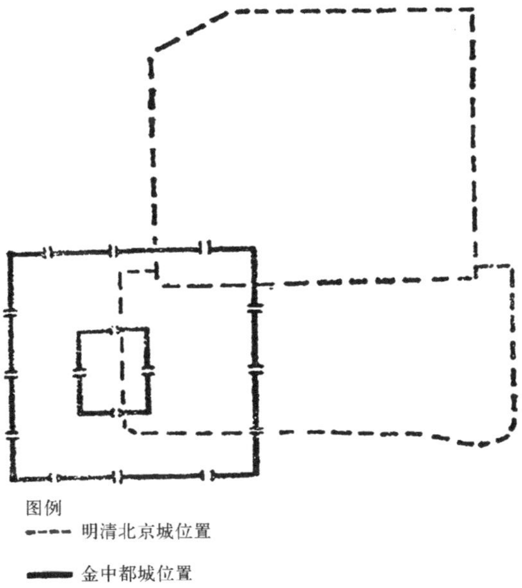

After seizing the throne, King Hailing moved his capital to Yanjing to further develop the Central Plains. Therefore, the central capital, Yanjing of Jin, was built on the foundation of Nanjing of Liao. The expansion plan followed the system of Bianjing of the Northern Song. In AD 1148, "the co-chancellors Zhang Hao and Zhang Tong, and aide Cai Songnian were ordered to take charge of rebuilding Yanjing by mobilizing its people to make it into a capital like Bianjing."[12] At the same time, artists were sent to copy the layout of Jingshi (Bianjing) and give these references to Zhang Hao, so his team could complete these drawings."[13] In

11. Yang Kuan, *Studies on Ancient Chinese Capital System History* (Shanghai: Shanghai People's Press, 2003), 461.

12. *Verifications of Beijing History*, vol. 37, *Introduction: The Unification of Yuan.*

13. *Verifications of Beijing History*, vol. 29, *Introduction: The Chronicle of Jin Dynasty.*

AD 1153, King Hailing officially moved to Yanjing and changed his reign title to Zhenyuan. The capital was renamed Zhongdu.

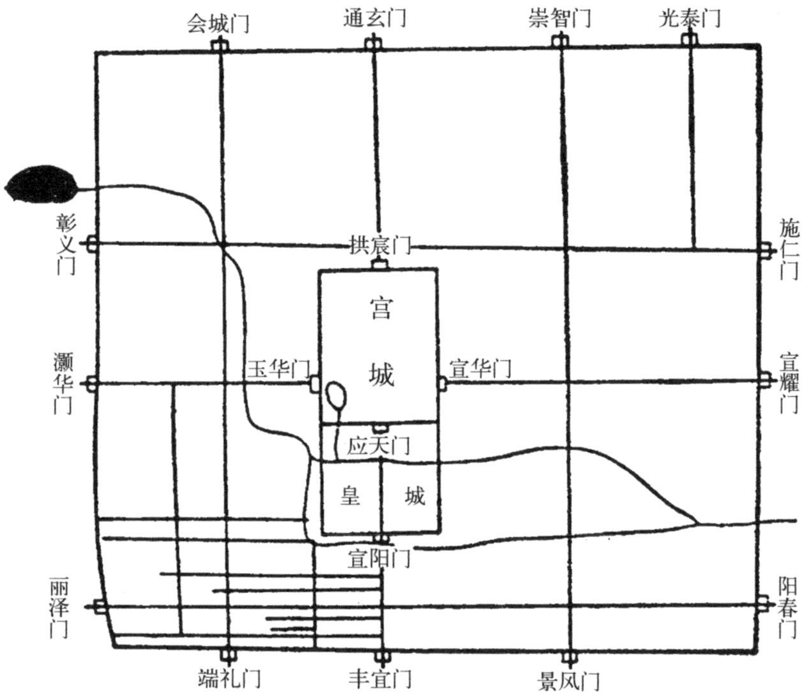

Fig. 4-6: Layout structure of Zhongdu (the Central Capital) in Jin[14]

The imperial city of the central capital of Jin mostly followed the structure of Nanjing (the southern capital) of Liao and used the older palaces as its main palaces. However, in the structure of Nanjing in Liao, "the sub-city was located in the outside southwest city wall," and the imperial city was located in the southwest corner outside the city wall. The west city wall needs to be moved further to the west if the city structure were to be changed like the three sets of square cities in Bianjing. The imperial city of the Jin Dynasty was located in the middle of the outer city wall and slightly to the southwest, which means that the area between the western wall of the imperial city and the western city wall of the outer city

14. Liu Jiaqian, ed., *Encyclopedia of Chinese Archaeology* (Beijing: China Encyclopedia Publishing House, 1986), 238.

was built by the Jin people, while the eastern and southern parts of the outer city were also widened during the expansion. Archaeological findings showed the central capital was roughly a square with the width a bit longer than the length. Presently, the remains of the east, west, and south walls of the outer city still exist. According to the actual measurement, the west wall is 4,530 meters, the south wall is 4,750 meters, and the east wall is 4,510 meters. In today's Beijing, there is still a Huichengmen Village, which should be the gate of Huichengmen on the west side of the northern area. The central capital of Jin still existed at the beginning of Ming, called the South City during this time. In August of the first year of Hongwu, the general Xu Da once measured it, about 5,328 *zhang* (17,660 meters) and 35 *li* in Song Dynasty's regulation.

There were three gates each on the east, west, and south sides of the outer city, and four gates on the north side. The three gates on the eastern side—Shiren, Xuanyao, Yangchun from north to south. For the western gates, there were Zhangyi, Haohua, and Lize from north to south. The southern wall had Jingfeng, Fengyi, and Duanli from east to west. For the northern wall, there were Guangtai, Chongzhi, Tongxuan, and Huicheng from east to west. The imperial city was located in the center, slightly southwest of the outer city facing the southern gate of Xuanyang. Two-thirds of the imperial city was the palace city with Yingtian Gate in the south, Xuanhua Gate in the east, Yuhua Gate in the west, and Gongchen Gate in the north. One could go through the city through Fengyi Gate in the south of the outer city, Xuanyang Gate in the south of the imperial city, Yingtian Gate of the palace city, the Gongchen Gate of the palace city, and the Tongxuan Gate in the outer city. This was the boulevard from south to north of the city.

It was also the middle dividing line of the central capital of the Jin Dynasty. The most important buildings were placed either in the middle of this line or on each side of the dividing line. It was obvious the central capital assumed capital functions in terms of both city planning and function.

3. Imperial Guards of the Capital

The Ling (陵) District is a kind of special district in Western Han—set around the vicinity of emperors' mausoleums. The architecture of these and the rituals of sacrifice were important aspects of ancestor worship, which was promoted to new heights during Western Han. Ling Districts were arranged near emperor mausoleums and people from the whole district were ordered to assist them in serving their imperial ancestors. This system was unique to the Western Han; thus, it is a special case in Chinese history.

The formal name of a Ling District was Lingyi. Superficially, the Ling Districts were set up for worship, but in fact, they were used to guard the capital. This was clearly demonstrated in the *Book of Han · Geographical Annals*. After the establishment of the Han Dynasty, the capital was built in Chang'an. The emperor migrated the war heroes surnamed Tian in the Qi State, surnamed Zhao, Qu, and Jing in Chu State to Chang Ling. Later he moved the officials who earned a salary of more than two thousand *dan* (石), wealthy business people, and other heroes to different Ling Counties. It is probably also used for state centralization, not just for the Ling. The establishment of the Ling Districts was not just about allocating a piece of land and some guards to serve the emperor's mausoleum. It had other issues—disgruntled old nobles from the previous six states in Guandong and some wild, recalcitrant, rich paladins (people who were adept in martial arts and given to chivalrous conduct) were relocated to Guanzhong, centering on the capital, Chang'an. This was a stone to kill many birds: increased monitoring of the capital to prevent uprisings and dissent, and an improved economic and cultural situation.

The first Ling District was established in 197 BC (the tenth year of Emperor Gaodi) when Emperor Liu Bang (Gaozu) buried his father in Beiyuan, Yueyang County. He set up Wannianyi in the city of Yueyang to serve his father's mausoleum. Although Wannianyi was the first district specially set up for serving this, it could not be considered a real Ling District.

A total of seven Ling Districts were established in Western Han, including the Changling of Emperor Gao, Anling of Emperor Hui, Baling of Emperor Wen, Yanling of Emperor Jing, Maoling of Emperor Wu, Pingling of Emperor Zhao, and Duling of Emperor Xuan. Besides Emperors, there were also two Ling Districts for the Empress Dowagers: Nanling for Empress Dowager Bo and Yunling for Zhao Jieyu. According to the original system of Western Han, the Emperor and his queen should be buried together. Therefore, the queen did not have a separate Ling District. However, Emperor Gao was already buried with his first wife, Empress Lü, in Changling. So Emperor Wen had to build Nanling to bury his mother, Empress Dowager Bo. Zhao Jieyu is a different story. She was buried in Yunyang County when she was dead. Her son, Emperor Zhao of Han, came to the throne. He honored his mother as the empress dowager and set up Yunlingyi, especially for her.

Moreover, Fengming District is also a quasi-Ling District, which Emperor Xuan set up for his father, Shi Huangsun. Shi Huangsun was the son of the abolished crown prince of Emperor Wu in the Han Dynasty. He had no chance of becoming Emperor. Later, his son Emperor Xuan succeeded, so Emperor Xuan honored him with Ling in Fengming District. Although Fengming District can not be called Ling District, its nature is no different from other Ling Districts. Therefore we believe it is a quasi-Ling District.

Among the nine Ling Districts and two quasi-Ling Districts, eight were established during the Han Dynasty. For instance, Maolingyi was the Mao Town of the Huaili District. Ba Lingyi was renamed Zhiyangxiang, Yun Lingyi was located in Yunyang County, and Emperor Jing's Yangling was renamed Yiyang. Therefore, these Ling Districts are relatively narrower than normal counties. Maybe because of the special status of these Ling Districts, they were under the administration of Courts of Imperial Sacrifices—although geographically, they were located in Guanzhong. The Ceremonial Temple was the department established by the central government in Western Han to administer the imperial ancestor temple rites, while the local administrative institution was called "Three Guardians" (metropolitan area). It was clear the Ling Districts were not under the governance of the metropolitan area, but the Chamberlain for Ceremonials, indicating they were not restricted by the local administrative institutes. This showed the Ling Districts' main function was religious for Western Han.

Nevertheless, this system somewhat changed later. No more Ling Districts were established after Emperor Yuan, and previous districts were put under the administration of the metropolitan area. In the Han Dynasty, a District leader with a population of more than 10,000 households was given the title of *Xianling* (District Magistrate), and those with less than 10,000 households were called district leaders (without title). However, every Ling District leader has a title, and income is much higher than a normal District leader, one thousand *dan* to six hundred *dan* income. For example, in the third year of Gao's reign (185 BC), the income of the Chang District Magistrate increased to 2,000 *dan*, which is the same as the *Jun* Magistrate.

In addition, the status of the Ling Districts can be illustrated by the considerable scale in the construction of city walls. According to the *San Fu Huang Tu*, a geographical work, the city, Changling, was built in 182 BC (the sixth year of Empress Lü) with "a circumference of seven *li* and one hundred eighty steps." Archaeological investigations showed the southern wall was 1,245 meters long, the western wall was 2,200 meters, and the northern wall 200 meters.[15] The northern wall of Emperor Hui's Anling City is also on a large scale; the northern wall is 1,223 meters long.

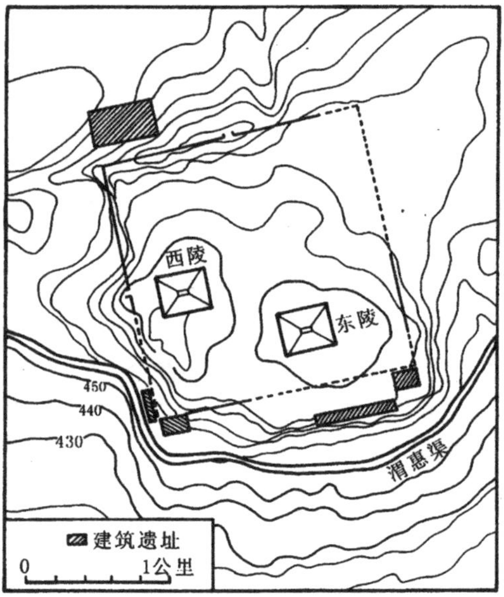

Fig. 4-7: Plan of the Changling Site, Western Han[16]

The inhabitants of the Ling Districts were not the original residents of Guanzhong, but those who came by forced migration, including nobles of Guangdong, merchants, and cavaliers. *A History of Guanzhong* recorded in the city, Changling, 10,000 households migrated from Guandong to make the Lingyi here. This migrated population was a considerable size as recorded in the

15. Xu Pingfang, "Chinese Mausoleums and Cemeteries in Qin, Han, Wei, and Jin Dynasties," *Archaeology*, no. 6 (1981).
16. Shaanxi Provincial Institute of Archaeology, "Briefings on Changling and Yangling GPS Measurement," *Archaeology and Cultural Relics*, no. 6 (2006).

Rites of Han Dynasty, where Wuling, Zhaoling, and Xuanling each had 30,000 households. The 30,000 households were the number when Ling District was first established. By the end of the Western Han Dynasty, Changling had grown to 50,000 households and Maoling to 60,000 households. Therefore, Changling and Maoling are very large counties with large populations. However, there were also some Ling Districts with fewer households. For example, Fengming District had only 1,600 households when it was first registered in the first year of the Yuankang reign (65 BC), which was much worse than Changling and Maoling.

These populations of the Ling Districts migrated in groups, changing the regional culture of Guanzhong in Western Han. Chang'an and these Ling Districts became places where intellectuals gathered and, in turn, attracted more talented people; it even became a custom for paladins to tour these areas. When historian Ban Gu wrote his *Book of Han*, he had a special volume—*Biographies of Rangers*—to record these intriguing people, their characters, and their deeds.

Nine Ling Districts or quasi-Ling Districts of the eleven were clustered around Chang'an—except Wannianyi and Yunlingyi, which were somewhat further away. Changling, Anling, Yangling, Maoling, and Pingling were located next to each other on the north bank of Wei River in the northern region of Chang'an, forming spectacular scenery. Besides these five famous districts, Baling, Nanling, and Duling were established in the eastern suburbs of Chang'an. The last one, the Fengming District, was also close to the suburbs of Chang'an. North of the Wei River, there was a Weicheng District located between Chang'an, Changling, and Anling. This district has a more famous name—Xianyang, the capital of Qin.

Liu Bang established the capital in Chang'an on the southern bank of the Wei River and then ordered Xianyang of Qin to become part of Chang'an. In 114 BC, some parts of Weibei were made separate from the others and renamed Weicheng. Here, these 11 districts are clustered in an area of 30 kilometers in length by 50 kilometers in width. Due to Ling District's unique functions and status, as well as its highly concentrated population, it is even difficult for today's metropolitan cities to match. Ban Gu's *Odes to the Western Capital* praised its spectacular scenery: "Look at Du and Ba in the south, and five Lings in the north. Mansions and royal pavilions are adjacent to each other." Therefore, Zhou Zhenhe believed that this region was made up of Chang'an and ten satellite cities.

Although the area of bigger Chang'an was narrow, it had a large population. According to the *Book of Han: Geographical Annals*, Chang'an had 80,800 households, a population of about 246,000. Changling had more than 50,000 households and a population of about 180,000. Maoling had 61,000 households and a population of about 277,000. These three counties together would total 703,000. Although it's hard to tell the exact population of the rest of the eight counties, with rough estimation, from Maoling to the end of the Han Dynasty, more than 60,000 households doubled from 30,000 when they first settled. Pingling and Duling are roughly the same. When Anling was first established, there were 5,000 households. The situations in Baling, Nanling, and Yangling were similar to Anling, while the number had increased to 10,000 by the end of the Han Dynasty. When Fengming was first built, there were only 1,600 households, and by the end of the Han Dynasty, it was about 3,000 households. Only the number in Weicheng is completely incalculable. But even excluding it, there are probably 150,000 households in the remaining seven counties. If each family has five members, the total number is about 750,000. In this way, the most conservative estimate is that the population of Chang'an and its ten subordinate counties was more than 1.5 million, then the population density is 1,000 per square kilometer. When we compare today's data, the population density is quite astonishing. The metropolitan city of Shanghai is the most densely populated and most urbanized area in China. According to the statistics in 2008, Shanghai's population density was 2,931 people per square kilometer, which is only three times the population density of Chang'an two thousand years ago. Let's take into account that the majority of the population (1.5 million) are urban consumers who are not engaged in production, and there is a large area of palace gardens and ponds near Chang'an. We can imagine the population density and prosperity in this area.

Therefore, Ban Gu of Eastern Han, in his *Xi Du Fu (Odes to the West Capital)*, recalled the prosperous scene of the city and its metropolitan suburbs.

The streets in the city are well-connected, and there are nearly a thousand alleys; nine markets have opened simultaneously, and different goods stores are listed on different roadsides. The city is jam-packed with dazzling crowds. Pedestrians fill the city, overflow the city walls and flow into hundreds of shops. Rolling red dust diffused everywhere in the city, rolls of mist connected to the sky. The city's population is vast, and the society is more prosperous than ever. People are filled with joy. Men and women in the capital were different from those in other places. Travelers' clothing can be compared with that of wealthy dukes, and business women's clothing is better than that of noble girls. The country boys are brave and handsome, have an air of chivalry, their integrity is close to Lord Pingyuan and Lord Mengchang, and their fame is second only to Lord Chunshen and Lord Xinling. They made friends, united with disciples, and often galloped across the capital. If you observe the city of Chang'an and wander around the nearby counties, you will see Du and Ba in the south and five Lings in the north. The famous capital is opposite the city wall, and the mansion is adjacent to the royal pavilion. That is where the heroes lived, where the great men built their towns; Officials who wear fancy hats travel in the city like clouds in the sky. The court selected seven ministers and five princes of the country, talented men of the prefectures, and wealthy business people from the country. It moved these three groups of families to the Seven Lings of the Han family to undertake the critical task of enshrining the imperial tombs. Presumably to strengthen the central government's rule, weaken the local government, reinforce the capital position, and show the state's power across the world.

However, the formation of the bigger Chang'an area was not a natural result of economic and population growth, but a result of human administration intervention. Therefore, once the policy was changed, the prosperity dispersed like a mirage. After Emperor Yuan, no more new Ling Districts were established, and the existing Ling Districts went under the supervision of the metropolitan area, an indication of the decline of the status of Ling Districts. In the Yuanshi period, Emperor Ping ordered the destruction of Fengming's garden and lowered the rank of Fengming District, Nanling, and Yunling as ordinary counties. Finally, Ling District lost a large population during the turmoil at the end of the Western Han Dynasty. After the Wang Mang period, the population of the Changling area was less than one-tenth of its original size. In the Guanghe era, Eastern Han Dynasty, the number of households was less than 4,000. This is understandable because Chang'an and its Ling District had a large population who did not work on farmlands, so food supply could not be guaranteed in turmoil. Therefore the population decrease is a natural result.

When the Eastern Han Dynasty moved the capital to Luoyang, Chang'an and the other Ling Districts further declined. Their glory became the past. Even the *Xi Du Fu* (*Odes to the West Capital)* by Ban Gu was written on observations of the remains and interviews with older generations. The Eastern Han respected the Western Han as their origin. Hence, the seven emperors' Ling Districts were preserved. Still, as time went by, the ritual ceremony gradually became very perfunctory. Even Changling for Gaozu was not well maintained. The guards would steal sacrifices offered because of the sharp population decrease, while the situation in the other Ling Districts can only be imagined.

The Nanling and Yunling district system went further and was removed at the beginning of the Eastern Han. Wannianyi was not revoked, but the Yueyang District was not retained, and Wangnianxian became a part of the Yueyang District—meaning the Wannianxian was no longer specially designed to serve imperial tombs.

When it came to the Three Kingdoms Period, the seven Ling Districts were revoked, and Duling was renamed Duxian. Baling, due to its location at the eastern pass of Chang'an, was renamed Bacheng. By this time, the eleven Ling Districts around Chang'an were reduced to three, and their past glories had faded considerably and irrevocably.

CHAPTER FIVE

INNER CITIES AND OUTER CITIES: THE EVOLUTION OF CAPITAL FORMS

"When the craftsmen build the capital, there should be nine *li* along each side and three gates. Within the city, there should be nine roads from south to north and another nine from east to west. The Imperial Ancestor Temple should be on the left and the Altar to the God of the Land on the right. The government offices should be in front and the market at the back. The palaces and the markets should be about one hundred *mu*."

This is from the city planning records in the *Rites of Zhou · Record of Trades*. Aside from specific descriptions, *Record of Trades* demonstrated the importance of centralization theory during the Warring States Period (475–221 BC), when people attempted to represent the central power of feudal emperors through architecture.[1] Originating very early, this concept took nearly 2,000 years to materialize in the capital design of Dadu (grand capital) of the Yuan Dynasty (AD 1206–1368). Nevertheless, all capitals built by feudal dynasties in ancient China were influenced by the ideal capitals described in *Rites of Zhou · Record of Trades*. In other words, the change of capital was a continuous balancing process between realistic local conditions.

1. Hou Renzhi, *Theories and Practice in Historical Geography* (Shanghai: Shanghai People's Press, 1979), 209–210.

1. Capital Construction Rules for the Craftsmen

Rites of Zhou is one of the classics of Chinese Confucianism, focusing on the regulation of morals and behavior. Rules about the emperors' construction of capitals are found in the *Record of Trades* section. Now, academia generally believes the *Rites of Zhou* was written during the Spring and Autumn and Warring States periods.[2] Thus, the book's descriptions are considered the benchmark for people of the time. During subsequent centuries, as Confucianism continued to rise in status and gradually evolved into the dominating ideology of the Chinese ruling class, capital construction rules for the craftsmen described in the book became the golden rules for later emperors in building their capitals.

The section on "Jiang-ren Ying-guo" (Capital Construction Rules for the Craftsmen) focused mainly on the city's building rules. The word "guo" means capital and "ying-guo" means constructing the capital. In the enfeoffment system of the Western Zhou Dynasty, this not only included building moats, cities, palaces, ancestor temples, and god's altars, but also planning territorial boundaries, including fields and nearby towns—so-called "governing the field." It was the Western Zhou system in which the state was surrounded by fields. Therefore, capital construction meant establishing a city-state in this way. Whether the King of Zhou, the dukes, or the high officials, they all have their city-states.

Based on this, the descriptions of "ying-guo," as recorded in *Record of Trades,* can be divided into three levels: (1) the King's City, that is, the capital of the state; (2) the city of the dukes, or the capitals of the dukes; and (3) "Du," namely the imperial clan and feudal bureaucrat fiefdoms.

Record of Trades described the King's City in more detail whilst the others were only mentioned fleetingly, using city corners and roads as examples to illustrate their differences. No direct descriptions of specific internal planning were provided. Therefore, scholars across generations based their interpretations on the planning of the King's City. Specific planning of smaller cities was through these estimates.

In its planning, what *Record of Trades* described can be summarized as follows:

---

2. See He Yeju, "The Nature of *Record of Trades* and its Production Time and Location," in *Studies on City Building System in "Record of Trades"* (Beijing: China Industry and Architecture Publishing House, 1985), 171–180.

> The city should be nine *li* on each side and three gates on each side. Within the city, there should be nine roads from south to north and nine roads from east to west. The nine south-north roads should allow nine-horse carriages to pass abreast with each other. The Imperial Ancestor Temple should be on the left and the Altar to the God of the Land on the right. The government offices should be in the front and the market at the back. Palaces and markets should be about 100 meters on each side.
>
> There should be nine houses within the palace for the Emperor's nine concubines and nine houses outside the palace for the nine high-ranking officials to work.
>
> The nine south-north roads should allow nine-horse carriages to pass abreast with one another. The roads around the city should enable seven-horse carriages abreast, and the roads outside the city should enable five-horse carriages to go abreast.

Here are the clear Confucian standard capital design principles in the *Record of Trades*. The first is to confirm the palace as the core of the city's planning. Other important buildings would be constructed in locations related to the palace, the residence of the Emperor. The palace had to be the center of important buildings—this was a core principle of the regime. The front of the palace area would handle major national affairs, while markets were established at the back. The gates, the main roads, and the planning of residential areas would be distributed symmetrically with the palace in the center.

There is a very specific design for the capital's planning. For instance, the palace and market would be one *"fu,"* which means about 100 meters on each side. The King's City's walls were about seven *zhi* (one *Zhi* is about 2 meters), and the city walls' corner tower was about nine *zhi*.

Each city wall had three gates, a total of 12 gates. The height of the palace wall was five *zhi* (丈, *zhang)*, the palace corner was seven *zhi*, and the palace gate was five *zhi*; the whole city used a *Jing-Wei-Tu* (i.e., chessboard format) boulevard network that was composed of three north-south and three east-west main roads (One-*Dao*-Three-*Tu)* as the backbone. Along the city wall, *Huantu*, a ring road was added. It connected the *Jing-Wei* boulevard and formed the leading road network. *Yetu*, the Zhou Dynasty expressway, communicated the inside and outside of the city. The breadth of *Jing-Wei-Tu* was nine *gui* which was seven *zhang* two *chi* in the measurement of Zhou Dynasty. *Huantu* was seven *gui*, equal to five *zhang* six *chi*. Moreover, *Yetu* was five *gui*, four *zhang*. The width of temple door was two *zhang* one *chi*. Meanwhile, *Weimen*, the central door of temple, was six *chi*; *Yingmen* was two *zhang* four *chi*; *Lumen*, the door of the road, was one *zhang* six *chi* five *cun*, etc.

It was clear this way of building put much emphasis on the rites. Showing such strict hierarchy was expected in this era—the end of the Spring and Autumn Period when all types of systems went to the edge of bankruptcy. It should be noted the King's City scheme as described was not the ideal plan for feudal capitals, but the capital building for the slavery system of the Zhou Dynasty.[3]

The planning concept of ancient capitals described in the *Rites of Zhou* was not practiced before the Song Dynasty. Scholars in later generations took this concept and designed a wide variety of display forms. For instance, The King's City map described in the *Three Rites in Illustrations* by Nie Chongyi presented a direct image. The problem is that Nie only paid attention to the spatial relationship between the road and the city gate, but neglected the capital's important landmark buildings, such as the Ancestor's Temple; their locations were obscure, which made Nie's drawings unsatisfactory.

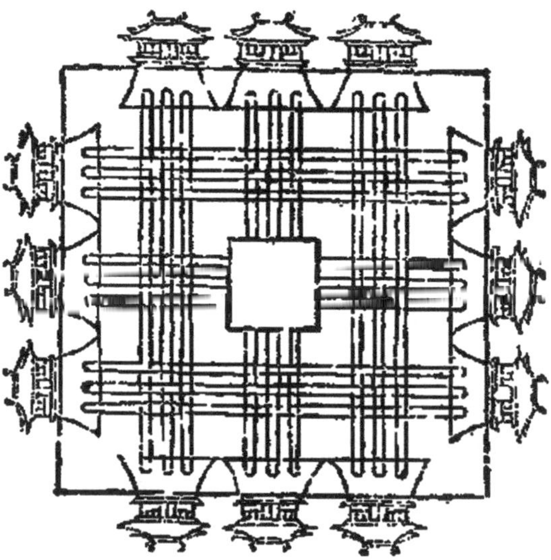

Fig. 5-1: The King's City in "Three Rites in Illustrations" by Nie Chongyi

3. See He Yeju, *Studies on City Building System in "Record of Trades"* (Beijing: China Industry and Architecture Publishing House, 1985), 37.

Dai Zhen, a famous empirical scholar during the Qing Dynasty, modified the map of the King's Capital. In his version of *The Maps of "Record of Trades,"* Dai Zhen put the Ancestors' Temple and the Altar of the God of Land on the east and west sides of the palaces. This actually did not originate from Dai Zhen but had been proposed by a school since the Song Dynasty. Because of Dai Zhen's influence, this version of the King's City map was very popular during the Qing.

A contemporary scholar, He Yeju, conducted a thorough study of the construction rules of *Record of Trades,* and drew detailed, specific maps.

These maps were a concise summary of the construction planning concepts indicated in the *Rites of Zhou · Record of Trades* underlining Confucian influence on the Chinese capital system. The actual situation was more complex.

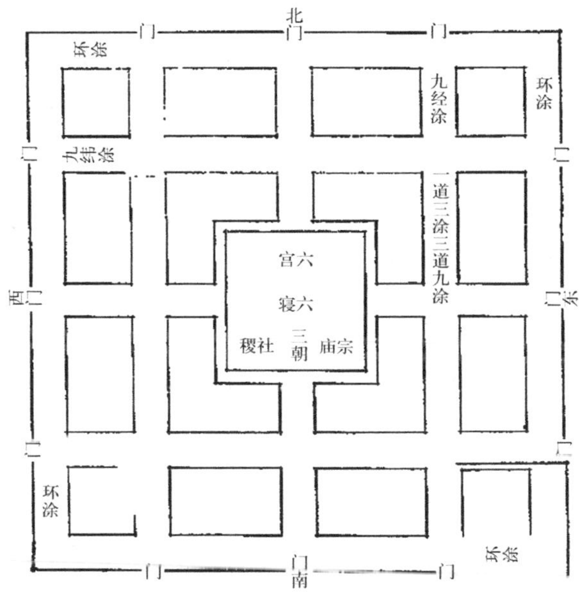

Fig. 5-2: The King's City in "The Maps of Record of Trades" by Dai Zhen

2. Living in the Southwest, the Most Respected Location

Little is known about the capital systems of both the Xia and Shang dynasties because it was so long ago. The earliest record of capital construction was Chengzhou, the eastern capital of the Zhou Dynasty. The significance of the Chengzhou construction has been discussed. Chengzhou and its counterpart—

the original capital of Western Zhou—Haojing, coexisted. This system of two capitals strengthened the rule of the central government and was copied by later generations. This also began the "small inner city, big outer city" concept inhered by all capitals before the Qin era. Some historians also regard "small inner city, bigger outer city" as "inner city in the west and outer city in the east." The king's palace was located in the entire western part of the city, while the commoners and merchants lived east of the city. The city's layout was closely related to the legal system of the Zhou Dynasty in the Spring and Autumn Period and the Warring States Period. For this story, we shall begin with the ancient capital city of State Lu, which is considered to be the only living evidence that was built during the Western Zhou Dynasty and is well preserved today.

- ***Qufu, the Capital City of State Lu***

Located in today's Qufu, Shandong, many parts of the capital city's walls, especially in the east and south corners, are still standing today. The remaining walls are about 10 meters. Based on these and the archaeological reports, we can project the basic layout and nature of the city during this time.

According to these, State Lu's capital was rectangular, with the south-north section a little longer. In the western and northern parts of the site, water from the Zhu River was used as a moat. In the eastern and southern parts, a man-made moat introduced water from Zhushui; thus, forming a circular defense system. There were 11 gates in the city's walls. Their design and the main street layout were in an east-west direction.[4] The setting of city gates and the layout of traffic roads prove that the layout of the city is in an east-west direction.

Excavation results indicate the palace areas should be located near the north gate of the eastern walls extending to the west, slightly in the northeastern part. That is, they should be the rammed earth foundation in today's highland area of the Duke of Zhou Temple. As recorded in *Commentary on the Water Classic*: "Zhou Gongtai is five *zhang* in length, it takes 50 steps to measure the circumference" was described here. To the north of the palace area, the area of today's Shengguo Temple is the largest residential site in the city. The cultural sites in the western part are more than two meters thick which lasted from the early Western

4. See Yang Kuan, *Studies on the Ancient Chinese Capital System History* (Shanghai: Shanghai People's Press, 2003), 44.

Zhou Dynasty to the Han Dynasty. The city's early crafts workshops were mainly scattered along the north and the northwest. Bronze metallurgy was found in the Shengguo Temple and Yaopu (today) in the northwest, while the north of Yanpu and the spring factory were obviously pottery-making sites.

Judging from the layout of the gates and traffic roads of the ancient city of Lu, the main residential areas were in the west and the central and northern parts of the city, and the whole layout was also in the west-east direction, with the palace area in the northeast part of the central part.

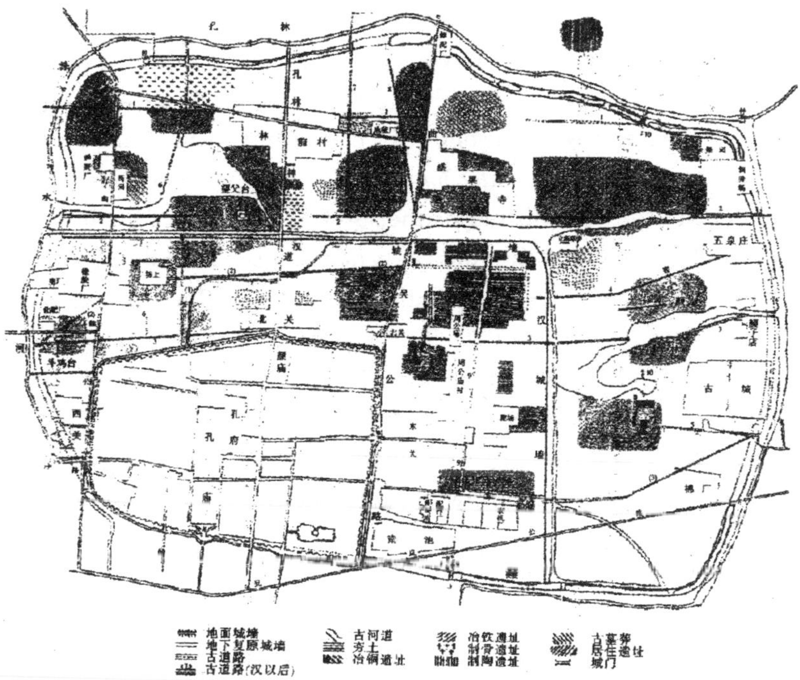

Fig. 5-3: Plan of Qufu, the capital of State Lu[5]

From the Western Zhou to the Spring and Autumn and the Warring States, most Chinese capitals would show the evolution from a single city to a city connected with an outer layer, from the Western Zhou to the Spring and Autumn and Warring States. This was a result of political and military demands. In the eastern capital, Chengzhou, a new outer city was constructed east of the King's

5. From *Qufu, the Capital of State Lu* (Jinan: Jilu Publishing House, 1980).

City, mainly for citizen settlement, migration from the Yin, and also military stationing (see Fig. 5-5).

Many of the big states in the Central Plains would adopt such layouts to strengthen their reigns. Another reason for constructing a bigger outer city was to meet the demands of economic development, particularly handcrafts and business. With social-economic change and the increasing advancement of handcrafts and business, the inner city could not contain everything. The outer city became the main residential area too. Gradually, this layout spread to other states in the Central Plains.

The layout was designed according to the rite system of the Zhou Dynasty. The palace sat in the west and faced the east. In other words, the palace was built in the west or southwest direction, with the main gate in the east or north. The most striking part was the southwest corner of the room was reserved for the respected. *Code of Rites · Rites for Trivials (Part One)* said being a son, one could not live in the *Ao*. This means the southwest corner of the house (*Ao*) is reserved for the elders, and the younger generation should not occupy it. When funerals were held, Zhou people would consider the southwestern corner of the room as the place for gods and *Shi*. The gods here referred to the spirits of the hosts' ancestors, and *Shi* was a representative of the spirits of the ancestors in a sacrificial ceremony, mostly selected from the youngest generation. *Code of Rites · Rites of Sacrifice Offering* described ceremony procedures in which officials made sacrificial offerings to their ancestral temples. The entire ceremony is as follows:

When hosts made sacrificial offerings to ancestors, they would order the *Sigong* (a rite official) to prepare feast food in the southwestern corner of the temple room and *Zhu* would place a rectangular desk southeast of the food table for the gods.[6] When the gods' seats were well-arranged in the southwestern corner, *Zhu* would invite *Shi* to come to the temple and into the room. During this time, the *Shi*, who represented the gods, would sit in the southwestern corner, facing northeast to accept the offerings and kowtow of the *Zhu* and hosts.[7] Thus,

6. *Codes of Rites · Rites of Sacrifice Offering* (No. 16): "*Sigong* prepared the feast in the *Ao* area, while *Zhu* put the desk on the right." Zheng Xuan's annotation: "This was the preparation for the seats of gods. The southwestern corner of the room is called *Ao*. A measurement of the east and the location in the south would be considered as more respected."

7. *Codes of Rites · Rites of Sacrifice Offering* (No. 16): "After *Shi* got seated, *Zhu* and the host stood facing the west. *Zhu* was on the left. Both *Zhu* and the host bowed."

temple and palace rooms considered the *Ao* in the southwestern corner as the place for respected elders, who would face east, since this was considered the most honorable position.

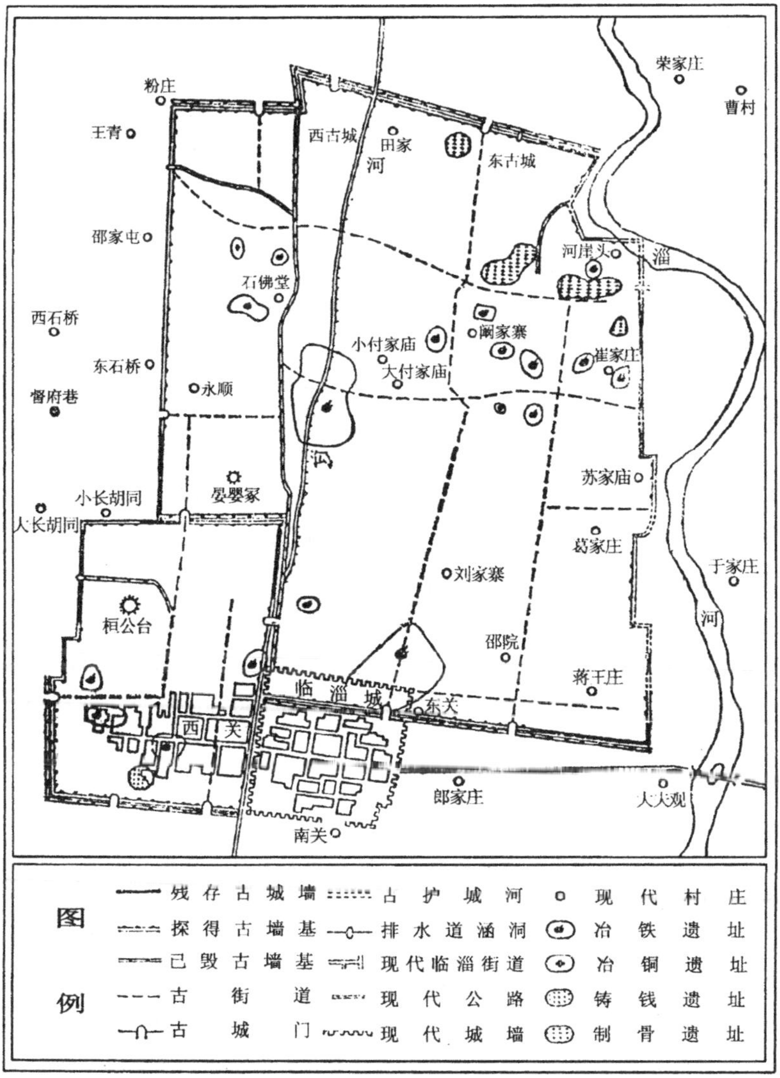

Fig. 5-4: Plan of Linzi, the capital city of State Qi[8]

8. See Yang Kuan, *Studies on the Ancient Chinese Capital System History* (Shanghai: Shanghai People's Press, 2003), 63.

The designers of ancient Chinese capitals considered the entire city as a room. Therefore, they would build the palaces or elite residential areas in the southwestern corner. The entire city was located in the west and faced to the east, it was clearly the custom of Zhou. When Zhou's ancestor Gongliu built the city in Bin, "Gongliu took a trip to watch the sunset, he found the land of Bin is really vast." Sunset refers to the west. If they build the palace in the western region, they naturally consider the west is the honorable position. The lofty status from facing east did not only apply to ancestor worship, but also to the rituals held indoors. During this time, the palaces faced the south, but the east was considered honorable until the Qin and Han dynasties. In the Banquet at Hongmen, Xiang Yu and Xiang Bo sat east, Yafu (Fan Zeng) south, Pei Gong north, Zhang Liang west, and Fan Kuai later west. Han Xin defeated the forces of Chen Yu of Zhao and captured Lord Guangwu (Li Zuojun) alive. "Han Xin broke his shackles and sat down with Guangwu. Han treated him as a guest, so he let him sit in the east, looked at him from the west." In this context, Han Xin respected Guangwu and let him sit in the honorable position.

One example from Western Han was when Emperor Wen (Prince Dai) was welcomed to Chang'an, and his officials asked him to ascend to the throne seat. Emperor Wen "declined to sit facing east three times and to sit facing north two times."[9] Prince Dai first declined to sit facing east to show his modesty by not daring to be in the elders' position. His decline to sit facing north was an indication to show his modesty of not daring to be the Emperor. Because of such rules, the capitals of vassal kings were mostly a combination of the inner city in the west and outer city in the east.

During the Spring and Autumn and the Warring States periods, it was based on this etiquette that the capitals were almost always a combination of "city" in the west and "city walls" in the east. From the relatively intact and well-investigated cities such as Linzi (now Linzi, Shangdong), the capital of Qi; Xinzheng (now Xinzheng, Henan), the capital of Zheng and Han; Xintian (now Houma, Shanxi), the capital of Jin; Anyi (now Xia County, Shanxi), the capital of Wei; Handan (now Handan, Hebei), the capital of Zhao; Ying (now Jiangling, Hubei), the capital of Chu; Yong (Fengxiang, Shaanxi), the capital of Qin. The cities above seem to apply the layout until Chang'an, the capital of the Western Han Dynasty.

---

9. *Records of the Grand Historian · Annals of Xiaowen.*

• ***Linzi, the Capital of State Qi***

According to historical records, Lü Shang (Taigong Wang) established his capital in Yingqiu in order to control the Lai minorities in the east. (There has been some controversy about the capital's location—with some arguing it is today's Linzi, while others disagree. Some scholars think Yingqiu is Linzi, while others think it is somewhere else. However, it does not change the fundamental point.) It was not until the seventh generation that the Xiangong, whose expedition to the east and establishment of Linzi as its capital, reestablished its status as the most powerful state in the Shandong Peninsular.[10]

The Qi State continued to use Linzi as its capital for over six hundred years until 221 BC, when it was destroyed by Qin. As an important settlement to control the east, Linzi's layout demonstrated the combination of Zhou rites and military defense. The scale and layout of this spectacular city gradually took shape after the excavation of the remaining walls and underground by archaeologists.

With the Zi River in the east and the Xi River (called Dirt River today) in the west, the old city of Linzi was on the tip of the alluvial fan of the Zihe, which slightly tilted northward. The old city consisted of a small inner-city in the southwest and an outer city in the northeast. It was more than four *li* from north to south direction and nearly three *li* from east to west direction. The big city was an irregular rectangle with many turns. The southern end of the west wall was connected with the north wall of the small city, and the west end of the south wall was connected with the east wall of the small city. It was nearly nine *li* from north to south and more than seven *li* from east to west. The total area of the two cities was more than sixty square *li*. The small inner-city was rectangular and embedded in the southwest section of the outer city.

Judging from the layout of its gates and main streets, the inner city, located southwest of the outer city, faced east. The main entrances were the east and north gates, with the east gate particularly important. There were five gates in the small city, one on each of the east, west, and north sides, and two on the south side. Among them, the east and north gates were the passages leading to the big city, and there were gate buildings. The palace's foundation was in the northwest part of the small town, with the so-called Huan Gong Tai as the center. The traffic avenues of the small town were also built around the palace. In addition to

10. *Records of the Grand Historian · Annals of Qi.*

the ruins of palace buildings, the small town also found many ruins of iron and copper smelting workshops serving the palace. More importantly, there were also the ruins of the money-making workshops monopolized by the rulers.[11]

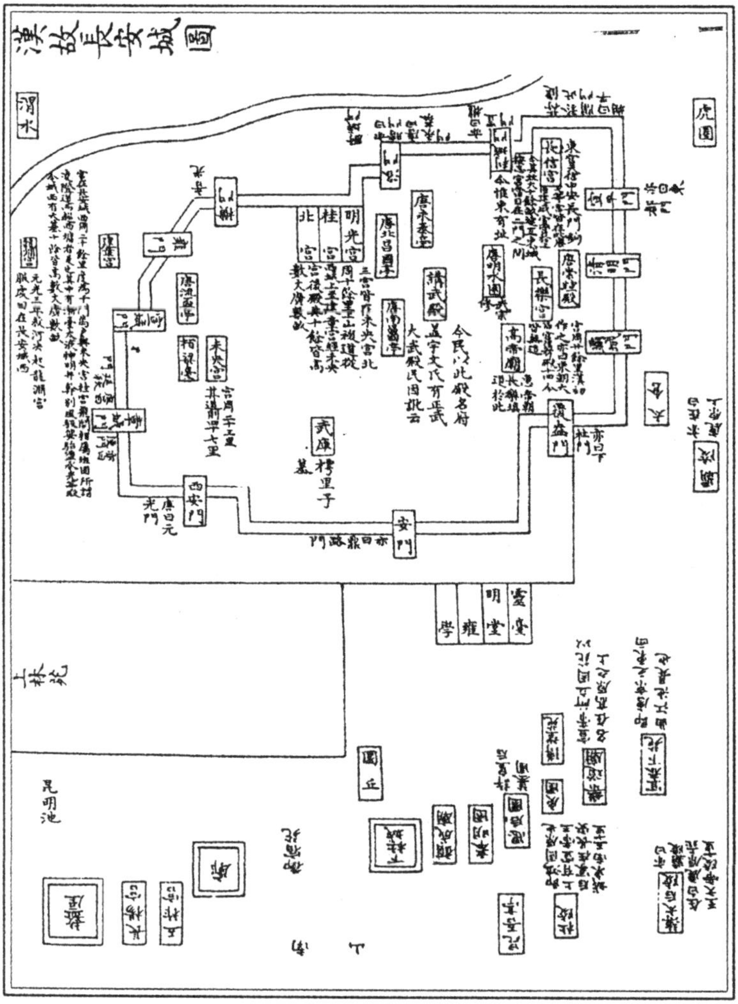

Fig. 5-5: Li Haowen, "Map of Chang'an in the Han Dynasty"[12]

11. Hou Renzhi, "The Origin and Development of the Main Towns of Linzi," in *Theories and Practice of Historical Geography* (Shanghai: Shanghai People's Press, 1979), 348.
12. Yang Kuan, *Studies on Ancient Chinese Capital System History* (Shanghai: Shanghai People's Press, 2003), 108.

There were eight gates in the big city, three gates on the east wall, two city gates on each of the south and north wall, and one gate on the west wall. There were two avenues traversing the east and west, which were inclined to the north, and there were also two avenues that run through the north and the south, which were inclined to the east.

At an intersection near the highland of Han Xin Ridge around the vicinity of Heyatou and Kanjiazhai villages, a large accumulation of workshop remains, including iron and copper smelting, was found. Bone ware was unearthed, indicating these were the most prosperous parts of the outer city.[13] It should be noted the east wall of the outer city was dramatically different from the other three walls. Instead of going as straight as possible, it curved randomly and was very irregular. In fact, these irregular convex or concave changes were not aimless but had a specific design concept. If the threat came mainly from the east, the entire city's defense system must be based on the shape of the Zi River in the east.[14]

- ***Chang'an of the Western Han Dynasty***

The famous scientist and writer, Zhang Heng of Eastern Han, described the construction of Chang'an by Xiao He as the "improvement of the Qin system and Zhou's rules" in his work *An Ode to the West Capital,* a memoir of the prosperity of Chang'an of Western Han. In fact, we consider the construction of this city as a product of makeshift and make-do strategies.

At the beginning of Western Han, the throne had just been established, and reinvigoration was required. Everything was dealt with as simple as possible: even four horses of the same color could not be found for the Emperor's carriage. Thus, the construction of Chang'an was mostly a simple maintenance job on the original foundations of Qin.

During Emperor Gao's time, the Qin provisional palace, Xingle, was remodeled into Changle Palace. Then Weiyang Palace, the North Palace, and artillery storage were also built. It was not until the time of Emperor Hui of the Han Dynasty (194–188 BC) that started the construction of the surrounding city walls and the construction of the West City. By Emperor Wu's time, society had fully recovered

13. Yang Kuan, *Studies on Ancient Chinese Capital System History* (Shanghai: Shanghai People's Press, 2003), 66.
14. Hou Renzhi, "The Origin and Development of the Main Towns of Linzi," in *Theories and Practice of Historical Geography* (Shanghai: Shanghai People's Press, 1979), 346.

because of rehabilitation policies. In addition, due to the luxurious lifestyle of Emperor Wu, many palaces were built in Chang'an, such as Jianzhang Palace in the west of city, Mingguang Palace in the north of the Changle Palace, Gui Palace in the north of the Weiyang Palace, added building North Palace, etc. The remaining walls of Chang'an built by Emperor Hui of Han can still be found today. The east wall is 5,940 meters long, the south wall is 6,250 meters, the west wall is 4,550 meters, and the north wall is 5,950 meters, with a total area of about 36 square kilometers. It is also said in the *Book of Han*: "The city of Chang'an is 63 *li* in length, 15 *li* in longitude and latitude, having 12 gates, and covering 973 hectares."

Chang'an City in the Western Han era was mainly occupied by gigantic palaces, temples, office buildings, affiliated institutions, and the residences of officials, princes, dukes, and princesses. From a contemporary view, Chang'an is an inner city—the outer city areas in the northeast. Judging from the gates and street layout, the entire inner city faced east. The city of Chang'an had eight boulevards and 12 gates with three gates in each wall. Archaeological reports showed only the gates in the eastern walls were designed to have gate towers. In the excavated Xuanping Gate (East Wall and North Gate) and Bacheng Gate, the city walls on both sides of the gate had outwardly protruding parts, just like the east tower gate of the small town of Linzi in the capital of Qi. It means that the east gate of Chang'an City was the main gate. In addition, among the eight streets in the city, from the north gate of the east wall (Xuanping Gate) to the west, it led directly to the middle gate of the north wall (Chucheng Gate) and the north-south Luocheng Gate (east gate of the north wall) Street, the junction between the Luocheng Gate, An Gate, and Chucheng Gate Street was the leading traffic road from the northeast of the city to the east, and it was also known as the most important city channel in Chang'an. Looking at the entire city, this inner city was built to protect the royal palaces, official buildings, barns, and residential houses of the nobles and officials. Therefore, the inner city could only hold a small portion of the people: residential districts of the common fold were distributed in the northern and eastern parts of the outer city.[15]

---

15. From Song Minqiu, *Records of Chang'an, Waterways of China · River Wei,* and *San Fu Huang Tu (Historical Geography in the Qin and Han Dynasties).*

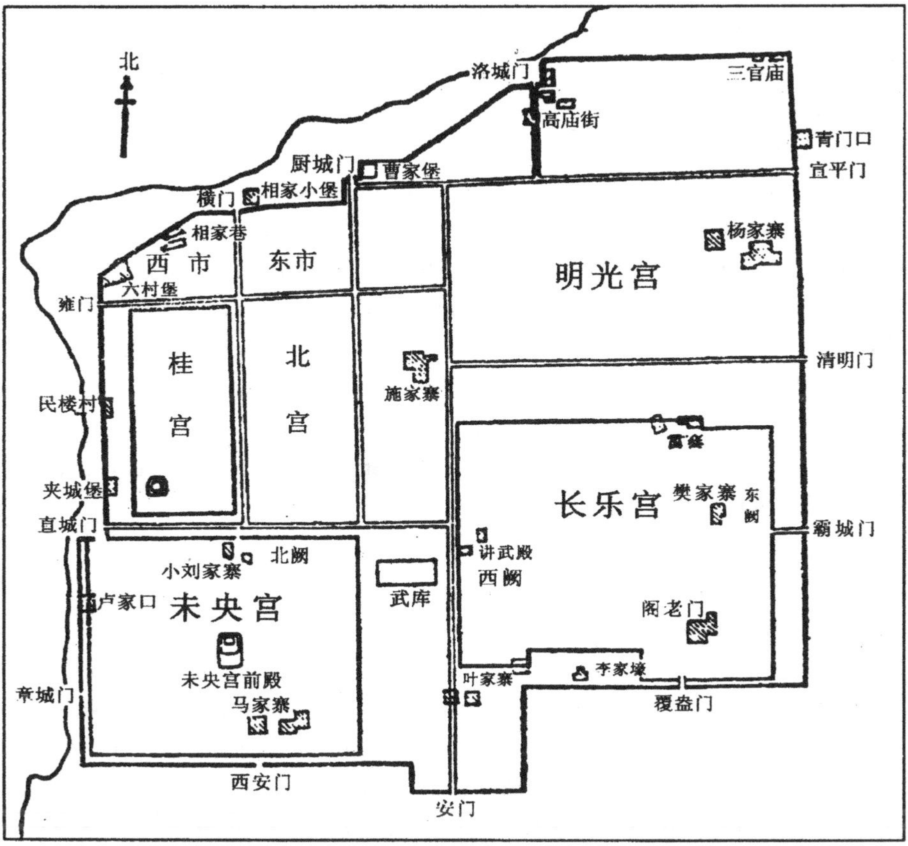

Fig. 5-6: Layout of Chang'an in Western Han[16]

According to *Historical Geography in Qin and Han,* "Chang'an had nine markets, and each was about 266 *bu* (step). Six markets were located on the west side of the main street, and three were on the east side. There would be one market in every four *li.* People from all over would gather along the Hengqiao Boulevard, while the market administration occupied the grand houses."[17] Hengqiao Boulevard, the main road, extended from Heng Gate (western gate in the north wall) to Hengqiao, a threshold of Chang'an and five countries north of

16. Yang Kuan, *Studies on Ancient Chinese Capital System History* (Shanghai: Shanghai People's Press, 2003), 133.

17. *Zhaoming's Selected Works · Ode to the West Capital.* In the "opening of the nine markets" part, Li Shan made annotations by quoting *Hangong Queshu*: "There were nine markets in Chang'an, with six in the west of the boulevard and three in the east."

the Wei. Therefore, Hengqiao Boulevard became an advanced business area, and the west markets were established here. This symmetric layout of the east and west markets in the outer city had a great impact on the market development for later capitals.

This layout of connecting the inner and outer cities in the Western Han followed and was built on the pre-Qin and Qin era capital system. The inner city of Chang'an was constructed in the southwest, and the outer city was located in the northeast, which copied the popular capital layout of the Central Plains. However, this style of ancient capital began to change during the late stage of Western Han. The shift from the tradition of younger generations not living in the southwestern section of the room, and the change from facing east to facing south—following the order of Heaven—was not achieved until the construction of Luoyang in the Eastern Han Dynasty.

3. Following the Order of Heaven

The capitals before the Western Han Dynasty would face east. However, with the establishment and consolidation of central power, the worship of imperial power became a core demand of national rites. The Emperor's worship of heaven gradually replaced ancestral worship and became the most important ritual of rulers. Heaven worship was held in the southern suburbs of the capital—a key reason for the change in capital layout. This activity of Heaven worship in the suburbs can be traced back to the Western Zhou and was known as suburb worship. There was a saying that, "the most important business for the Emperor was to carry out Heaven's orders and the most important business to carry out Heaven's orders was to conduct Heaven's worship ceremonies."

Since the Shang (Yin) Dynasty, people considered the God of Heaven (god, emperor) to be the master of nature and human society. The Emperor was a representative of the God of Heaven on earth, and he administered his reign by accepting this destiny. Therefore, in the Zhou only the King (Heaven's son) had the privilege of worshipping Heaven. None of the vassal kings were allowed to do so.

Early sacrificial ceremonies were mostly conducted in the eastern suburbs. Because the sun rose in the east, the sunshine was sufficient. After the royal Zhou family moved eastward, the authority of the King deteriorated, and the previous religious system weakened. The vassal kings fought for independence: they even started their own worship of Heaven; this change began in the Qin State.

At the beginning of the Spring and Autumn Period, Qin Xianggong, granted a duke title, thought he should exclusively occupy western China. Hence, he offered sacrifices to Bai Emperor, a legendary god of the west. Later, with the growth of the Qin State, another three gods were added: Qing Emperor, Yellow Emperor, and Yan Emperor. The change of gods from one to many reflected the situation of division on earth. After Qin Degong moved the capital to Yong, Yong became a religious center. At the beginning of Western Han, this rite continued and Emperor Wen established the Five Emperors' Temple in Weiyang. Of course, the Five-Emperor theory was a product of national disintegration. After the unification of China, one god on top of the hierarchy—Taiyi—became the norm.

However, the chaotic ritual system for worship did not meet the demands of the unified political system. Hence, after Emperor Cheng of Han came to the throne, a great Confucian scholar, Kuang Heng, proposed reorganizing the religious system by changing Chang'an into a standardized religious center. Heaven worship should be conducted in the southern suburb and earth worship in the northern suburb. But this rule was abolished soon thereafter. It was not until the Yuanshi period of Emperor Ping of the Han Dynasty that Wang Mang again stipulated that the sacrifice of heaven and earth should be in the southern suburbs.

This ritual of annual sacrifice offerings in the southern suburbs met the needs of the political system and was adopted by Emperor Guangwu in Eastern Han. In AD 25, Emperor Guangwu came to the throne in Gao (north of Bo County) and offered sacrifices by using the story of Yuanshi, who started the ritual.[18] On January AD 26, he continued to adopt the story and built a sacrificial offering place seven *li* south of Luoyang. Later, Pingcheng Gate was opened in Luoyang, making it convenient for officials to come to the palaces to meet the Emperor. More importantly, it was easier for the Emperor to hold sacrificial offerings in the southern suburbs. Since then, others followed suit and it became a custom.

- ***Luoyang during the Eastern Han and Northern Wei***

The site of Luoyang as the Eastern Han capital, the so-called Old City of Han and Wei, is located 15 kilometers from present-day Luoyang. The old city was an

18. *Book of Han Continued · Records of Worshipping*, vol. 1.

irregular rectangle with a length of 9 *li* and a width of 6 *li*. Thus, it was named "Nine-Six City." After Emperor Guangwu established the capital in Luoyang, he inherited the inner-city system of Chang'an of Western Han. The palaces were constructed in the middle and took up about one-third of the entire city. It was clear the whole of Luoyang faced south, which could be judged from several aspects.

First, the palaces that ranged from south to north had the southern gate as their main entrance. Second, there were three gates each on the eastern, western and southern side of the city and two gates only on the north side. However, there were four gates in the south, and the Pingcheng Gate was the main entrance on the south slightly east. Pingcheng Gate faced the southern gate (Zhuque Gate) of the Southern Palace, which was mainly used for the emperor to offer sacrifices in the southern suburbs. Therefore, "Pingcheng Gate was the main entrance gate and the entrance to the palaces, the gate used for Heaven worship. Hence, the most revered."[19] Besides the function of being used as the entrance for sacrificial offerings of Heaven, it was also used when officials went to the front palace to meet the Emperor. This was the only gate guarded by the royal guards.

Within Luoyang, there were 24 streets and three markets. The main market (gold market) was within the city and located southwest of the Southern Palace. The horse market was established in the eastern part, and the southern market originated close to the Luo River (in the south). Luoyang's three-market system began during this time. Most official residential buildings were in the southeast, close to the Hao Gate of the eastern wall. In the northeastern part, barns and arms stores were constructed.

At the end of Eastern Han, Dong Zhuo, a top official, burned Luoyang's palaces. When the Cao Family of Wei rebuilt the city, the northern palaces were maintained, and the layout of Yecheng was adopted—the home base of the Cao Family. The northern part of the bigger city was as a restricted entrance, and the southern part was the market and common residential areas. A central axis was also designed with the main palaces sitting on the axis. The southern entrance gate of the palaces faced the southern entrance gate of the bigger city. Between these two entrances, a special road for the emperor was built.

---

19. *Book of Han Continued · Records of Wu Xing (No. 1).*

After the southern movement of Jin, Tuoba Xianbei, a minority leader from northeast China, moved to the Central Plains and established the Northern Wei Dynasty. In AD 493, Luoyang was built as the capital, and the Emperor moved there two years later from Pingcheng. The planning map of the Northern Wei shows how the original layout of Luoyang was greatly adjusted. The southern palaces were discarded, and the northern palaces became the principal buildings. The palace-city was located northwest of the central part of the city. The palace wall was rectangular, about 1,398 meters from north to south and 600 meters from east to west. It covered an area of about one square kilometer, accounting for one-tenth of the area of the city. Because the palace was established slightly northwest of the Luoyang City, the city's central axis deviated to the west. This axis starts from the north of the city, passes through the palace, Tongtuo Boulevard, Xuanyang Gate, and from the south of Luo River, reaches the Yuanqiu, which is outside of the South Gate of the city wall.

Fig. 5-7: Palace layout of inner city of Luoyang, the Eastern Han[20]

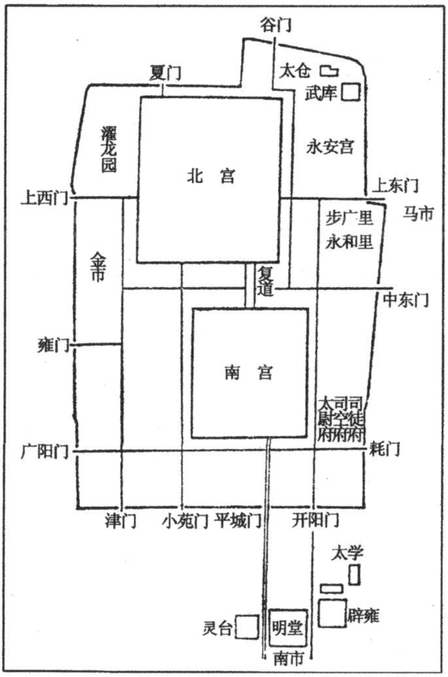

20. Yang Kuan, *Studies on Ancient Chinese Capital System History* (Shanghai: Shanghai People's Press, 2003), 131.

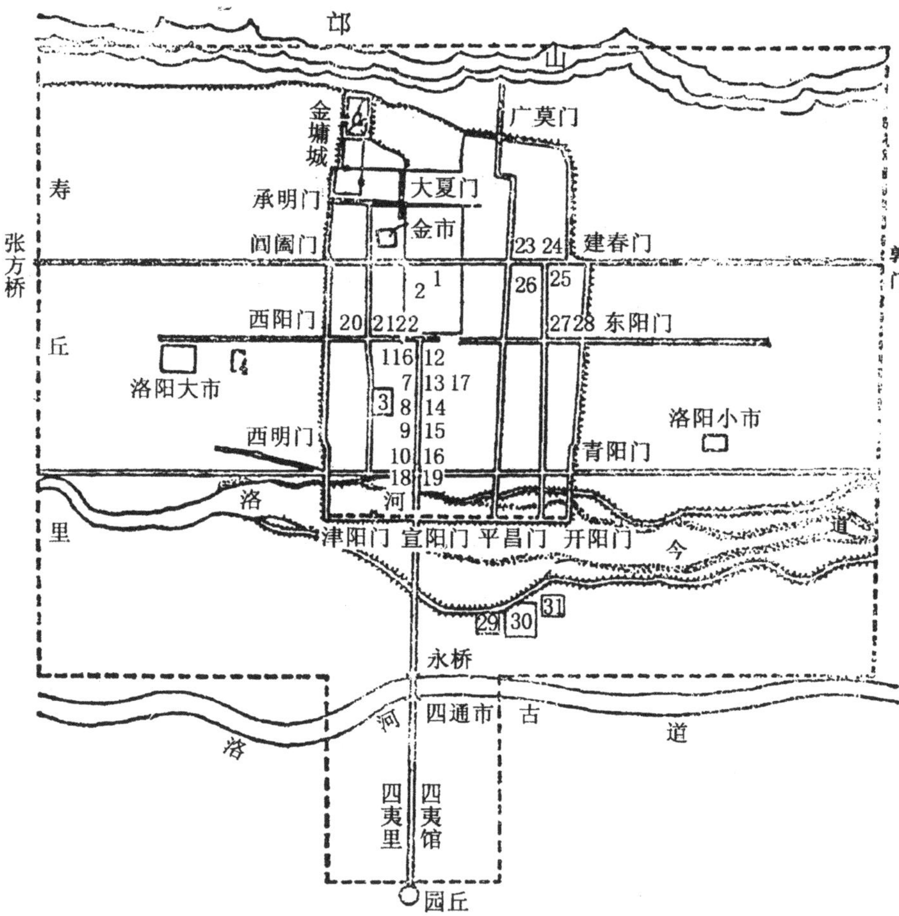

Fig. 5-8: Plan of Luoyang, Northern Wei[21]

21. Yang Kuan, *Studies on Ancient Chinese Capital System History* (Shanghai: Shanghai People's Press, 2003), 133.

On the left side of Tongtuo Boulevard, the main street in front of the palace, was the Imperial Ancestor Temple. On the right was the Altar to the God of the Land, while the official residences were spread along the street. Archaeological detection showed the Taiji Palace, where the Emperor administered national affairs, was to the south, and the residential quarters and the Xiyou Garden were to the north. The other main streets of the city were chessboard like. The markets were not in the northern part of the palaces, but spread out across the outer city.

If measured by the King's City system recorded in *Record of Trades*, Luoyang in the Northern Wei would roughly fit the plans in *Rites of Zhou*, except the site and city system, which copied previous generations. Therefore, it would be appropriate to consider Luoyang, built by the Xianbei in Northern Wei, as closest to the ideal capital construction since the end of Western Han.[22]

- ***Chang'an during the Sui and Tang Dynasties***

The predecessor of Chang'an in the Tang Dynasty was Daxing in the Sui. Hence, the planning for Chang'an of Tang was actually completed in the Sui Dynasty. In AD 582, Emperor Wen of Sui ordered the building of new capital in Longshouyuan, southeast of the old Chang'an. This new settlement was divided into the inner and outer cities, and the latter was further divided into the Palace and Imperial cities.

This is illustrated on the structure map of Chang'an in the Tang drawn by Li Haowen in the Yuan era (Fig. 5-10). The special structure is very clear: the inner city was located in the central and northern area with the palace city to the north and the imperial city to the south. The outer city embraced the inner city from east, south, and west. The whole area was symmetrical, with the palace city and the imperial city located on the axis of the entire city. In addition, the roads were designed like a chessboard, and residential quarters were allocated by taking advantage of the spaces evenly divided by these chessboard roads.

This feature was verified by contemporary archaeological findings. According to archaeological reports, the outer city of Chang'an in the Sui and Tang dynasties was rectangular with a width of 9,721 meters and a length of 8,651 meters. From documents, we know Chang'an was not only symmetrical on this axis, but also

---

22. See He Yeju, *Studies on City Building System in "Record of Trades"* (Beijing: China Industry and Architecture Publishing House, 1985), 15–16.

separately administered according to the division line—the axis street, Zhuque Street. The east side was administered by Wannian County and the west by Chang'an County.

The palace design of Chang'an also produced far-reaching impacts on later generations. In the middle was the Taiji Palace, where the Emperor dealt with national affairs and the so-called outer royal office. Eastwards of the Taiji was the East Palace, the residence of the crown prince. On the west side was Yeting, where the palace maids lived. The main building of the Taiji Palace was called Taiji Hall. In front, there were provincial offices on the east side and regional offices on the west side. These were also central government departments to assist the Emperor. Chang'an was the first capital to gather all central government departments to the south of the palace city.

Five gates were designed around the palace city of Chang'an, with the most important being Chengtian Gate in the middle. Chengtian Gate faced Taiji Hall in the north and was on the same axis as the Zhuque Gate in the imperial city and Mingde Gate in the outer city, thus forming three important points on the axis of Chang'an. The side street in front of Chengtian Gate is 300 steps in width, approximately 411 meters, and is the widest street in Chang'an City, with the feature of a square, commonly known as Sky Street. Every New Year's Day, Winter Solstice, and Qianqiu Festival (the emperor's birthday), the court would hold a grand ceremony in Chengtian Gate, and on the side street, the ministers would be arranged here in the order of their titles rank. The award ceremony of granting amnesty and receiving tributes was also held at Chengtian Gate. In fact, many of Chang'an people's popular events were also arranged here. As recorded in the *Biography of Li Wa* by Bai Xingjian, Chang'an east and west cities of the elegy competition was held in Sky Street. The side street in front of the Chengtian Gate and its connected Zhuque Street formed palace square had a great influence on the design of the later capital cities, such as the Tian'anmen Square in the Ming and Qing dynasties was designed with this concept in mind.

South of the Chengtian Gate was the outer royal office. Taiji Hall was where the royal ritual occurred at the beginning of every month. Liangyi Hall (back of Taiji) was where the Emperor dealt with daily affairs, known as the Inner Court. In addition, an award ceremony and banquets were often held at Liangyi Hall. Chang'an Palace walls were very close to the northern part of the city, which meant it was also a part of the outer city wall with three gates, Xuanwu Gate and

Xing'an Gate in Taiji Palace, and Zhide Gate in the Eastern Palace. The Emperor's royal guards were stationed just outside the Xuanwu Gate, which explained the Xuanwu Coup by Li Shimin.

4. The Ever-Lasting State

Since the construction of Chang'an in the Sui and Tang dynasties, China's capital system has been altered. During this period, the unified dynasties did not construct new capitals but mostly took advantage of existing cities and restructured them. Therefore, there was no attempt to apply the "ideal" capital in practice. Strangely, the ideal capital as described was realized by the Yuan Dynasty—by the Mongolians who "only knew about shooting the eagles with arrows." This was Dadu (Grand Capital), built by Kublai Khan, Emperor Shizu of Yuan.

Located at the intersection of the Huabei Plains and Inner Mongolian Plateau, Dadu, or Beijing of the Ming and Qing eras, can trace its written history to the Spring and Autumn and Warring States periods. During this time, the city was called Ji and served as the State of Yan capital, one of the seven major states of the time.

In 221 BC, Qin Shi Huang, the first Emperor of Qin, unified the entire country and divided it into 36 counties. Ji became the administration center of Guangyang County. From the Qin to the Tang, the city of Ji became an important location and also a strategic military town to conquer northeastern China. Being a transport hub of the Han and nomads in the Mongolia Plateau, it subsequently became an economic center in northern China.

During the Five Dynasties Period, Liao rose in the north and confronted the Northern Song. In this expansion to the Central Plains, Emperor Liao Taizong, originally named Yelü Deguang, acquired the Sixteen Prefectures of Yan and Yun from Shi Jingtang, and Youzhou was renamed Nanjing (the Southern Capital), as one of the Five Capitals of Liao. It was considered an important station in conquering the Central Plains. Shortly after the destruction of Liao by the Jin, King Hailing moved the capital from Shangjing (Acheng in Heilongjiang today) to Yanjing and renamed it Zhongdu of Daxingfu. Since this time, Zhongdu was the capital of Jin, coexisting with the Southern Song and Western Xia until AD 1214, when the capital was moved to Kaifeng to avoid Mongolian harassment.

In AD 1215, Zhongdu was occupied by the Mongolian army and was subsequently renamed Yanjing. In the beginning, the Mongolians did not intend to build a capital here, so they burned down all the city's palaces. In AD 1264, Emperor Kublai Khan decided to move to Yanjing and resumed the name of Zhongdu (Middle Capital) on advice from his Han official, Liu Bingzhong. He also rebuilt a new capital in the northeast suburbs of Zhongdu. In AD 1271, Kublai Khan changed this and Zhongdu became Dadu (Grand Capital). Since then, Dadu/Beijing officially became the political center of China.

The Ming Dynasty built its capital in Nanjing at the beginning of its reign. In AD 1368, Zhu Yuanzhang, the first Emperor of Ming, expedited to the north and after occupying Dadu of Yuan, renamed it Beiping. After a series of reconstructions, the city became an important military town in defending against the remaining Mongolian forces. Zhu Di, the Emperor's fourth son and the most valiant, was enfeoffed.

Fig. 5-9: A geographical map of Khitan[23]

23. *Ancient Chinese Atlases: From the Warring States Period to Yuan Dynasty* (Beijing: SinoMaps Press, 1990).

Zhu Di successfully seized the throne from his nephew, Emperor Jianwen, and changed the era to Yongle. In AD 1421 (nineteenth year of Yongle), Zhu Di successfully promoted his territory, Beijing, into Jingshi and declared it the capital. The previous Jingshi was changed to Nanjing and demoted to an alternate capital. During this time, the Ming made some modifications and created the layout of Beijing as we see it today.

The following Qing Dynasty mostly inherited the architecture of Beijing from the Ming, but the Qing made a few striking imprints on the city. One was a separate government of the inner and outer city under the Eight Banners System. Another was the construction of gardens in the west suburbs.

In the history of Chinese capital construction, Beijing, a capital first established by a non-Han feudal dynasty, became the capital that most strictly followed Confucian rites and rituals. Beijing also comes closest to the ideal capital as described in *Rites of Zhou · Record of Trades*. Its layout and plan design were influenced by this. How did Dadu combine traditional design concepts with a realistic geographic situation effectively and what changes did it experience?

- ***The Superior Capital of Celestial Empire: Dadu***

As mentioned previously, the construction of Yuan's Dadu came as close as possible to creating the ideal capital. Thus, it holds a significant position in Chinese history. The Mongols originated from the deserts in the north, unified China by force, and ended the north-south divide apparent across China over the past hundred years. After unification, the Mongol ruling class featured internal disagreements between conservatives and reform proponents.

Emperor Shizu of Yuan, or Kublai Khan, was against the old system and advocated for political reforms with rules from the Han Dynasty. To counter the stubborn forces of the conservatives, Kublai Khan adopted Liu Bingzhong's advice and moved the capital from Shangdu to Zhongdu in AD 1264. In AD 1267, Kublai Khan gave up the old Zhongdu as the capital and established a new capital centered around the Daning Palace in the northwest suburbs of Zhongdu of Jin. This would later be Dadu (Grand Capital). Why did the Yuan rulers wish to move to Zhongdu and then later abandon the idea and build a new capital? Was this because Zhongdu was destroyed by fire during the wars? If so, why should the Daning Palace in the northeast suburb be selected as the new site? There are a number of reasons, the most important being the water supply of the city.

Zhongdu of the Jin Dynasty was located in the northern part of the North China Plains, where rainfall was insufficient, and water came mainly from surface water sources, such as the Lotus Flower Pond southwest of Beijing today. However, the water supply from the Lotus Flower could only meet the demands of local households and palace gardens. It would be of no use for grain transport—an integral part of the Jin Dynasty. The Jin failed to solve this issue during their entire reign.[24] Thus, the Yuan took the problem seriously, especially the water supply of the waterway in the south-to-north transfer of grains.

However, in the northwest suburbs of Zhongdu, there were once lakes and swamps. After the construction of Zhongdu, they were gradually transformed into scenic sights, later known as Qionghua Island. There was also Daning Palace, an alternate palace for the Jin royal family.[25] After Mongol soldiers conquered the city at the beginning of the thirteenth century, Zhongdu suffered severe destruction (as it was not considered a potential future capital). Daning Palace survived the fire and later became a sojourn palace for Kublai Khan.

In AD 1262, Guo Shoujing, a water supply expert, suggested that the old sluice stations of Zhongdu could be restored to bring water from the Yuquan Mountains, thereby improving the grain supply via the transport canal. This modified waterway went past Daning Palace. It is a wise choice for the new city planners to design the new capital around the lake of Daning Palace to solve the water transportation problem. In other words, moving from the old city of Zhongdu to the new town of Dadu is moving the city from the Lianhua pond water system to the Gaoliang River water system.[26] This is the most laudable aspect of choosing the Yuan capital's location. This is one reason it has remained a capital after several hundred years.

After the new site was chosen, the central axis of the city needed to be clarified, in order to build a new capital for this purpose.

As discussed previously, since the Capital of Ye built by the Cao family of Wei, a central axis located through the city center appeared in the layout of Chinese capitals. This was considered representation of the emperor in the center of the universe. Because this was related to the rites and rituals system of the nation,

24. See Hou Renzhi, *Theories and Practice in Historical Geography* (Shanghai: Shanghai People's Press, 1979), 162.

25. Ibid., 160–161.

26. Ibid., 164.

it was of vital importance to determine the central axis of the capital. To avoid the central axis of the new capital being blocked by Jin's old capital and to go through the city smoothly, the specific location of the palaces was planned on the east bank of the lake on the south side of the previous Daning Palace (see Fig. 5-13). Legend said the designer of Dadu, Liu Bingzhong, used a tree in the south of the third bridge outside of the Lizheng Gate. The axis that crossed the tree was the central axis of the entire city, and palaces were constructed first on this line. However, if we observe the archaeological restoration map of Dadu in the Yuan Dynasty, we can see the palaces were actually on the southern part of the axis instead of being located strictly in the center. This layout feature was deviant from the traditional ritual concepts of "the superiority of the Center"[27] and "the Doctrine of the Mean." The planners of Dadu deliberated on this choice.

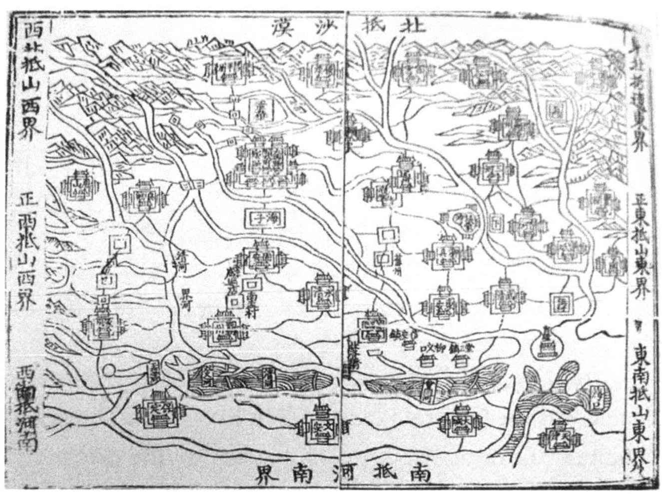

Fig. 5-10: "Map of the Capital's Surroundings"

After the palace site and the meridian direction were decided, the proposal of putting palaces in the center were considered first. However, this meant the new capital would overlap with part of the old site of Jin's Zhongdu. Thus, part of the old city would have to be demolished; this was against the wishes of Dadu's planners. As a result, they gave up the plan of constructing the palaces in the

27. (Song Dynasty) Shao Yong, "Observing the External," in *Huang Ji Jing Shi Shu* (*Book of the Imperial Supreme on Worldly Affairs*), vol. 12.

middle, instead the palaces were constructed in the central-southern part of the whole city. Naturally, this decision narrowed the distance between palace walls and imperial walls, and did not highlight the meridian sufficiently. Thus, they made Dadu somewhat similar to Lin'an (today's Hangzhou), the capital of the preceding Southern Song Dynasty.

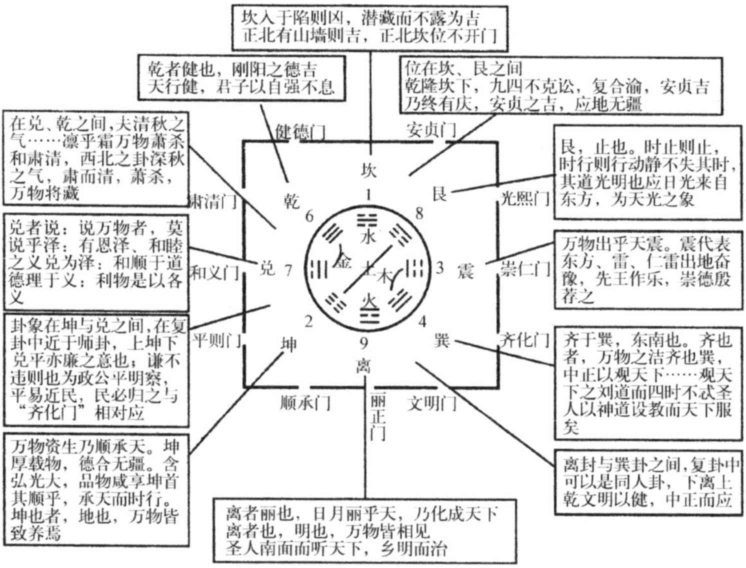

Fig. 5-11: Speculated plan of the "putting palaces in the center" of Dadu, Yuan[28]

After the meridian location and the palaces were decided, another symbol to decide was the Central Platform. Liu Bingzhong chose a place in the northeast of Jishuitan (meaning water pools) located on the extended axis of the meridian as the central point of the layout of the whole city. He erected a stone measurement and sculptured the words, "Central Platform." Fifteen *bu* to the east or about 23 meters east, another central pagoda was erected, with its position where the Drum Tower is located today in Beijing. This is the first time actual measurement technology was applied to design cities, which guaranteed regularity and an exact square of the plan of Dadu.[29]

28. Huang Jianju, *Studies on the Choice and Planning of Chinese Ancient Capitals* (Xiamen: Xiamen University Press, 2004), 210.
29. See Hou Renzhi, *Theories and Practice in Historical Geography* (Shanghai: Shanghai People's Press, 1979), 165.

With the center of the city decided, the next was to determine the boundaries of city. The east and west walls were built using the distance between the Central Platform and the west bank of Jishuitan as the radius. The south and north walls were determined, based on the distance between the Central Platform to the south end of the imperial city. Afterward, Liu Bingzhong organized palaces, palace towers, and other functional architecture by strictly following the principles of *Record of Trades* where the construction (relative to the imperial throne) would have government offices to the fore, markets to the rear, the Imperial Ancestral Temple to the left, and the Altar to the God of the Land to the right.

Based on this principle, the market was located along the port connecting the Jishuitan at the back of the palace and the canal waterway. The Imperial Ancestral Temple would be located in the north of Qihua Gate at the south gate of the east wall; the Altar to the God of the Land was located a little south of Heyi Gate, the middle gate of the west wall of the outer city, south of today's Xizhimennei Street. The Imperial Ancestral Temple and the Altar to the God of the Land were located, respectively, on the east and west sides of the outer city. It is similar to Bianjing in the Northern Song Dynasty, which built the Imperial Ancestral Temple (place for worshiping ancestors) and the Jiaoshe (place for worshiping heaven) respectively on the east and west sides of the wall. It was clear the significance of the construction of Dadu lay in its innovative application of the ideal designs from ancient China to real life. This was inherited by the Ming and Qing dynasties.

- ***The Ever-Lasting State: Beijing in the Ming and Qing Dynasties***

Beijing City of Ming was renovated and expanded on the foundation of Dadu of Yuan. The Ming developed extreme feudal rites, and their capital design was heavily influenced by this, laying the blueprint for the basic pattern of Beijing today. The Qing rulers adopted an attitude of inheritance towards Beijing but left some marks of their own.

While the Ming and Qing inherited the city planning of Dadu, there are still differences. One of these was the moving of the city site further south. At the end of the Yuan, there were very few inhabitants within Dadu due to the chaotic wars. During this time, the Mongol nobles of the Yuan were still eyeing the Central Plains, ready to attack in spite of their defeat, and retreat to the Mongolian Plateau. Shortly after the Ming seized Dadu, they chose to give up the obsolete northern areas of Dadu for defense purposes and build new walls five *li* south of the original northern walls. And because the western section was blocked by Jishuitan, which was used as a moat, it formed a corner-shaped terrain.

To counter the threat from the north and further control northeastern China, Zhu Di promoted his base of Beiping as Beijing (the Northern Capital), the alternative capital in AD 1403 (the first year of the Yongle era). It is the first time this name is used. In AD 1406, Zhu Di began building palaces in Beijing. The southern walls were pushed two *li* south. As a result, Beijing of the Ming era was located slightly further south, with the palaces now closer to the geometric center. Obviously, compared with the capital of the Yuan Dynasty, the idea of "palace city in the middle of the city" was better applied in the Ming Dynasty. However, this layout was problematic due to the continued threat from Yuan forces—Mongol cavalries often invaded and looted suburbs of the city, occasionally even breaching the city walls.

Eventually, Beijing grew in prosperity, as underlined by the construction of ritual architecture, such as the Temple of Heaven, and the Temple of Agriculture. Yet, the city was still vulnerable to Mongol invasions, especially in the districts not protected by the city walls. In AD 1564, the building of the outer wall was completed.

Robbery by the Mongolians left this area extremely vulnerable since it was unprotected by walls. Therefore, after the Tumu Crisis (a frontier conflict between the Oirat tribes of Mongols and the Chinese Ming which led to the capture of the Emperor Zhengtong on September 1, AD 1449 and the defeat of an army of 500,000 men by a much smaller force), the Ming decided to add an outer city around Beijing. In AD 1564, the outer wall surrounding the southern suburbs was completed; thus, forming the symbolic layout out for Beijing as indicated by the Chinese character, "凸."

When we examine details of wall construction, there are many stories to tell. For instance, by looking at a map of Beijing after the mid-Ming era, we find many neglected details. The new southern wall expansion was not in a straight line, but slightly curves north. Different scholars have different interpretations of this. Huang Jianjun put forward the theory of Feng shui. According to Feng shui, straightness would lead to misfortune, while curves lead to good luck. Therefore, in city planning, the mechanical repetition of geometric forms like rectangle or squares were avoided, while the combination of rectangles and circles (e.g., rectangles within circles) was sought to achieve aesthetic effects.[30] The southeast of the outer city was in angular shape. It is said that the purpose of doing so is to achieve a symmetrical image with the north-western corner of the inner city to echo the shape of the corner.

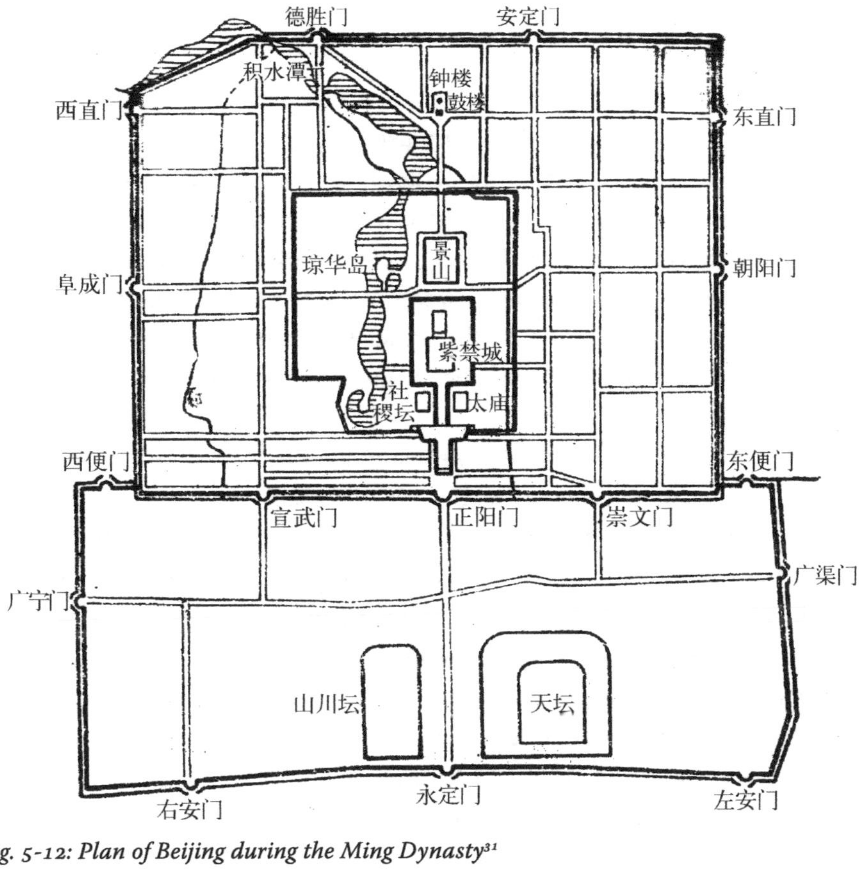

Fig. 5-12: Plan of Beijing during the Ming Dynasty[31]

Shifting the entire city south meant a change to the city's core. One of the most important tasks was to rebuild several of the palaces. Emperor Yongle decided to move the capital to Beijing and used all the financial, material, and

30. Huang Jianju, *Studies on the Choice and Planning of Chinese Ancient Capitals* (Xiamen: Xiamen University Press, 2004), 238.

31. Hou Renzhi, *Theories and Practice in Historical Geography* (Shanghai: Shanghai People's Press, 2003), 214.

human resources of the country to build his new capital. During the beginning of the Ming when it seized Dadu, all palaces of Yuan were demolished to destroy the "emperor's influence" of the previous dynasty. Emperor Yongle decided to move the capital to Beijing and started to build using all the financial, material, and human resources of the country. Beijing was constructed in the center of the feudal empire by integrating experiences in the construction of Nanjing and Zhongdu.

Like previous capital constructions, the remodeling of Beijing focused on the city's central axis. Although Beijing used the axis of Dadu of the Yuan, it redesigned all buildings south of the Center Pavilion. Ming palaces were moved 400–500 meters to the south, and a moat as wide as 52 meters around the palaces was dug to strengthen defense. Thus, Fengxian Hall—the emperor's chief hall and front Imperial office—was built on top of the previous Chongtian Gate, the main gate of Dadu of the Yuan. The three back Imperial offices were constructed on top of the main hall. This symbolically guaranteed conquering the previous dynasty.

The imperial city was renovated by expanding three walls outwards, with only the west wall remaining intact. As a result, the space between the palace and imperial cities was expanded and this new space outside the Wu Gate was used to build the Imperial Ancestral Temple and the Altar to the God of the Land on each side of the central axis—copying the layout of Nanjing of Ming. This better connected two previously isolated compounds on the west and east with the imperial city, stressed the importance of the boulevard of the central axis, and increased the depth between Tianan and Wu gates. On the other hand, it also restructured the layout of Dadu which strictly followed conventional principles. Besides, the newly built Duan Gate between Wu and Chengtian gates, and the walls surrounding the palaces along the Emperor's Boulevard greatly enhanced the magnificence and mystical atmosphere of the palace city.

After renovation, the city was roughly square, with the southwest corner slightly curving inside—a reconciliation to reduce disturbance for residents. Simultaneously, a new lake was dug to expand the water and add natural scenery. Today, it is the Southern Sea.

The second change was to move the northern and eastern walls outwards to reduce interference from the residential quarter for the palace. However, this change made the Tonghui River part of the city's interior. As a result, the canal waterway to Jishuitan of the Yuan was disconnected and ceased operation. Consequently, thriving Yuan business areas around the eastern and northern shores of Jishuitan lost prosperity during the Ming era. Later, even Jishuitan (literally means water pool) dried up.

Fig. 5-13: Layout between Wu Gate and Zhengyang Gate[32]

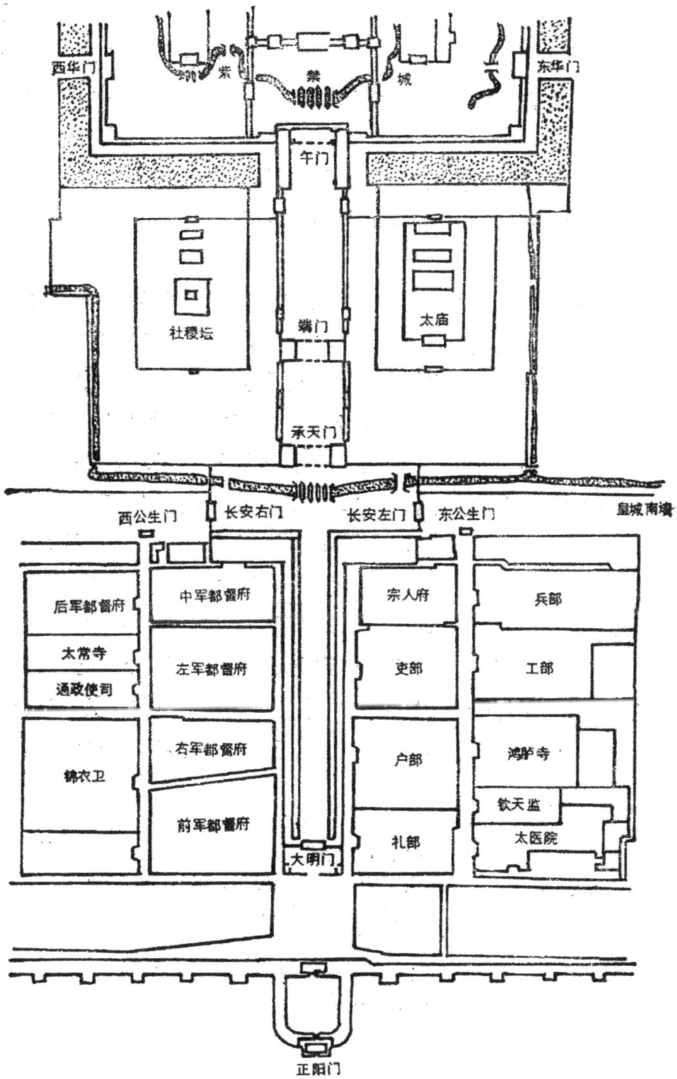

32. Hou Renzhi, *Theories and Practice in Historical Geography* (Shanghai: Shanghai People's Press, 1987), 239.

As a third change, a palace square and central official residential quarters were formed in the expanded area between the Chengtian and Daming gates. Palace walls on the west, east, and south sides were built on the square between Chengtian and Daming gates during the Ming, forming an enclosed square of the letter T. There were three gates on this enclosed square, two on the east and west wings and one on the protruding side at the south end. Since "a thousand-step corridor" was built along the inner side of the east and west palace walls from the Daming Gate, while outside the palace walls followed the architectural traditions of the Tang and Song dynasties—The central government offices for the imperial service were arranged symmetrically in the east and west along the central axis. This layout completely changed the city design of the Yuan Dynasty, in which central government offices were scattered throughout the city. This change reinforced the importance of the existing central axis.

During the Qianlong reign (AD 1736–1795), the east and west sides of the royal square in front of Tian'an Gate were further expanded. The palace wall paralleled the southern wall of the imperial city, enclosing the square's two wings into one section. This further enhanced its closeness. Regarding the short distance between the Daming and Zhengyang gates, as planned, it became a channel to connect traffic between the eastern and western parts of the city; known as Chessboard Street. It became a thriving business area in Beijing during the Ming and Qing dynasties.

In addition, Jingshan was built north of the palace city at the beginning of the Ming by taking advantage of dirt accumulated from the man-made South Lake and moat. As the highest point of the city, Jingshan, later called Coal Hill, replaced the position of the Center Pagoda of Dadu. Jingshan became the new geometric center of the renovated Beijing. Thus, ensuring that the layout of the city was square and symmetrical.

Maybe Jingshan, as a *feng shui* symbol of the Guardian Mountain, was a favorite name of the Ming rulers, since it not only represented the heart of the city but also sat on the original Yanchun Pagoda. Maybe the Ming wanted to use this as a symbol for the downfall of the previous dynasty and salute their own eternal rule; unfortunately, it did not bless the reign of the ever-lasting Ming. Instead, its last Emperor, Chongzhen, hung himself here at Jingshan after he failed to resist a rebel attack. Thus, it became the termination point of the Ming Dynasty. A cruel twist of fate perhaps.

The southern move of the palace, imperial, and outer areas extended Beijing's axis south. In the Center Pagoda of Yuan, the Ming also built the Drum and Bell Tower and shifted south towards the Chengtian and Zhengyang gates. After the outer city was built, the central axis passed between the Temple of Heaven and the Temple of Agriculture, and extended straight to the Yongding Gate. Thus, Beijing's distinct axis began south at Yongding Gate, through the exact center of the palace city and the central peak of Jingshan, and finally ended at the Drum and Bell Tower—a distance of eight kilometers. This was rare in city planning history, both at home and abroad, and also the most striking feature of the city's design from this period.

Fig. 5-14: Zhengyang Gate

- ***City Gates: Symbols of a Ritual City***

A look at the archaeological restoration map of Dadu (Fig. 5-18) shows the concept described in *Record of Trades*: "When the craftsmen construct the capital, it should be nine *li* on one side, with three doors on each side. There should be nine south-north streets and nine east-west streets. The ancestral temple should be on the left and the Altar to the God of the Land on the right. The market and the royal palaces should be about one *fu*." However, the designers of Dadu did not follow these principles strictly and only opened two gates at the northern wall; thus, Dadu had 11 gates.

Some scholars thought the 11 gates designed for Yuan came from the *Iching* (*The Book of Changes*), a result of categorizing odd numbers as *Yang* and even numbers as *Yin*. The number for heaven includes one, three, five, seven, and nine; the number for earth includes two, four, six, eight, and ten. When five, the middle number of heaven's numbers, and six, the middle number of earth's numbers are summed, the result is 11. This can be interpreted as the integration of earth and heaven. Therefore, there were three gates—an odd number in the south, and two gates—an even number in the north, to show the corresponding meaning of *Yin* and *Yang*.[33]

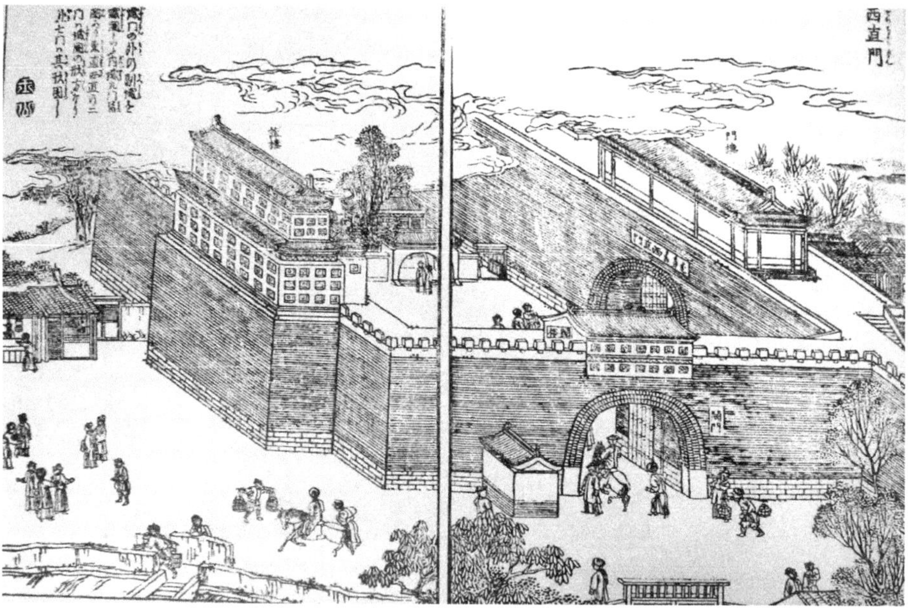

Fig. 5-15: Xizhimen

Alternatively, a group of scholars thought this design was related to a monk named Liu Bingzhong. When he was young, his extensive reading of Confucianism, Taoism, and Buddhism had a profound impact, which can be seen from the gate design and naming of Dadu. There was one gate less in the northern wall because Liu Bingzhong believed in the Shaoyong theory—that the North should

33. See Huang Jianju, *Studies on the Choice and Planning of Chinese Ancient Capitals* (Xiamen: Xiamen University Press, 2005), 213.

not be seen completely. North implied "hidden" and "serious risks," according to the *Iching*. Thus, the main entrance of the northern gate was avoided. In fact, this also fits the climate of Beijing, which is part of the continental monsoon climate, with northwestern winds prevalent in winter. Likewise, northern Chinese houses do not open their windows to the north in order to avoid the cold, northwest winds.[34]

The naming of the gates of Dadu in the Yuan Dynasty also originated from the *Iching* with a deep cultural meaning. The Lizheng Gate, the main entrance door of the capital, came from the *Li* (离) Hexagram "*Ri Yue Li Hu Tian*" (the sun and the moon in the sky, meaning eternity), expecting the "saint would face the south and be wise in governing." By studying the hexagram of the *Iching* and the map of the Dadu gates, plus referring to studies by scholars,[35] it seems we can look into this mystery.

Since the mid-Ming era, Beijing was a combination of inner and outer cities which appears like the Chinese character "凸" from the previous rectangle. The gates changed from the previous 11 to a pattern of nine gates in the palace city; seven in the imperial city; and four in the outer city, which continued for about 500 years without much change. Even most of the gate's names are the same today.

The so-called "inner nine" refers to Dongzhimen and Chaoyangmen in the east, Xizhimen and Fuchengmen in the west, Deshengemen and Andingmen in the north, and Chongwenmen, Zhengyangmen (Qianmen), and Xuanwumen in the south. A very well-known phrase—Nine Gate Supervisor—refers to the man in charge of the inner city's security. The nine gates each had their own functions, and as the Beijingers said, "the nine gates had nine kinds of carriages go through."

Zhengyangmen was the gate of the "dragon carriage." Called Lizhengmen during the Yuan, the middle gate in the south wall was renamed Zhengyangmen during the Ming and Qing. This gate was exclusively for Emperors and was also called the "national gate." The Emperor would go through Zhengyangmen twice a year: once during winter to offer and again to the Waking of the Insects (one of

34. Yu Xixian and Hou Renzhi, *History and Geography of Beijing: The City Planning and Construction of Beijing in Liao, Jin, and Yuan Dynasties* (Beijing: Beijing Yanshan Press, 2000), 101.

35. Ibid., 102–104.

the 24 solar terms in the Chinese Lunar Calendar) to plough the land in Xiannong Tan (Altar of Agriculture). Because of its location at the front of the imperial city, it received another name—Qianmen (which means front gate). The well-known "Da Qianmen" cigarette was named after this.

Chongwenmen was the wine carriage entrance. Chongwenmen and Xuanwumen were the two gates on the southern wall of the inner city. "Chongwen" means "reverence for culture" and "Xuanwu" means demonstration of forceful power. The two city gates were juxtaposed with the east and west, which was to take the meaning of "Arts on the left, Military on the right" and "Arts make people civil, Military make country safe." Chongwen Gate was the name in Ming and Qing dynasties, and it was called Civilization Gate in Yuan Dynasty, with similar meanings. Chongwenmen, also known as "Hademen," was the capital's tax collection headquarters. During the Ming and Qing, wine consumed by high officials and noble lords came mostly from Hebei, Zhuozhou, and other places, passing from the Grand Canal to Tongzhou, and then entering the city from Chongwenmen. The wine would be checked and taxed in the vicinity of Chongwenmen. In addition, according to the *Yin* and *Yang* of the five lines of argument, the east was in charge of wood, which oversaw life. For this reason, candidates who came for the imperial national examinations would also enter the capital from Chongwenmen.

Xuanwumen (宣武门) was the exit for prisoners' carriages. Xuanwumen was called Shunchengmen in Yuan Dynasty. It was renamed Xuanwumen (玄武门) in Ming Dynasty. Later, in order to avoid the taboo of Emperor Kangxi's name Xuanye (玄烨), it was changed to Xuanwumen (宣武门). The execution of convicts took place in Caishikou, outside of Xuanwumen. After the Justice Department convicted prisoners, they were taken to Caishikou for beheading. It was said that three Chinese characters—"regret too late"—were engraved in Xuanwumen, with its meaning clear at a glance. According to the theory of the five elements, the west direction concerns gold and death, so funeral participants would also pass through this exit. Hence, it is called "the gate of death" too.

Chaoyangmen was the entrance for grain carts. Chaoyangmen was the south gate of the eastern wall of the inner city. It was called Qihuamen in the Yuan. During the Ming and Qing dynasties, the city's grain mostly came from south of the Yangtze along the Grand Canal to Tongzhou. After unloading grain from the ship, it was transported by land to Beijing within Chaoyangmen and stored in the official depots: "Shipping warehouse," "East Warehouse," or "Lumicang." To this day, the names are still retained, and Chaoyangmen is called the "Grain Gate."

Fuchengmen was the entrance for coal carts. Fuchengmen was the south gate of the west wall of the inner city, it was called Pingzemen in the Yuan Dynasty. The coal was produced in Mentougou, an area west of Beijing. A plum blossom was carved at the top of Fuchengmen gate. Plum is a homophonic of "coal" in Chinese, and was used to indicate the coal entrance.

Xizhimen entrance was used for water tankers and was the northern gate of the western wall. It was called Heyimen in the Yuan Dynasty. Because the water quality from the city wells was not good, drinking water for the palaces was brought from the Western Hills and Yuquan Mountains in special water tankers. All royal water tankers went through Xizhimen into the city. Therefore, ripples of water were carved at the top of the gate.

Dongzhimen was used for bricks and wood carts. This door was the poorest among the nine gates because the kilns in the past were located in Dongzhimen. Wood from the south also came to the city through Dongzhimen. In fact, Dongzhimen Street during the Ming and Qing dynasties was the distribution center for people's daily necessities and supplies—a hub of the working classes.

Deshengmen was the exit for army carts—the western gate in the northern wall. It was called Jiandemen in the Yuan Dynasty. According to the constellation, Xuanwu oversees the northern territories, so the north gate of Chang'an in the Tang Dynasty was called Xuanwu Gate (玄武门). However, it's said that the God Xuanwu blessed Zhu Di when he seized power, so when he built the city of Beijing, Zhu Di deliberately placed the Xuanwumen in the south of the capital. But Chinese tradition believed that Xuanwu represented the military, so if he sent troops to war, the army should still be sent out of the city through the north gate of Xuanwumen. This gate was also called Deshengmen based on the following story: At the beginning of the Ming era, Xu Da conquered Beijing. He found the Yuan Emperor had fled from the western gate, Jiandemen, of the northern wall to the Mongolia Plateau. To commemorate this victory, Xu Da renamed Jiandemen to Deshengmen (得胜门). Later, it was renamed Deshengmen (德胜门, virtue victory gate). This gate was the exit point for all armies during the Ming and Qing, so it was also called the military gate.

Fig. 5-16: Deshengmen

Andingmen was the exit for human waste carts, located east of the northern wall. This gate, like Deshengmen, was originally for victorious soldiers returning to the city. In fact, because the gate was near the Earth Altar, the main farm manure area of Beijing, it would naturally become a channel for waste carts to pass through. Still, it was called Bingche huicheng (meaning the army comes back) as a euphemism.

"The Outer Seven" refers to a total of seven outer city gates added in AD 1553 by Emperor Shizong of Ming to strengthen the city's defense. In the north and paralleled with the three front gates of the inner city were Dongbianmen and Xibianmen, in the east and west there were Guangqumen and Guang'anmen, and in the south there were Zuoanmen, Youanmen, and the Yongdingmen, directly below Zhengyangmen.

Through photos, we can see the outer city gates were not as grand as those of the inner city, an indication of their relative position. Only Yongdingmen, at the center of the southern city, was considered an important outer city gate. The reason for this was very simple: Yongdingmen was the end point of Qianmen

Street, which extended from Zhengyangmen. As the terminal of the central axis of Beijing, it would assume a higher status than most other gates.

The "Imperial Four" refers to the four imperial Forbidden City gates. There was Dong'anmen in the east (now the Donghuamen), Tiananmen in the south, Xi'anmen in the west, and Di'anmen in the north. These gates were established by feudal rulers to protect themselves and had little to do with the common people.

Fig. 5-17: A Map of the imperial city

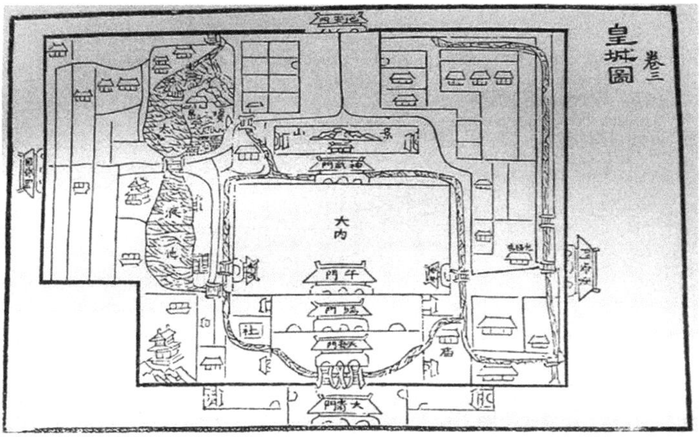

- ***Markets: Vitality of a Ritual City***

Speaking of markets in Beijing, people often think of Wangfujing, Qianmen, Dongdan, Xidan, and other well-known places. These markets only developed after several dynastic changes. To understand where the modern markets emerged from, we must begin with the Yuan Dynasty.

During the Yuan, due to the Grand Canal and developed land and water transportation, merchandise from all parts of the country could reach the city directly. According to research, there were more than 30 special markets in Dadu, forming a market spread centered on the vicinity of the Drum and Bell Tower and the slanted street of the north shore of Jishuitan.[36] This layout further influenced later generations.

---

36. Gao Songfan, "Historical Studies on the Market Evolution of Beijing and its Districts," *Geography Journal*, no. 2 (1989).

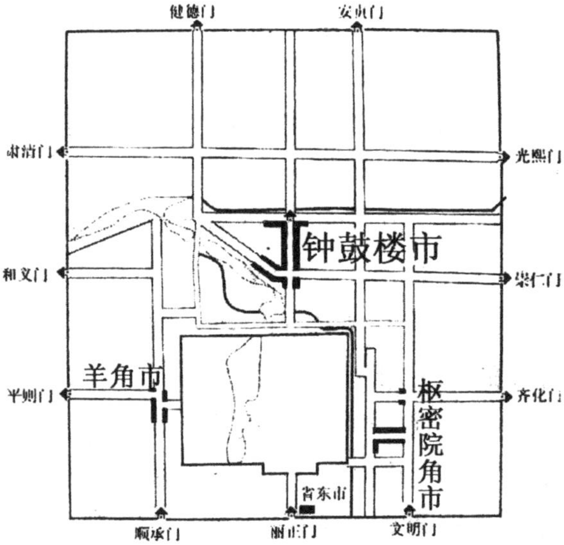

Fig. 5-18: The distribution of main markets in Dadu of Yuan

As we know, the business district is usually located in the geometric center and can be reached conveniently by many to access and provide goods and services. Located in the northeast of the city, the Bell and Drum Tower held a key position. As mentioned before, the Bell and Drum Tower of Dadu in the Yuan Dynasty was located in the geometric center of the city, where several main roads intersected. Jishuitan served as the terminal of the Tonghui River and Ba River waterway transport. Water and land transportation was highly convenient, so it was natural that Dadu became the city's commercial center. This also makes Dadu the capital that most follows the ideal capital system described in the *Rites of Zhou*. Besides the Drum and Bell, markets such as Yangjiao, located near Shunchengmen (today's Xuanwumen) in the southwestern part of the city, formed a business center west of Dadu, roughly in the location of today's Xisi. This shows Xisi had long history as a trade center. In addition, the Privy Council Corner Market and the Eastern Commercial Center were located in today's Dengshikou area.

The three markets mentioned above were the most important and largest at the time. But for ordinary people, they also needed to acquire daily life necessities near their neighborhoods. As a result, there were also smaller markets distributed within Dadu to provide these. For instance, in Shishikou (today's Dongsi) there were grocery stores, firewood, and cart markets. Near Shunchengmen in the west (today's Xuanwumen), there were grass, charcoal, fruit, and workers' markets. In Wenmingwen, there were also grass, pig, and fish markets. Inside Lizhengmen (today's Qianmen), there was Shengdong market, where books and papers were sold.

In fact, apart from the principal of balanced distribution within the city, the social strata of the urban population also affected the layout of urban commercial networks. Since high-ranking officials and rich families of Dadu mostly lived in the southern and central parts, large markets that could provide quality commodities, were mostly located in the center. The majority of the poor, lower class residents lived in the previous locations of Zhongdu—the southwest suburbs of Dadu.

Although Beijing markets developed on the foundation of Dadu, market distribution somewhat changed due to large-scale city renovation conducted at the start of Ming. One of most important tasks was the moving of the royal office to the front of the palace and the markets to the back. During the early Ming, northern Dadu, empty and difficult to defend, was contracted and the city expanded its southern wall. As a consequence, the Grand Canal was no longer directly connected with Jishuitan further north in the city. Therefore, the business districts around the Bell and Drum towers lost commerce and status. The second consequence was the formation of a new market in the newly expanded space.

Fig. 5-19: A sketch map of main market distribution

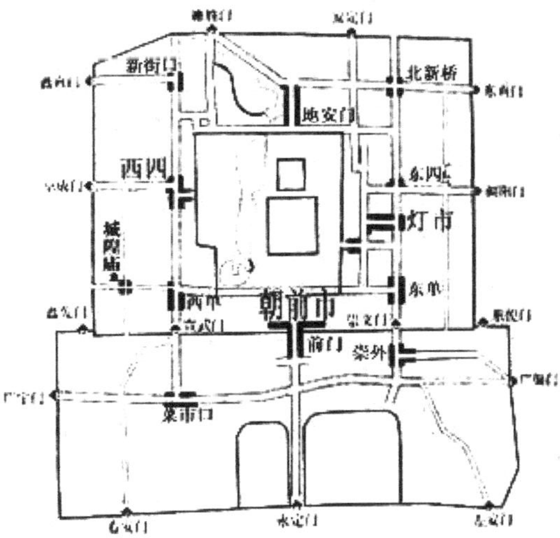

The market in front of the royal offices was composed of the Chessboard Street area, in front of the Daming Gate, and the street outside of Qianmen. It was the busiest downtown area of the inner city and the commercial center for all of Beijing. According to statistics, there were more than 1,100 shops and 320 high-end shops, providing a glimpse of the size and status of this market.[37]

Besides this, other markets were mostly inherited from the original site, such as the Lantern Market outside Dong'anmen. In the Ming Dynasty, the entire street was two *li* in length, and six famous imperial stores, including Baohe. On the fifth, tenth, and twentieth day of each month, according to the Chinese lunar calendar, regular markets were held. At the end of the Ming, the Interior Market, held three days every month, was moved to the Lantern Market.

The main market in the western part of the city was Xisi Pailou Market, which was also developed on the basis of Yangjiao Market in the Yuan Dynasty. Beijingers called this market "West Market" in the Ming Dynasty. Halls were built during Emperor Yongle's reign, which underlined their importance. There were also other markets, such as horse, goat, and fruit markets, etc. Even an entertainment district was formed in the Goulan Hutong. There was Di'anmen Market in the northern part of the city, which included the area from the outside of Di'anmen to the street of the Drum Tower. This area eventually lost its prosperity due to the rerouting of trade routes, but still remained a commercial hub for northern Beijing. In addition, there were many shops and other markets in Dongdan, Xidan, Dongsi, Caishikou, and Chongwen, which are thought to inherit the market system from the Yuan.

There was another feature of commerce in Beijing during the Ming: fair markets. These markets began as regular markets that developed into traditional temple fairs, characterized by commercial and trade activities, and folk entertainment. The temple fair, like other fairs, became a supplementary form of the established commercial market and played an important role in urban life. Among them, the temple fair in Chenghuang Temple was the largest in Beijing during the Ming Dynasty and was held regularly on the first, 15th, and 25th days of each month.

Obviously, commercial activities in Beijing centered on Chessboard Street and the market in front of the royal offices at Qianmen. Lantern Market was in the

37. Gao Songfan, "Historical Studies on the Market Evolution of Beijing and its Districts," *Geography Journal*, no. 2 (1989).

east and West Market (Xisi today) was in the west, plus other markets in Dongsi, Caishikou, and Chongwenmenwai. Fair markets represented Town God's Temple Fair and other regularly held markets. This seems complex, but was an orderly market system pieced together by the Beijing market structure of the time.

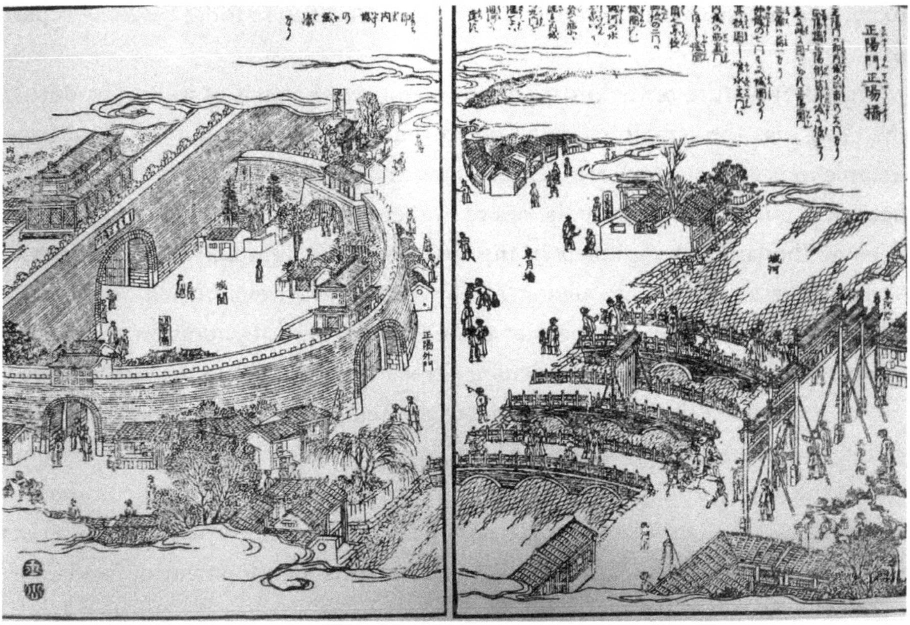

Fig. 5-20: Pailou (ceremonial arch) in Xisi

Beijing's market system during the Qing Dynasty experienced two stages: decline in the early stage and recovery and development during the middle and later periods. In the beginning, the government imposed a segregation policy on the Man and Han ethnic groups, and divided the inner city into Eight Banners territories—this devastated the city's markets. This separation policy was relaxed gradually and by the Qing mid-era, commercial life had begun to thrive again. The establishment of trade associations and guilds, as well as the development of a commodity economy, promoted market prosperity and diversification.

Based on the city's layout from the Ming, the Qing formed a system with Qianmen (the front gate) as the commercial center. This commercial district started in the north from Chessboard Street in front of Daqingmen, then went south in the area of Zhushikou, extending east to Changxiangertiao, and west to Meishi Street. It was the financial center of Beijing during the Qing Dynasty, the most luxurious and prosperous district. Because of Chessboard Street's location, it enjoyed convenient transport links. However, it was also restricted by densely distributed offices, residences, and limited transaction space. In this context, commercial activities further extended south, integrating with Qianmen to become the top business center. The famous Dashilan in today's Beijing is part of it.

Another feature of the prosperity of commercial activities in Beijing during the Qing was the temple fair market. In the early Qing Dynasty, Chenghuang Temple moved south to Ciren Temple, now known as Baoguo Temple, and soon became a bustling bazaar. By the era of Emperor Kangxi (AD 1662–1722), it had become the largest temple fair in the city. The Land Temple Fair, Nanyaowang Temple Fair, and the Lingyougong Temple Fair, which were formed in the Ming Dynasty, were also very prosperous in the Qing Dynasty. In addition, there were temple fairs in Dongzhimen, Jiugulou Street, and the Dongyaowang and Beiyaowang Temple Fairs on the northeast of the Temple of Heaven. During the start of Emperor Yongzheng's reign, the Longfu and Huguo temples rose to become two of the most prominent as well. Since the inner city had few fixed commercial stores before the late Qing, temple fairs became the main venues for residents seeking daily necessities. However, with the gradual development of fixed commercial stores in the inner city, temple fairs were relegated to a subordinate position. This feature can be showcased by the development of the Liulichang Market.

At the beginning of the Qing era, fixed temple fairs arose around the Ciren Temple. However, this area soon declined and commerce moved to Liulichang, located further south. With bookshops clustered around Liulichang, the district thrived as a cultural and commercial center. The situation of Liulichang markets demonstrates the basic commercial development pattern in inner-city Beijing in Qing Dynasty—the regular markets in the early period were transformed into fixed commercial shops, therefore forming the hierarchical urban commercial system. The same situation also occurred in Dongda market, which was the most important commercial center in the east, also known as the Dongsi Pailou market, one of the "Four Great Heng" money shops of the capital. Originally, it was a fixed trade fair because of its proximity to Gongyuan. After the middle of the Qing Dynasty, it developed into a commercial center in the eastern part of Beijing's inner city.

Even the main commercial centers of Xicheng (west city) and the Xisi Pailou Market evolved from a temple fair market. Besides these district commercial centers, there were more grass-root level commercial centers formed along the traffic intersections, such as Xinjiekou, Beixinqiao, Jiaodaokou, Donganmen, and Dianmen, became very bustling bazaars. Business markets were also found along passes, such as the Chaoyangmen, Andingmen, Deshengmen, Xizhimen, etc.

The commerce layout of the outer city during the Qing was slightly different from that of the inner city. This was because the outer city markets developed steadily on the foundation of the Ming, as residential areas for Han officials and commoners, as well as businessmen from around the country. The inner city was different because it was not until Emperor Kangxi and Yongzheng's reign during the mid-Qing period that commerce started to recover. Before this time, the two temple markets—Longfu and Huguo—served the function of commercial centers.

During the late Qing era, markets in Beijing included Zhengyang Gate Street, Dianmen Street, Donganmenwai and Xianmenwai, Eastern Xisi Pailou, and Eastern Xidan Pailou, along with the outer city's vegetable and flower markets. Together with the fixed temple fairs and some specialized bazaars, these became the basic layout for Beijing's market system.

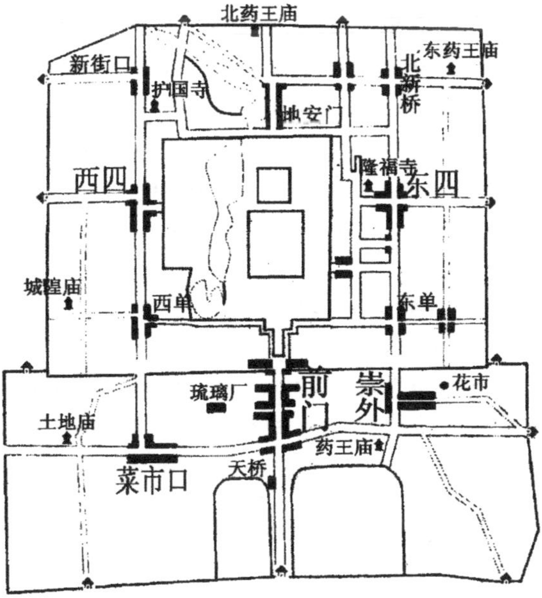

Fig. 5-21: Distribution of the main markets in Beijing during the Qing Dynasty

Because of the spread of Western ideas and culture, the improvement of urban transport as well as the interplay of political and economic factors, the market focus of Beijing shifted during the Republic of China (1912–1949). The formation of Wangfujing business center and the rapid growth of commerce in Xidan laid the foundation for the present market system of the city.

The political situation in the Republic of China has dramatically shifted Beijing's business landscape, Wangfujing Commercial Center became the largest comprehensive market and the most important business center in Beijing.

Wangfujing was located in the area between the foreign embassies and Donganmen, the main entrance of the imperial city. Two different yet important political forces of Beijing collaborated to build this business center. On the one hand, feudal rulers implemented the "New Deal," including the establishment of the market in Dongan. On the other hand, foreign capital funded a number of modern public institutions, including the Beijing Hotel, Union Hospital, banks, theaters, etc. Chinese and Western investment led to the development of commerce in this area, allowing Wangfujing to rise rapidly and become the city's commercial center.

If the successful construction of Wangfujing commercial center is the joint effort of Chinese and foreign parties, the formation of Xidan commercial center is the product of the Chinese national economy under Western influence. The creation of the Xidan market during the 1930s promoted the prosperity of commercial activities in the Chang'an Avenue area, whose openness further promoted the establishment of various stores. This made Xidan the largest commercial center in the western district of Beijing, replacing Xisi. Similarly, the Dongdan market was mainly influenced by foreign capital and its business services were more "westernized." As the Chinese saying goes, "lost here and gained there" and vice versa. The rise of Wangfujing and Xidan mirrored the corresponding downturn of the Dongsi and Xisi markets, and the markets within the Qianmen area.

After the formation of the Republic of China, the originally closed Tiananmen Square and Chang'an Avenue were opened, providing easy access for inner and outer city traffic flow. The position of Qianmen, previously the only channel connecting the inner and outer cities, declined as an important transport intersection. One direct consequence was the shrinking Qianmen business district where many shops moved to Wangfujing and Xidan Pailou.[38]

Additionally, the Caishikou and Chongwenmenwai markets became sluggish. Only Tianqiao Market bucked the trend. It developed and rapidly grew into the biggest common market in Beijing. The rise of Tianqiao reflected the obvious class differences in modern Beijing. Tianqiao positioned itself as the market to provide commerce services, which were considered inferior, and could not or would not be provided by Wangfujing or Xidan, to the lower-class people mostly living in the outer city.

Still, history and tradition have played a role that cannot be underestimated: old markets such as Dianmen Beixinqiao, and Xinjiekou continued to play a vital role in local commerce. Also, the Qiansanmen markets, though incomparable to their heydays of the Ming and Qing, still rivalled emerging business centers. Qianmen market was still considered an important business center in this age of upheaval.

38. Gao Songfan, "Historical Studies on the Market Evolution of Beijing and Its Districts," *Geography Journal*, no. 2 (1989).

CHAPTER SIX

LIS AND *FANGS*: THE DEVELOPMENT OF URBAN SOCIETY

1. Neighborhoods and Communities

In China, the basic unit for city residents was called *li* (里, community or village) from the Western Zhou to the Qin and Han dynasties. As the name in Chinese suggests, it is an area for a square *li*. Until the Northern Wei Dynasty, "an area with 300 steps on each side would make a *li*" as mentioned in the capital, Luoyang. Therefore, *li* was a typical dwelling unit in early Chinese cities.

As a unit of urban residence, certain administrative institutions were customarily needed. In the *lis* where the nobles of the capital gathered, a head, called *lijun*, was usually appointed as the lowest ranking person—roughly the equivalent to the director of a neighborhood community in China today. *Book of Documents · Announcement about Drunkenness* recorded that the Shang King persuaded his ministers to drink less alcohol, "Officials of all levels at court, *bailiao, shuyin, weiya, weifu, zonggong,* and *lijun.*" *Bailiao* is the general title of all the officers in court; *shuyin* refers to the leader of hundred officers; *weiya* includes adjutant officers; *weifu* means officers in general; *zonggong* is the kind of officer who works for the clan; *lijun* refers to the officers who work in nobles' communities. It can be seen that *lijun* is the lowest rank of officer. During the Spring and Autumn Period, people still called the head of *li* as "*lijun.*" As Guanzi said to the Duke

Huan of Qi in *Guanzi · Xiaokuang Section*: "Establish a unit of *li* higher than your jurisdiction, a *li* under the jurisdiction of the state, and a *li* under your jurisdiction, and divide the kingdom into three divisions as three armies. Select talented commander as the leader of *lis*." In the Warring States Period, the states in the Central Plains adopted this *li* system. *Mo-tse Superiority of Centralization* discussed the three-level administrative system, including "state," "town," and "*li*." The town had a magistrate, and the *li* had a head, too. During the Warring States Period, the head of *li* in the Qin State was called "*lizheng*." During the Warring States Period, all the counties and townships in each State, including the capital, had officials who looked after the gate, called the Gate Officer. Shi Ju of Xiacai, the teacher of Primer of King Wu of the Qin State, was a Gate Officer of Xiacaili alley. Another example was Li Yiji between Qin and Han Dynasty; he came from a poor background and worked as a Gate Officer for a living. The officer of *lilü* was the lowest official rank, so it was regarded as a lowly position. Therefore, in the *Strategies of the Warring States*, the retinues of King Xuan of Qi said, "To an educated gentleman, the Gate Officer is a very lowly position." However, from this record, we can also observe that the layout of *li* was a closed loop, so there was a gate and Gate Officer to manage the gate.

We do not have much information about the *li* system in the Qin Dynasty. But one record worthy of attention is the *Records of the Grand Historian · The Heredity House of Chen She*. It states: "draft the left during the first year of Emperor Ershi of Qin," which meant residents living on the left side of the *lü* (the main entrance of the *li*) would be enlisted. From this, we can infer the residents of the *lü* were divided into left and right sections. We can further speculate the *li* in the Qin had an internal alley and the main entrance like before.

The Western Han inherited the *li* system from the Qin. For instance, *San Fu Huang Tu (Historical Geography in the Qin and Han Dynasties)* discussed the *lüli (lü* means the entrance of a *li)* in Chang'an like this: "there are 160 *lülis* in Chang'an, houses are packed densely, and the alleys were straight." Besides this description, there was no reliable data to refer to the *li* system in the cities during the Han Dynasty. Therefore, later scholars inferred through indirect sources, like markets, that *li* were surrounded by walls and had gates to pass through. More specifically, the interior layout of *li* was a narrow-shaped space in the north-south direction, with the main entrance on each side of the south and north walls. From the literature, it is likely the *lü* and *yan* already existed, since the South and North gates of *li* were mentioned in *Chunqiu Fanlu · Prayers for Rain*. Other works, such as Zhang Heng's *An Ode to the West Capital* and other literature, also mentioned *lü* and *yan*.

As explained in the *Book of Han · Biography of Zhang Chang*: "The thief chiefs marked thieves' plackets with reddish-brown pigments, prison officers sat at the alley to check those who come out in red and then grabbed him and tied him up, arrested hundreds of people in one day." This story tells us that Chang'an had many thieves at that time. The police officers were stationed at the gates of every town and would arrest anyone marked as a thief. It shows that the general residents' houses were built inside of *li* (residential area), and anyone entering and leaving the residential area had to pass through the front gate—*lü*.

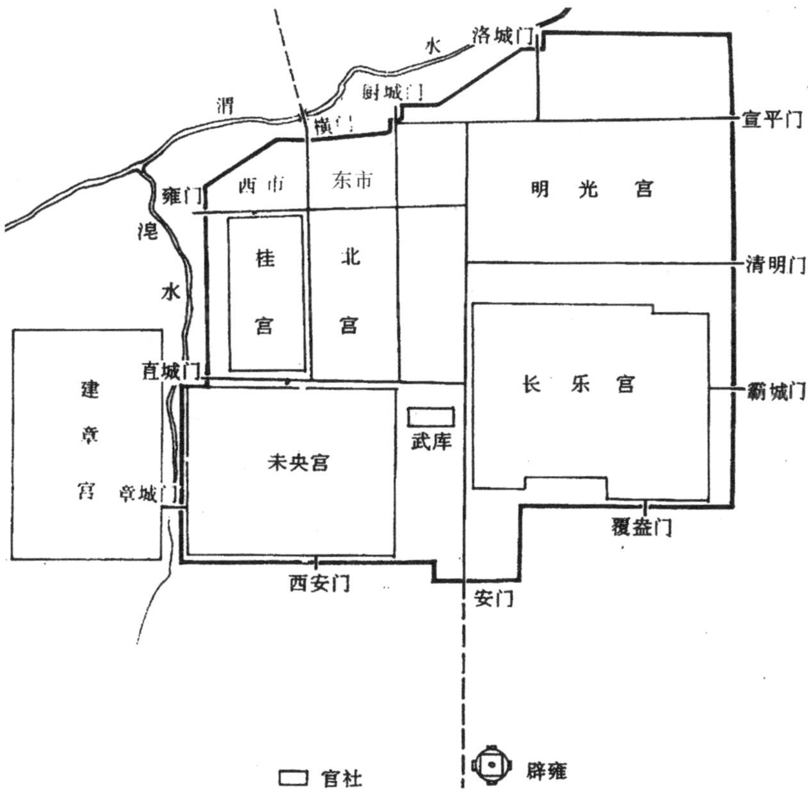

Fig. 6-1: Diagram of Urban Zones of Chang'an during the Western Han

This mode also led to another characteristic of the urban living style—ordinary people's house gates do not directly face the streets. This is due to the residential area being surrounded by walls. Residents must come in and out through the inner door, which is also easy to manage. Because of this, the senior officials and nobles can open their gates on the street, not from the inner doors. This became a privilege, and people called this kind of residence "*di*." Therefore, when the Han and Wei dynasties system was explained in *Chu Xue Ji*, there was a special rule: "Those who do not enter or exit through the inner gate and whose front gate open toward the street are called *di*. Furthermore, if the noble collects less than ten thousand household taxes, the noble's house still cannot be called *di*. His house cannot be called *di* if a person lives inside *li*." Today's term mansions "Fudi" come from this tradition. Chang'an in the Western Han Dynasty was built and perfected on the foundation of the old palaces of the Qin Dynasty. Even the court where the emperor lived was continuously expanded later, so it is unlikely that the ordinary people built their houses in one day.

Until the late Western Han Dynasty, new *li* was built in Chang'an. As noted in the *Book of Han · the Commentary of Emperor Ping*: In the second year of Yuanshi reign, five *li* were built for ordinary people inside the city of Chang'an, 200 districts in total."

2. The Enclosed "*Fangs*" and Strict Administration

Since the Eastern Han Dynasty, noble residencies in the palace became "*fangs*." For instance, "there was Prince *Fang* in Luoyang in the Eastern Han."[1] But this is only one case. Later, it was clear that *fang* had become a name for residential areas of Luoyang. *Palace and Pagoda Names in the Jin Dynasty* documented "in the Palaces of Luoyang, there were Xianchang *Fang*, Xiucheng *Fang*, Suifu *Fang*, Yanfu *Fang*, Xiuzhi *Fang*, Chengqing *Fang*, Guifen *Fang*, Jiaofang *Fang*, Shulan *Fang*, and Yiwen *Fang*." In fact, from a semantics perspective, *Fang* (坊) also means *Fang* (防, defense). For instance, there is an article *Fang Ji* in *Book of Rites*, a *fang* is read as a defense. *Fang* originally refers to the area surrounded by walls. In the Northern

1. "Palaces and Pagoda Names of the Han Dynasty," introduction in *Imperial Readings of the Taiping Era*, vol. 157.

Wei Dynasty, "*li*" (where the residents lived in the city) began to be called *Fang*.

When the Northern Wei Dynasty built Pingcheng, it imitated Ye and Luoyang to construct the outer city. In AD 406, "the outer city was planned with about 20 *li* on each side. Markets and *lis* were set up along roads and boulevards. Within 30 days, the planning was complete."[2] At this time, it was only planning and preparing to build the outer wall, which was used for the city's commercial district. And the inner-city area was for the city residents. The outer city of the Pingcheng was built sixteen years later, in the seventh year (AD 422) of the Taichang reign of Emperor Mingyuan. According to the records of that time, "The outer city was ordered to be built, and the total length should be 32 *li*." At that time, the structure of the outer city was "The city surrounded by the south of the palace city walls; there were alleys within the *fangs*. The big *fangs* could hold 400–500 households, and the smaller ones 60 or 70. They would sometimes be closed for search purposes to avoid misconduct."[3] This system of surrounding the southern districts of the palaces with an outer city and dividing the outer city into *fangs* and *lis* copied Luoyang and Ye from the Wei Dynasty (established by Cao), since the Eastern Han. In this record, we know *fangs* were built for the commoners in Pingcheng for the purpose of urban security administration.

After moving the capital to Luoyang, the Northern Wei brought this style of life to the Central Plains. After unified planning of the capital, 50,000 people were recruited in AD 502 (the first year of the Jingming era) and 320 *fangs* were built in one go. This was the first time entire residential areas were completed in one attempt with an orderly planning layout in Chinese history. The following was written at the end of volume 5 of *A Record of Buddhist Monasteries in Luoyang*:

> The capital was 20 *lis* wide and 15 *lis* long with more than 109,000 households. On the outside of the temples, altars, palaces and office buildings, *lis* were set up, each with 300 steps on each side and four gates around. There would be two *lizhengs* (supervisors), four soldiers, and eight gate keepers for each *li*. Altogether, there were 220 *lis* and 1,367 temples.

2. *Book of the Wei Dynasty · A Biography of Taizu.*
3. *Book of the Southern Qi · The Northern Wei Annals.*

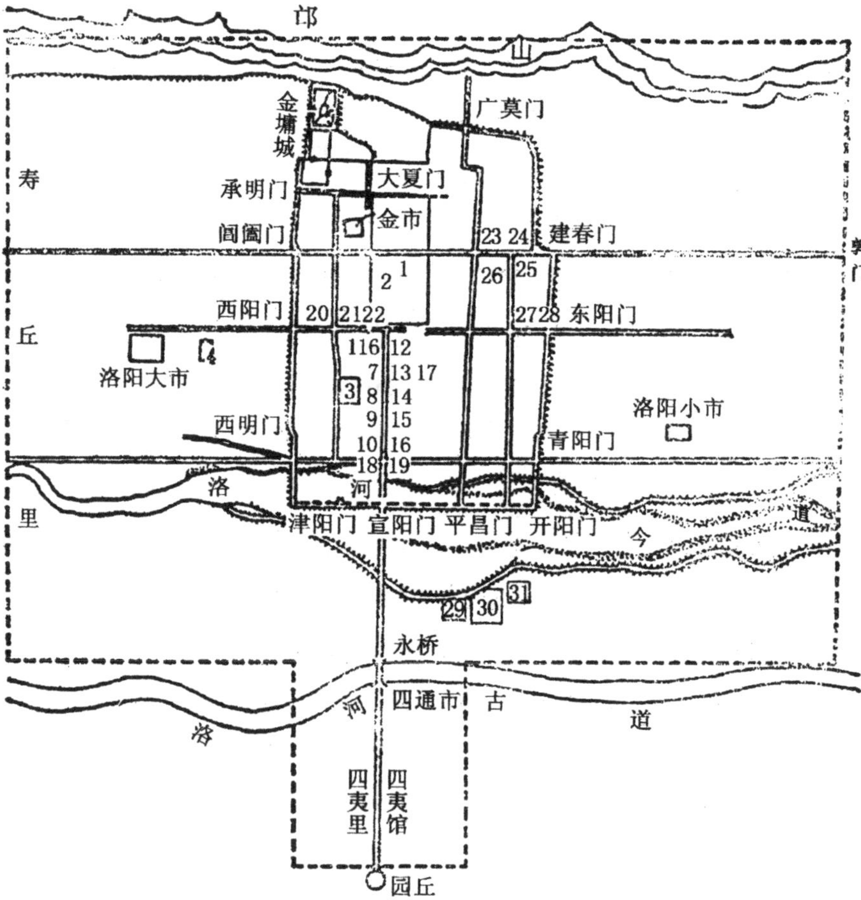

Fig. 6-2: Map of the fangs *in Luoyang, Northern Wei*

"An area of 300 steps on each side as one *li*"—each *fang* in Luoyang was just one square *li*, so people would use *li* and *fang* interchangeably. The commoners' *fang* was a square with a gate on each side and had two *lizheng*s as superintendents and four petty officers taking charge of the business of *fang*. To strengthen public security, eight gate guards were employed to supervise the residents who pass through the four main entrances of the *fang*. It's worth pointing out that the "220 *lis*" record should be 320 *lis*. According to the regulations at that time, the area of these 320 *lis* should be 320 square *li*. Luoyang City is close to Mang Mountain in the north, so the city is naturally mainly distributed in the east, west, and south. The famous archaeologist Mr. Su Bai painted the *Reconstruction of the Design of*

Luoyang Guocheng in the Northern Wei Dynasty, which paints the inner city of Luoyang into six *lis* from east to west and nine *lis* from north to south, paints the entire Luoyang including the urban area and the surrounding Guo District into 20 *lis* from east to west and 15 *lis* from north to south, and draws a rectangular protruding part in the center of the south with four *lis* from east to west and five *lis* from north and south, so it is precisely 320 *lis*. Most of these 320 *lis* are located outside the Guo District. This painting method is the most accurate restoration of Luoyang City in the Northern Wei Dynasty. *Fangs*, as formed in the Northern Wei as city residence areas, reached their peak during the Tang Dynasty. One of the main characteristics of the *fang* system during this era was its closeness, most typically represented by Chang'an, the capital.

The predecessor of Chang'an City in the Tang Dynasty was Daxing City in Sui Dynasty. In the second year of Kaihuang reign (AD 582), Emperor Wen of Sui ordered Gao Xi and Yuwen Kai to build a new capital city called Daxing in Longshouyuan, located in the southeast of the ancient Chang'an in the Han Dynasty. Daxing was divided into inner and outer cities, with the inner further divided into the palace city and the imperial city. Like Luoyang, this was another capital built step-by-step on a pre-designed plan. The palace city would be built first, followed by the imperial city, and the outer city would be built last. After the Tang conquered the Sui, they inherited the capital, Daxing, and changed the name to Chang'an.

As for Chang'an in the Sui and Tang dynasties, we have a better understanding of the layout and other details as more records become available. Walls were built in the *fangs* of Chang'an during the Tang. According to archaeological excavations, the walls were about 2.5–3 meters wide at the base. Viewing the whole city's layout, we can see the shapes of the *fangs* were slightly different. The four rows of little *fangs* on both sides of Zhuque Avenue south of the imperial city only had east-west streets and did not have passages from south to north. In addition to the *fangs*, east-west and north-south courses were crossed, and the whole square was divided into four independent neighborhoods. In these neighborhoods, there was a cross-shaped alley leading to each house. At that time, this kind of alley had a unique name called *qu*. For example, the famous entertainment area in Chang'an was Pingkang *Fang* which occupied three *qu*. Moreover, each *fang* was equipped with east, west, north, and south four gates, which were connected to Cross Street.

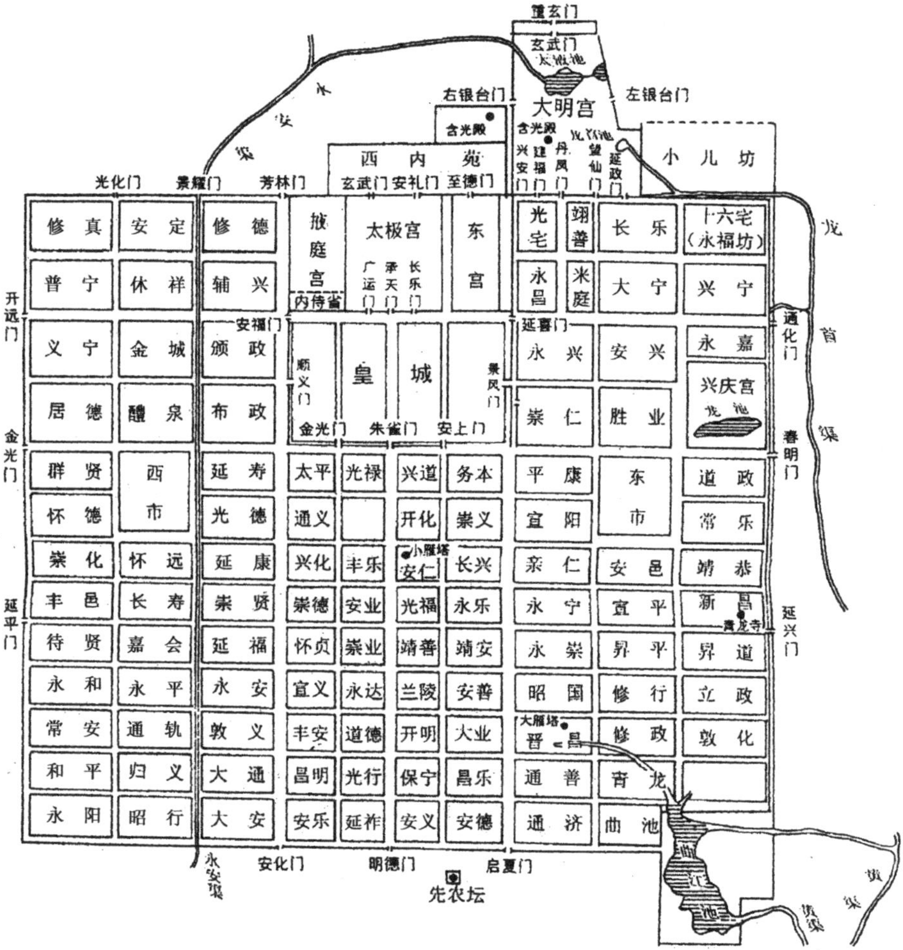

Fig. 6-3: Plan of fangs *in Chang'an in the Tang Dynasty*[4]

4. Yang Kuan, *Studies on the Ancient Chinese Capital System History* (Shanghai: Shanghai People's Press, 2003), 163.

The residential *fang* was not only enclosed by walls, but it was stipulated that *fangs* should be opened and closed regularly. In big cities, such as Chang'an, Luoyang, and other capitals, the gates for *fangs* would be opened and closed with 600 drum strikes. The drums used to signal the opening and closing were initially located outside the Chengtian Gate, the southern gate of the palace. In addition, several cavalrymen were arranged to call on each street. Later in the tenth year of Zhenguan (AD 636) reign, according to Ma Zhou's suggestion, the arrangement of cavalrymen was abolished, and drum strikes were set up in each street instead. This kind of drum was called "Dongdong Drum," commonly known as "Street Drum."

If we lived in the Chang'an of Tang, we would find that when dawn came, drums would be struck outside Chengtian Gate, and it would open immediately. Almost simultaneously, the street drums were hit 600 times and the *fang* gates would open: the city would wake up and begin the hustle and bustle of a day. At sunset, drums were again beaten at Chengtian Gate, which would close. Then street drums would beat 600 times and the *fang* gates would close. The entire city would become quiet as night approached.

Regulations for the *fang* gate system were strict: once the gates closed, ordinary people could not walk the streets. If they did, they would face a violation or curfew. One such punishment was being beaten 20 times with a wooden plank. The system was enforced until the final years of the Tang. We can find evidence of curfew in late Tang Dynasty novels such as Shen Jiji's *The Ren's Biography* and Bai Xingjian's *Biography of Li Wa*. In the *Biography of Li Wa*, when Zheng Sheng was penniless, the bawd and Li Wa designed and used the regularly open and closed doors to get rid of Zheng Sheng successfully. On special occasions, the Emperor could order the gates to be opened at irregular times. For example, to celebrate the Lantern Festival, Emperor Xuanzong gave special permission for gates to be open on the 17th, 18th, and 19th of the first lunar month. Additionally, families who hold events such as weddings or funerals were allowed to enter at night if they had a pass issued by the county government. Thus, the city was not completely asleep at night.

Nightlife in Tang cities was mainly confined to the *fangs*. After the *fang* gates were closed, people would conduct all kinds of activities within them—they could party or drink, but they could not go beyond the walls of the *fangs*. By the late Tang Dynasty, many small-scale bakeries, wine shops, and eateries cropped up.

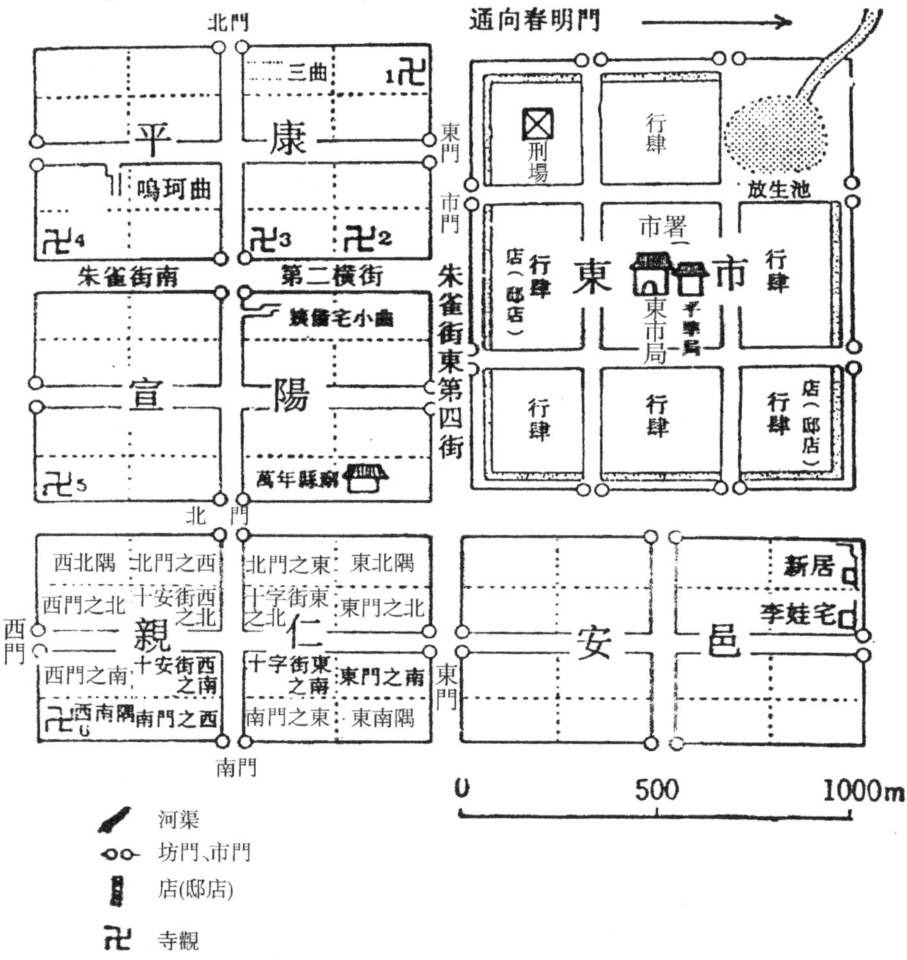

Fig. 6-4: Plan of the fang *interior in Chang'an*[5]

5. (Japan) Maio Dahiko, *Chang'an in the Late Tang Dynasty and Legendary Novels.* See *Japanese Young and Middle-Aged Scholars on Chinese History · The Six Dynasties, Sui, and Tang Dynasties* (Shanghai: Shanghai Ancient Books Press, 1995).

As described by Shen Jiji in his *The Ren's Biography*, he mentioned Wei Yin and his brother-in-law, Zheng Liu, went out and met to drink at a place called Xinchangli. Zheng Liu asked for leave a short while after he arrived at the south of Xuanping *Fang* and promised to return to the drinking place. Later, when it was dawn, Zheng Liu walked to the nearby gate of Shengping *Fang*, the third *fang* south of the East Market. At this time, the gate of the *fang* was not open yet, but "the bakery shops of the Hu people (minorities) started to make fires in their stoves" and prepare breakfast for residents in the *fangs*. We could infer there were several bakeries and wine shops set up to meet the daily demands of the residents.

Besides being closed, cities during the Tang inherited other characteristics from the *fang* and market arrangement. If we carefully observe the above sketch of Chang'an and Luoyang, we find there was separation not only between the Emperor's palaces and the imperial city, but also between the imperial and outer cities, where residents lived in the *fangs*. This characteristic determined peoples' daily lives in the Tang; thus, they were often more limited compared to capitals in previous dynasties.

Chang'an of the Western Han was not constructed through planning, and as a result there were no strict boundaries between the temples, offices, and residential *lis*. It was the same in Luoyang during the Han and Wei dynasties, where the temples, palaces, and residences of the higher class and commoners were intertwined. Such features did not fully change until Luoyang of the Northern Wei. Compared with past capitals, Luoyang was strictly planned and everything was placed in order. Even the residents would inhabit different *fangs* and the names of these *fangs* were very distinctive. For instance, near the Big Market of Luoyang, there were two *lis* named Tongshang (doing business) and Dahuo (the arrival of goods) in the east, and two *lis* named Tiaoyin (tuning) and Yuelv (melody) in the south.[6] From the names of these *fangs*, we know these places were occupied according to their professions, including merchants, musicians, wine makers, and funeral directors.

From the book, *A Record of Buddhist Monasteries in Luoyang*, we know there was still a mix of offices and private official residences in the palace areas, and in the inner city there was a mixture of commoner *lis*, office buildings, and private residences in the Northern Wei. However, it was completely different during the

6. *A Record of Buddhist Monasteries in Luoyang*, vol. 4.

Tang era. Both official private residences and commoner residences were constructed within the *fang*s in the outer city, while the central office buildings were isolated within the imperial city. The palaces the Emperor inhabited were even more strictly controlled, which further strengthened the closeness of the inner and outer cities.

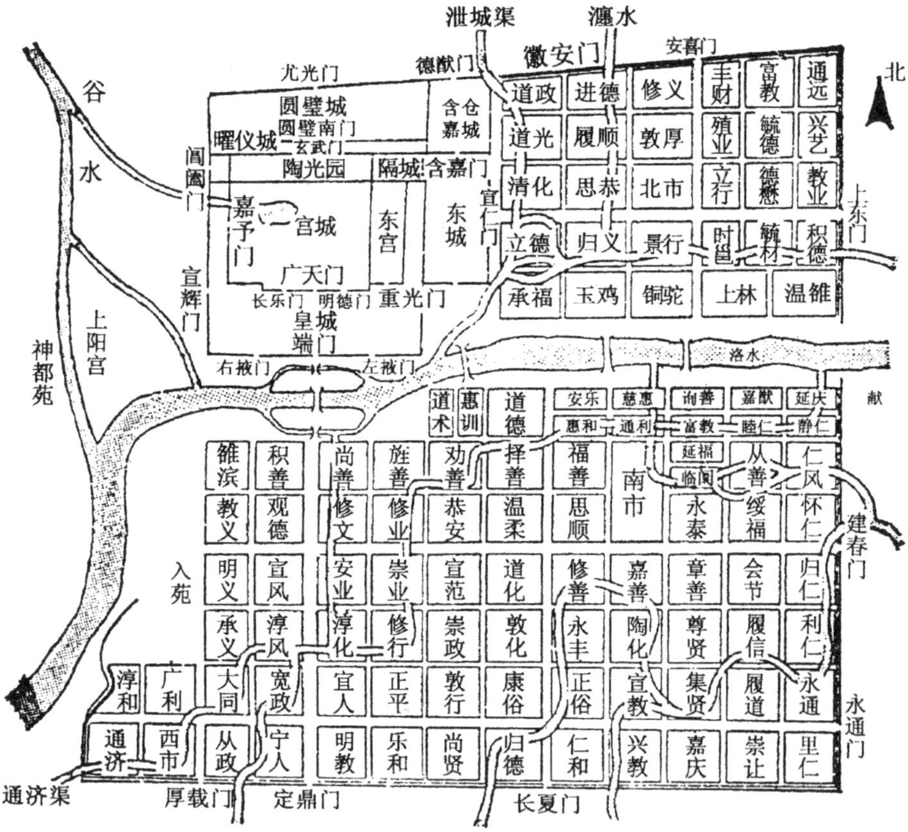

Fig. 6-5: Plan of fangs *in Luoyang*[7]

7. Yang Kuan, *Studies on Ancient Chinese Capital System History* (Shanghai: Shanghai People's Press, 2003), 173.

The primary purpose of such arrangements was to keep peace and security in the capital. Hence, although the Tang stipulated that officials with a rank of three or higher could open their gates towards the streets, many senior officials and even the Grand Counselor (Prime Minister) used the *fang* gates. In AD 815, a *Fanzhen* (military governorship) took advantage of this and used assassins to ambush the eastern gate of Jing'an *Fang* where the Grand Counselor, Wu Yuanheng, lived. When he passed through the *fang* gate on his way to the Imperial Court, assassins scared away his attendants by shooting arrows and then beheaded him.

Another example of an assassin's ambush at the *fang* gates was in AD 838. The eunuchs were dissatisfied with Grand Counselor Li Shi and decided to murder him. In January, the eunuchs attempted to shoot him with arrows on his way to the Imperial Court, but missed. His attendants scattered and when he rushed home on his horse he was intercepted again at the gate of a *fang*; he barely escaped assassination.

3. Waving Embroidered Pennants

Rapid population growth in the mid-to-late Tang era increased the demand for daily necessities. The city, known foremost as a political center, was becoming an economic center too. Many social organizations and economic transactions took place, for instance, guilds and markets sprouted and developed, stimulating prosperity. The closed urban landscape, inherited and largely followed from the Han and early Tang dynasties, began to gradually change.

Until the Tang Dynasty, closed markets were set up in the capital, restricting urban commercial activities in a fixed area. Like *fangs*, the markets would open and close regularly, and goods would depend on the supply of travelling merchants. It has been like this as early as the pre-Qin period. For instance, during the Spring and Autumn Period, there were both local merchants who conducted businesses in shops and other visiting merchants in the markets of Linzi, the State of Qi.

By the Western Han, Chang'an's visiting merchants mostly clustered in the vicinity of the Yong Gate in the northwestern corner of the city, close to the "Nine Markets." The visiting merchants in Luoyang of the Northern Wei mostly inhabited the Tongshang (business) *Li* and Dahuo (merchandise) *Li* east of the Big Market which was located west of the outer city. These names suggested the occupations of their residents. Similarly, during the Tang Dynasty, residents of the Xinghua *Fang* located southeast of the West Market were mainly merchants conducting silk cloth businesses.[8] However, this situation began to change during the Five Dynasties era and was completely transformed during the Northern Song.

In the Later Zhou, the urban population of Kaifeng exploded because of the large number of garrisons. Food and other daily supplies depended on water transport. Because there were so many visiting merchants gathered in Kaifeng, there was insufficient space for them and their goods. Therefore, Emperor Zhou Shizong adopted two measures to renovate Kaifeng: expansion of the outer city and increase of *didian* (hotels where the merchants could store their goods and stay). This would have a major impact and unexpectedly altered the capital system of ancient China.

The Eastern capital, Kaifeng, was originally the state capital of Bianzhou during the Tang. As a state capital, it was smaller than previous capitals and its streets were narrow. In addition, the inhabitants' continual expansion of their own residences by encroaching upon public spaces made the streets even narrower. The urban space of Kaifeng was insufficient for the demands of a capital. Therefore, in April AD 955, Emperor Shizong of Zhou (Chai Rong) ordered the outer city be built outside the original city. The outer city, called the new city or Luo City, was almost four times bigger than the original capital of Bianzhou.

In the Imperial Order of Emperor Shizong of Zhou,[9] an explicit explanation on the necessity of outer city expansion of Kaifeng was given. The purpose was not only to solve land shortages for barracks and government offices, but also to address limited hotels within the *fang*s. The rapid increase in population further deteriorated the living environment of urban residents. Therefore, this decision would not only solve the hotel shortage but also help improve residents' living quality. And pay extraordinary attention to fire safety.

The Kaifeng transformation by Later Zhou was divided into two steps. First, the government organized the building of Luo City. Then, in the newly built city, the rest was left for the residents to complete after the government had planned the streets and alleys, barracks, warehouses, and office buildings. This is clearly different from the construction of Chang'an during the Sui and Tang dynasties.

8. "A Biography of Wushuang," in *Imperial Readings of the Taiping Era*, vol. 486.

9. "Cities and Outer Cities," in *A Concise History of the Five Dynasties*, vol. 26.

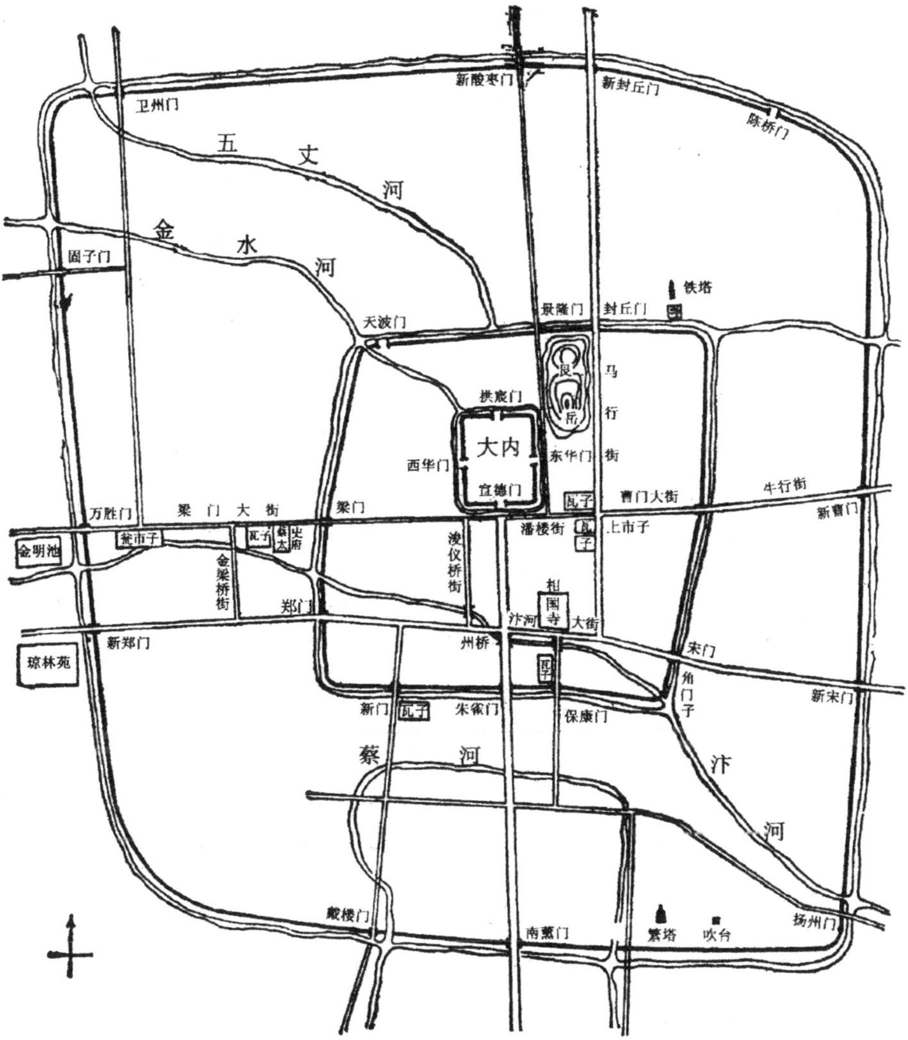

Fig. 6-6: Urban structure map of the Eastern Capital in Northern Song[10]

10. Yang Kuan, *Studies on Ancient Chinese Capital System History* (Shanghai: Shanghai People's Press, 2003), 279.

After outer city expansion and hotel construction, the government also pursued waterway transportation. In AD 957, "it was ordered for the Bian and Wuzhang rivers to be connected to the north, and thus ships from the Qi and Lu regions could reach the capital."[11] The following March, the Bian River was dredged and connected with the Huai. This opened water transportation to east and southeast China. Large numbers of merchants could reach the newly built outer city with large quantities of merchandise at much greater convenience. This further promoted urban development. By the beginning of Northern Song, the urban landscape of Kaifeng had totally transformed. Not only were large numbers of hotels built along the Bian, but many new guilds and markets for daily necessities emerged.

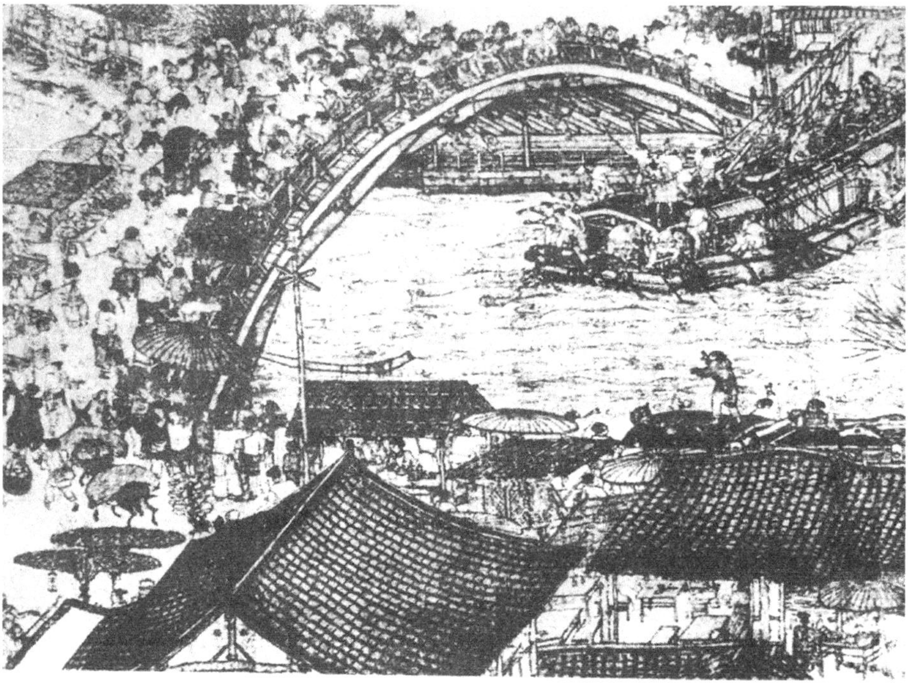

Fig. 6-7: The Bian River transport in "Along the River during the Qingming Festival"[12]

11. *A Mirror of History*, vol. 293–294.
12. Wu Tao, *The Eastern Capital of the Northern Song Dynasty*, illustration (Zhengzhou: Henan People's Press, 1984).

As mentioned previously, Kaifeng is not the best choice for a capital, since it's open to attack from all directions. However, since the middle of the Tang, the economic center shifted south towards the Yangtze and Huai River regions. The central government's rule largely depended on southeast water transport: Kaifeng became the inevitable capital choice for the Five Dynasties and even the Northern Song, due to this location as a land and water transportation hub. The city's status derived from the Bian River. The Northern Song understood this: Emperor Song Taizong once said in his later years, "thanks to the water channel, the Eastern Capital (Kaifeng) was able to support tens of thousands soldiers and millions of citizens."[13] The water channel here refers to the Bian River that connects Zhongzhou and Jianghuai region.

Daily supplies for millions of Kaifeng residents were shipped from the mouth of the Bian, mainly by a large number of merchants. The goods were first stored in hotels along the river and then sold to shops throughout the city. The closed city, with its rigid and inconvenient transport system, could not satisfy such large commerce. Thus, merchants organized themselves into guilds, which specialized in selling these daily supplies along vacant parts of the river. In this way, new guilds and markets came into being.

At first, these new markets were similar to temporary or regular bazaars, which means they would gather during trading times and then dissolve. Some merchants even made temporary deals directly at the ends of the bridges. Gradually, however, these temporary markets became regular. Thus, Kaifeng residents referred to these markets as "bridge markets."

Around the mid-Northern Song era, the government believed it was necessary to intervene with this continuous formation and fixation of these new markets. Policies were made and taxes were collected. At the same time, it was stipulated that transactions must be completed at the locations designated by the government. This meant that merchants had to rent shops built on government-owned land to establish permanently fixed markets. For instance, in September AD 1079, with the rectification of the government, government land was loaned to build *Chuangwu* as the flour market.[14] In fact, besides the flour market, there were

13. *Xu Zizhi Tongjian Changbian (A Complete History of the Song Dynasty)*, vol. 32, Item: June, Second Year of Chunhua Era and *History of Song: Records of Rivers*.
14. *Xu Zizhi Tongjian Changbian (A Complete History of Song Dynasty)*, vol. 300, Item: September, Second Year of Yuanfeng Era.

other newly built markets along the Bian, selling beans, vegetables, fruit, cows, horses, paper, etc., all taxed by the government. It was clear these new markets mainly dealt with daily necessities to meet the increasing demand of the urban population.

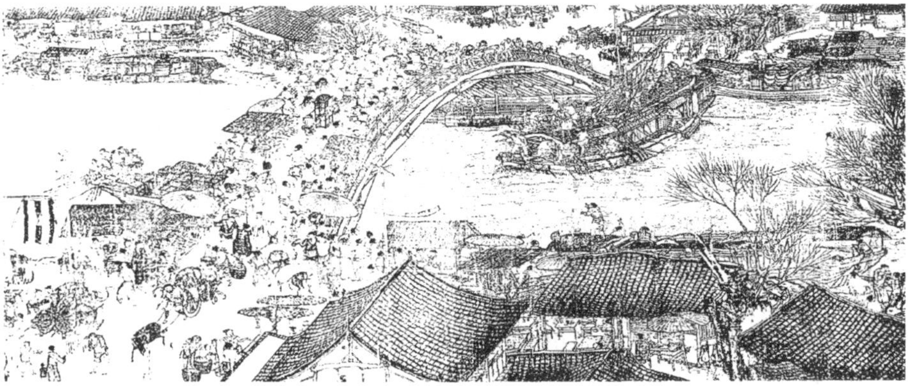

Fig. 6-8: Riverside bridge market in "Along the River during the Qingming Festival"[15]

However, government management of the new markets was ineffective. Eventually, government control evolved into a nuisance of tyranny. Therefore, in July AD 1085, Huang Jiang, a palace censor, created a petition for the Emperor to abolish this policy when he saw the consequences of the heavy tax burden. Interestingly, in the petition it states that, "renting vacant spots along the Bian River was permitted by the government initially." This suggests merchants had been using these spots for convenience before the government forced them to rent state-owned areas for storage and commerce.

This means many of the new markets started from the vacant places along the Bian River. Probably, this was achieved due to convenience—merchants needed to store goods along the Bian River and make transactions later. It was clear they conducted their businesses this way for a period of time before the government took control of the vacant places or forced them to rent government-owned places for transactions.

15. Yang Kuan, *Studies on Ancient Chinese Capital System History*, illustrations (Shanghai: Shanghai People's Press, 2003).

Fig. 6-9: Markets in "Along the River during the Qingming Festival"[16]

In addition to levying local taxes—thus robbing people of their income, the government also set up state-owned markets, such as fruit, flour, and meat markets. An imperial order issued in the eighth year of the Yuanfeng era mentioned, "Wanmu wood market, Tianhan Bridge market, and Sibi fruit market, the capital pig and sheep market ... and the west furniture market,"[17] were all under government administration. From this document, we know the government-owned markets included almost all daily necessities.

The newly emerged markets of Kaifeng were no longer restricted by fixed markets, due to transport limitations. Instead, these markets gathered around the riverbanks and bridges where transportation was more convenient. They became the new urban economic centers. According to *The Eastern Capital: A Dream of Splendor*, the fruit markets operated by the government and private merchants were both located around Zhou Bridge (Tianhan Bridge). Still, most business and trade activities were distributed along the inner city from the Zhou bridge to the East Water Gate along the Bian and the parallel streets.

16. Wu Tao, *The Eastern Capital of the Northern Song Dynasty*, illustration (Zhengzhou: Henan People's Press, 1984).

17. *Xu Zizhi Tongjian Changbian (A Complete History of Song Dynasty)*, vol. 368.

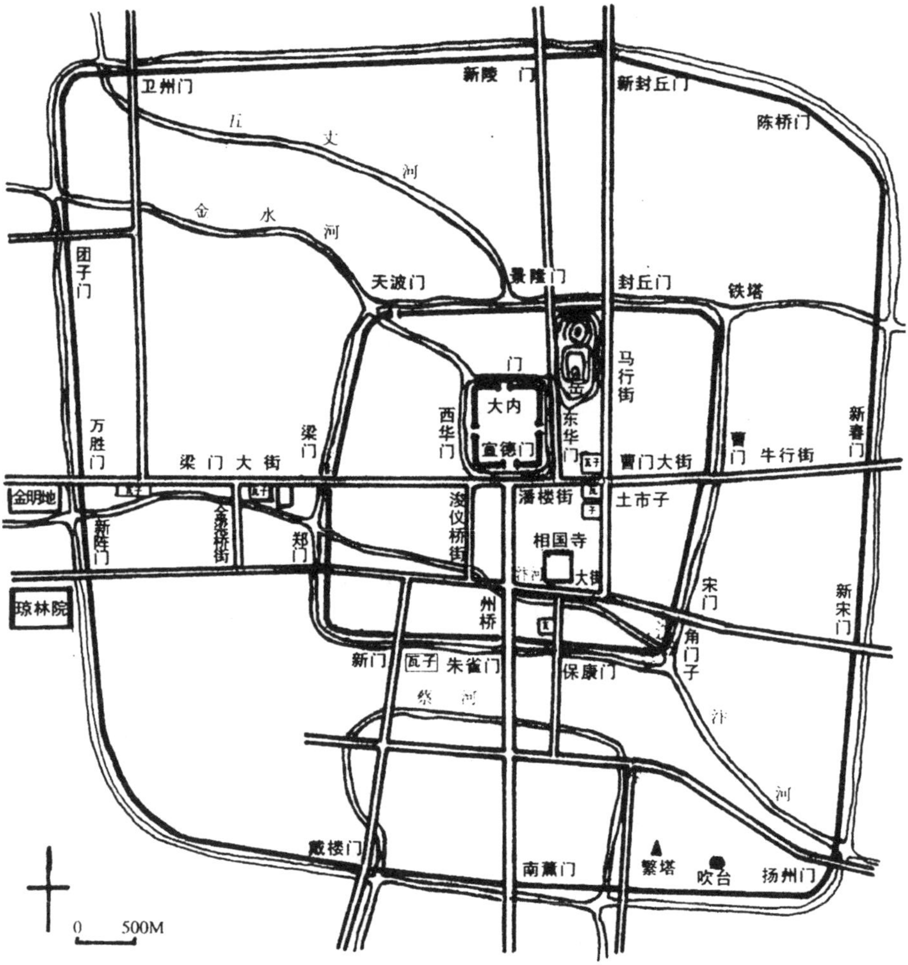

Fig. 6-10: Map of the gates and main markets of the Eastern Capital[18]

18. Wu Tao, *The Eastern Capital of the Northern Song Dynasty*, illustration (Zhengzhou: Henan People's Press, 1984).

In the Eastern Capital, wherever there were gates there would be boulevards spreading into the city. In addition, there were also water gates for convenience. The East Water Gate in the lower reaches of the Bian was the most famous among these. There were also the Tongjin and Shangshan gates along the sides of the East Water Gate, and the Xuanze and Datong gates along the sides of the West Water Gate. The streets connected to the city center through these gates—they were the main traffic lines for important supplies by land and water. Among them, the most prosperous street was Bian River street. It started from Zhou Bridge to the east, passed Xiangguo Temple Bridge, Dongjiaozi Gate, crossed upper Tu Bridge, lower Tu bridge, crossed Bian Bridge, and reached Tongjin Gate and Shangshan Gate. It was even far more bustling than the imperial street in the east.

The book *Eastern Capital: A Dream of Splendor* described many government warehouses, storage houses, and hotels providing services for visiting merchants to sojourn and trade.[19] Particularly, there were many grain warehouses around this area—the Yuanfeng and Shuncheng warehouses along the Zhoudonghong Bridge, and various warehouses such as Guangji and Lihezhezhong, inside the East Water Gate.[20] Simultaneously, places far from the main traffic routes also formed new markets following the rise in prosperity of the new guilds. Many street markets in Kaifeng developed because of this, such as the cattle street. Prosperous markets also formed on the city's main thoroughfares, such as the horse market.

The Mahang Market was initially for restaurants and hotels where guild heads met and traded. Later, because of the congregation of restaurants, they became centers for gatherings.[21] When the congregation reached a certain scale, more and more guilds joined to connect shops of the entire street; soon it was very long and the most prosperous of the four imperial roads in Kaifeng. There were many restaurants, tea houses, and eateries on Mahang Street. It was also said this was the only place that had no mosquitos, since at night the restaurants were so busy and the lights were as bright as day—and the mosquitos did not like the smell of oil.[22] Mahang Street business also catalyzed many other industrial and

19. "Alleys East of the Qianzhou Bridge outside the Grand Interior," in *The Eastern Capital: A Dream of Splendor*, vol. 3.
20. "External Ministries," in *The Eastern Capital: A Dream of Splendor*, vol. 1.
21. See Hong Mai, *Records of Chinese Supernatural Stories*, Part I, vol. 18, Item: A Servant of Li Shu.
22. Cai Xiao, *Reflections beside the Tiewei Mountain*, vol. 4.

commercial establishments. Many businesses also flourished in the nearby alleys: To the north, across Mahang Street, there were east and west alleys which were the location of many handicraft workshops. Further north, there were grocery stores, pharmacies, spice markets, and time-honored pharmacy brands.

Market formation along these streets completely changed the landscape of the Eastern Capital. This meant the old, closed *fang* markets were eliminated. According to scholars, the East and West markets disappeared around this time, as new guilds emerged and developed to a certain degree along the river, close to the bridges, and the gates.[23] At the same time, all kinds of bakeries and taverns opened everywhere in the city—unlike in the Tang era when these could only be opened in the *fang*s. Some restaurants became major shops on some of the important streets. Restaurants on the Nine Bridge Street faced each other with colorful decorations; there were so many embroidered flags and signs flying over the markets that one could not see the sky.

In *The Eastern Capital: A Dream of Splendor*, when street markets are mentioned, it often detailed the streets or alleys where stores were located, but never mentioned *fang*s. Instead, *fang*s were mentioned together with alleys. There would be a patrol house about every 300 steps within the alleys of a *fang*,[24] or there were meat stands in alleys of the *fang* and bridge markets.[25] Also, the rest were thousands of alleys of *fang* and courtyards.[26] These indicated that public spaces used by residents were alleys rather than *fang*s. In fact, alleys existed during the Tang and functioned as corridors within *fang*s,[27] rather than locales for public activities. During the Song Dynasty, however, alleys for *fangs* became important venues. This suggested the densely-packed shops and residential houses within the *fang*s were connected by alleys and utilized the urban space to a great extent.

Because of the removal of the *fang* walls, residents from Kaifeng could set up shops along the street. Therefore, the business district was no longer confined to

23. See (Japan) Kato Shigeshi, *The Development of Urban Societies in Song, Markets in Tang and Song, Business Associations "Hang" in Tang and Song and Guild Halls in Qing*, collected in *An Examination of Chinese Economic History* (Taipei: Huashi Press, 1981).
24. "Fire Security," in *The Eastern Capital: A Dream of Splendor*, vol. 3.
25. "Meat Markets," in *The Eastern Capital: A Dream of Splendor*, vol. 4.
26. "Shops on Mahang Street," in *The Eastern Capital: A Dream of Splendor*, vol. 3.
27. Jin Liuqi, *Jiuqian Zhi*, vol. 1, Wang Feibo, *A Tribute to the Birthday Celebration of Duke Miguo Wanyan Wangshou: "Liyulin Alley, Xuanping* Fang."

a fixed place in the city as before. Businesses were everywhere and intertwined with residential areas. Bustling streets emerged from many important convenient traffic alleys, with the four royal streets being the most prosperous. In addition, Xuandemenqian Street of the imperial city, Donghuamenqian Street, Jinglinggong East Gate Street, and Xiangguosi East Gate Street were also very busy with the emerging guilds, restaurants, tea houses, small eateries, *Wazi*, and other stores for daily necessities interwoven to present a vivid urban life scenery. This drastic change occurred during the Northern Song and was inherited and developed by Lin'an of the Southern Song. Hangzhou was called Lin'an in the Northern Song Dynasty. At that time, the population density was not high, "Four corners were empty, and no human traces can be found." The hill region in the southwest was "densely forested, and there was no human habitation." However, after the Southern Song Dynasty chose Lin'an as the capital, a large population moved south, which led to the rapid expansion of the city border and the sharply increased demand for daily necessities. Therefore, businesses from various industries flourished in the city: "From the city streets to small alleys, shops of all sizes were built one after another, and there was no vacant house. If you took a morning stroll, you would be surrounded by hundreds of traders and shops from both sides of the pavements. The city remained lively until dinner time."

In Lin'an, the distribution of markets also showed some clear patterns. The handcraft product markets that required large transport capacity were mostly located along the river and near bridges outside the city's gates. For instance, this was the reason why the firewood market was established along the Wood Market Bridge outside the southeastern Houchao Gate, the cloth market was located at the mouth of the Heng River outside the southeastern Convenience Gate, the fresh fish market was established along the southeastern outside Houchao Gate and the Bazi Bridge outside Dongqing Gate in the eastern part of the city. The markets that required relatively small transport capacity or those that needed to be processed were generally located in the town along the river and near the bridge.

For instance, the flower, comb, jewelry, and hair decoration markets were in Guan Alley in the middle of Imperial Street. The pearl market was located in the back-market street in the middle, and the silk market was located on the Salt Bridge in the northern part of the river. From the names of South *Fang* in the city and West *Fang* in the middle of Imperial Street,[28] we can infer these are closed city districts, which became common residential quarters over time.

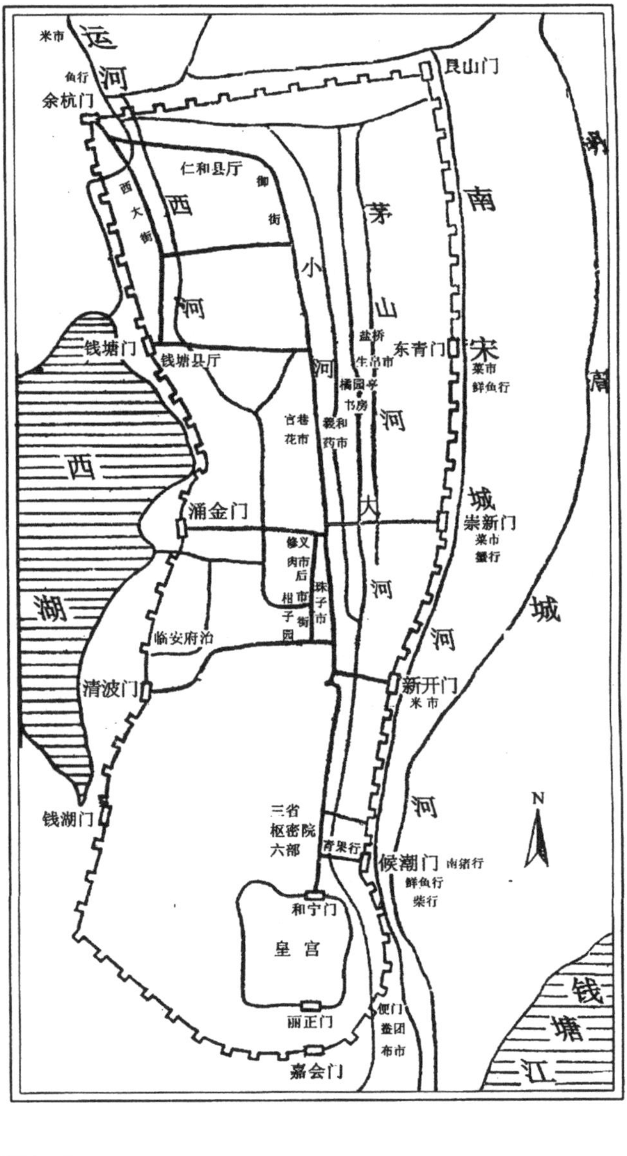

Fig. 6-11: Plan of Lin'an in the Southern Song[29]

28. *A Record of Lin'an in the Xianchun Era*, vol. 19.
29. Yang Kuan, *Studies on Ancient Chinese Capital System History* (Shanghai: Shanghai People's Press, 2003), 365.

Like Kaifeng, Imperial Street was the most bustling road in Lin'an. Although it was designed for political rituals—especially the New Year and Winter Solstice, and Jingling Palace tribute, it became the busiest business center because of its advantageous position. It began from Hening Gate of the Grand Interior and extended north until the Guan Bridge. Along this section, there were a variety of shops and different guild associations on both sides. "After all, Hangzhou (Lin'an) was the alternate capital with the gathering of many shops and guilds, which extended from the Cross Street of Hening Gate to Guan Bridge. Every household conducted business and there were numerous markets."[30]

Despite such descriptions, according to the literature, Imperial Street could be divided into three parts based on the different degree of business prosperity—the southern part ranged from Hening Gate to Chaotian Gate, the middle part was from Chaotian Gate to Shou'an *Fang* or Guan Alley, and the northern part was from Shou'an *Fang* to Guan Bridge.

The southern part of Imperial Street was very close to the palaces and Grand Interior. Therefore, these markets were used mostly for the palace and official needs. In the morning, palace officials and maids would send people to buy seasonal vegetables, freshly-made foods, and newly ripened fruits. In the afternoon, the eateries often provided food to the Grand Interior, bureaucrats, as well as the people who worked as liaisons for the government. Because of this, there were many kinds of well-known food, such as clove wonton sold in front of the Six Ministries, which were particularly tasty.[31] Many of the people coming to the markets were literati. Therefore, there were bookstores, framing shops, and pharmacies. Many important poems and novels were published here, such as, *Bei Hu Lu* (A Record of Customs in Lingnan), *Shu Yi Ji* (A Collection of Supernatural Stories), and *Qie Zhong Ji* (A Tang Poem Collection).

The middle part of the street was the busiest section of the Lin'an markets—especially the bustling night market in front of Zhong *Wazi*. In the book, *Capital Records*, it stated: "The night markets were everywhere except for the front of the Grand Interior. Among these, the front of Zhongwaqian was the most prosperous. All kinds of exotic, fancy items were sold. There was no difference from the daytime." Besides these temporary vendors, this was also where top restaurants,

30. "Associations and Guilds," in *Meng Liang Lu (An Introduction of Lin'an)*, vol. 13.

31. "People on Markets at Dawn," in *Meng Liang Lu (An Introduction of Lin'an)*, vol. 13.

tea houses, and famous opera houses sat. Some important business organizations, guilds, and trade shops for gold, silver, and salt note markets were also located here. Salt notes referred to the permission slips granted by the government to the chartered merchants, so they could acquire and sell salt and tea—items under government control. Of course, most businesses here were necessities, such as grocery stores, fabric stores, bookshops, etc.

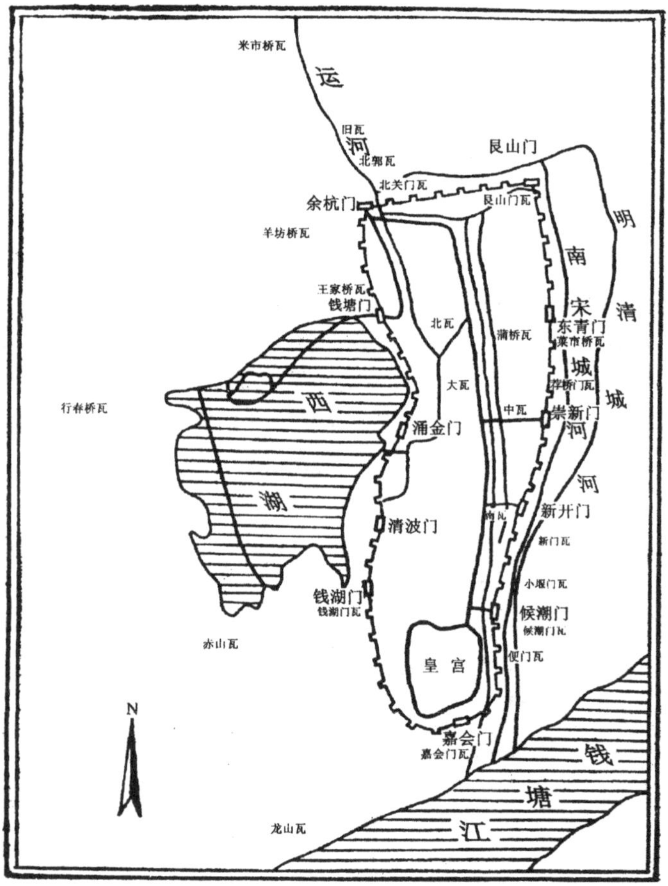

Fig. 6-12: Map of main Wazis *of Lin'an in the Southern Song*[32]

32. Yang Kuan, *Studies on the Ancient Chinese Capital System History* (Shanghai: Shanghai People's Press, 2003), 414.

The northern section of Imperial Street had relatively few famous shops. The only shop worthy of mention was the Lower *Wazi*, southwest of the Zhong'an Bridge. The Lower *Wazi* was the largest *Wazi* in Lin'an. With 13 theaters, it was a famous gathering place for folk artists.

Besides Imperial Street, the second most prosperous district of commercial activity was the market area close to the City River, Salt Bridge Canal, and Clear Lake River. These three waterways were the major water transport lines within Lin'an. Many supplies were first shipped to Linxun and then transported to the city by human labor. Therefore, many goods shops were located along the rivers near bridges, forming unofficial markets.

In fact, these types of markets were formed during the Northern Song. The famous poet, Su Shi, was appointed Vice-Governor of Hangzhou from AD 1071–1073 and Governor from AD 1089–1090. He wrote many poems describing civic life in urban Hangzhou. Among these, the poem *Evening Views from the Seaside Pavilion* described the scenery of Sand River Pond:

> *Mountains brightened by the lights of rowing ships,*
> *Drums and songs along the Sand River were interwoven with laughter.*
> *Is there anything in the youngsters' minds?*
> *Their hair was loose, thick, and black flowing in the air.*

Besides these busy streets, there were other shops that supplied daily groceries in more usual markets. There were even around government buildings.

An important change here was that closed markets were replaced by new guilds and markets along the rivers, near bridges, and outside the city's gates—not only in the capital city but also in some large cities in China. Take Pingjiang (Today's Suzhou) as an example; according to Fan Chengda's *Wu Jun Zhi* and the *Pingjiang Map Tablet*, the original closed east and west market and the famous market in the Southern Song Dynasty has been changed into *fang*, the big market into Xiujin *Fang*, the west market into Xishi *Fang*. In addition, there are Yuxing Bridge, Gushi Bridge, Silk Xing Bridge, Fruit Xing Bridge, and other bridges, indicating that new professions and markets along the river have also emerged. In addition, rice shops in Hefeng *Fang* and fruit shops in Guowa *Fang* indicate that the closed market initially has been abolished and formed open spaces for economic activities. Yet, it should be noted this change was preserved in the works and picture steles of the Southern Song when it should have been completed in the Northern Song. Capital Luoyang of the Northern Song also experienced a similar situation. The southern market was changed into Dongcheng *Fang* and Tongli *Fang*, while the northern market was changed into Linde *Fang* and North Market *Fang*, and the western market was changed into Tongji *Fang*.[33] These new names retained the meaning of benefiting from business activities, but no more than this.

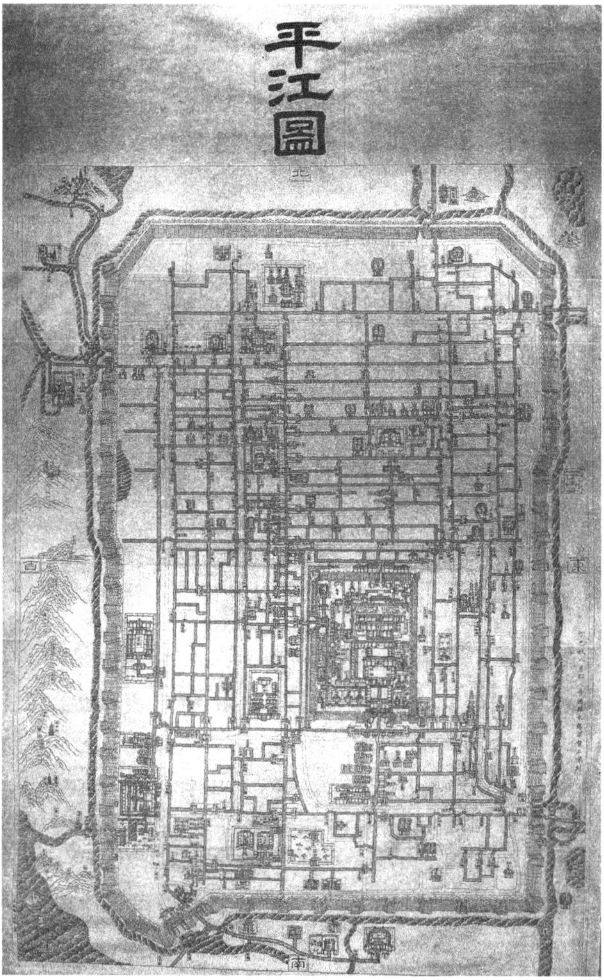

Fig. 6-13: Picture stele of Pingjiang[34]

33. *Annals of Henan, the Yuan Dynasty.*

34. *Ancient Chinese Atlas: Warring States to Yuan* (Beijing: SinoMaps Press, 1990).

4. Theaters and Entertainment Houses

In ancient China, mass recreational activities were usually held only during the Land God Altar offerings in spring and winter. Festivals of all kinds would take place at this time. Often the entire country would be thrown into the carnival spirit. Due to the large numbers of consumers in the city, there were normally daily recreational activities besides these annual celebrations.

For instance, in Linzi of the Qi State, people played all sorts of musical instruments such as flutes and harps, and enjoyed activities like cockfighting, dog walking, chess, football, etc.[35] These activities became popular after the Qin and Han dynasties, and even the palaces hosted such activities, open to the public. During the summer of 105 BC, the people in the capital observed wrestling in Shanglin Pingle Hall.[36]

After the Eastern Han, with the spread of Buddhism, many temples attracted the masses through wrestling tournaments and other novel shows. In the Northern Wei, the temples of Luoyang held Buddha parades on the birthday of Gautama every April 8. As part of the activities, the Buddha statues would be paraded out of the temple. The shows in Zongsheng Temple were, "exquisite and skillful talents performed almost as well as those of Liu Sheng ... that ... the noble ladies of the eastern part of the city visited this place."[37] Liu Sheng refers to the Long Autumn Temple established by Liu Sheng.

Besides the opera shows, there were many temples with gardens, often visited by city residents. The Treasure Light Temple "became a very popular destination during holidays when nobles and educated scholars often came here to meet friends and relax in their leisure time, since it had a lake in the garden."[38] The recreational activities of urban residents centered on the temples.

By the Sui and Tang dynasties, the areas for recreational activities had changed. Although Chang'an's residents in the Tang still used temples for entertainment during holidays and leisure time, large-scale entertainment was held on the broad streets. In AD 606, Turkic peoples visited, and all kinds of shows were performed in Luoyang, the Eastern capital. From the Jianguo Gate

35. *Strategies of Warring States · Strategies of Qi*, Part I.
36. *Book of Han · Annals of Emperor Wu.*
37. *A Record of Buddhist Monasteries in Luoyang*, vol. 2.
38. *A Record of Buddhist Monasteries in Luoyang*, vol. 4.

to the Duan Gate, "the theater stages lasted about eight *li* and the officials sat in the boxes, watching the performances from dusk to dawn and then again to midnight. Nearly 30,000 people performed in these shows,[39] beginning the tradition of large-scale gala shows every January when the Emperor would meet with ambassadors. More important to urban development was the usage of streets as stages for shows. It made a huge impact on Tang Dynasty's urban spatial layout and the later generations.

During the Tang Dynasty, there were often music and opera contests in Tianmen Street of Chang'an. Duan Anjie's *Pipa* article in *Yuefu Miscellanea* introduced such a story: "When drought hit Chang'an, the emperor ordered the people in the east and west market to pray for rain. In Tianmen Street, people were competing and singing." People from the east and west cities of Chang'an gathered on Tianmen Street to play pipa as part of a rain praying activity. These street music shows were described in the *Biography of Liwa* by Bai Xingjian: "Mr. Zheng, a singer of the West Market, was the champion of the Tianmen show. He was then found by his father who came to the capital to offer suggestions to the government." Using urban streets for entertainment performances laid the foundations of the *Wazi* of Song. The opera or drama shows, with the masses forming the audience, would take place in a vacant space within a *fang*, on a street, or in front of the temple—the common feature was that they were temporary and had no special housing. However, in the Northern Song, fixed theatres targeting the masses formally began.

Wazi, sometimes called *Washe*, *Wasi* or *Washi*, was an easy means to gather and then disperse. Still, as the early artists, who roamed the streets, switched to performing in fixed places with fences or ropes, it became customary that *Goulan* or *Wazi* were used to refer to entertainment venues for singing, dancing, and drama show performances. As we mentioned earlier, the cattle, horse, and fruit shops in the Eastern Capital of the Northern Song Dynasty were originally located in empty spaces without fences. Later the government forced these shops to set up accordingly and taxed them according to the amount of land they occupied. It is called "fenced the cattle, horses, and fruit shops." To be more specific, it was simply an enclosed temporary market. Because of this, we could use the written records to imagine the biggest *sang* (theatre) in the Eastern Capital at that time:

---

39. *Book of Sui · Records of Music.*

"If you step into the theatre, you can see the pharmacy, fortune tellers, singers, doctors, restaurants, hair salons, paper paintings, music composers, and so on." It's not just a place for entertainment. Since early wandering street performers used fences or ropes to enclose a space as a temporary stage when the theatre was developed into a fixed place, audiences gradually accustomed to songs, dances, and dramas performed on stage, which was called *Goulan* or *Wazi* at that time.

The emergence of *Wazi* and *Goulan* galvanized the recreational life of the urban residents and promoted the development of drama shows and performance skills. According to the *Eastern Capital: A Dream of Splendor*, there were many types of show in the capital city, including novels, history telling, *piao* singing, puppet shows, and acrobatics, etc. Among these, history telling evolved from the speeches of the Tang Temples. It could be seen that drama shows were rich in form and greatly influenced the dramas of the Yuan, Ming, and Qing dynasties.

Still, the appearance of *Washe* and *Goulan* did not drive the roaming artists from town. There were still large numbers of "vacant road performers"—artists who performed on the streets. The venues they performed at were still the road, which means vacancies in the markets. The appearance of *Wazi* and the active performances of folk artists in the city changed the dreary urban life drastically, with daily existence becoming increasingly colorful. Therefore, the urban landscape was also characterized by openness.

PART III

CITIES

CHAPTER SEVEN

CITIES AND TOWNS: TRADE AND ECONOMY

After the mid-Tang Dynasty, several military towns originally set up for defense purposes were transformed into commercial centers for the local economy, prosperity, and development expansion. This caused the emergence of many *Caoshi* (grass markets) on the periphery of settlements, which were considered the harbingers of prosperity for cities and towns during the Ming and Qing dynasties.

Since the Western Zhou, clear distinctions were made between urban and rural areas. The establishment of the Western Zhou Dynasty originated from a small populated tribe, which conquered the more populated Shang Empire as well as small, scattered tribes. To consolidate their rule over this vast land, the Zhou clan rewarded its people and others with various territories in different regions. These actions established a variety of fiefdoms with the family name of Ji (family name of the Zhou clan), or different family names to achieve rule over the Shang territories and their inhabitants, and provide safeguards against any rebellions.

These rewarded lords would find a suitable location within their fiefdom to build strongholds and guard their vassals or serfs. The people who lived in the city were called people of the state. The land outside the city was reserved for local indigenous people and those conquered for their farming abilities, who were referred to as "savages" or "inferiors." The division between the people of the state and the savages was also the dividing line between the races and the professions.

People of the state engaged in administrative management and business in the city, with a few involved in agricultural production; the "savages and inferiors" outside the city mainly engaged in agricultural production. This division of urban and rural areas was very strict in Western Zhou because it was a political division between the ruling tribes and the ruled tribes. But during the Warring States Period, when this strict division gradually became blurred and mixed, urban and rural areas could exchange more freely.

When the country strictly divided its people, there was no market available for commodity trade in rural areas; all markets were located in the city and rural folk had to visit to buy handcrafts and other goods they required. Besides, to buy daily necessities, rural people first needed to transport their surplus grain to the city market and convert it into currency. During this time, there were strict regulations on the establishment of markets. As recorded in the *Rites of Zhou · The Market Management,* "The big market would start around noon mainly for the citizens, the morning market would start earlier, mainly for the merchants, and the evening market would start around dusk mainly for the small vendors."

Later, with the gradual increase of population and expansion of agricultural areas, some people started to live and farm far away from the city. Then it became very inconvenient for them to buy and sell goods and it was impossible to return home within a day. Thus, there was a need to establish markets for trading goods outside the city. Some intellectuals in the Spring and Autumn and the Warring States periods realized this. According to *Guanzi,* six square of *li* was named *bao,* five *bao* area was named *bu,* and five *bu* area was named *ju.* There must be a market in every *ju,* otherwise, people would be short of daily necessities. *Li* was a village organization unit in the pre-Qin period, which meant that a village fair should be set up within 150 *li.* This was the ideal state conceived by Guan Zi, but it also showed that in the pre-Qin period, people already had a considerable understanding of the role and spatial distribution of the rural market.

From then to the Tang Dynasty, the markets set up by the government could only be found in the city. Peasants from outside had to take their surplus produce into the city and sell it in exchange for daily goods. Around the same time, agricultural and sideline product trading were also done in the suburbs. This was the market near the outer city. For instance, there was such a market in the suburbs of the capital of State Zheng—probably the earliest record of a market near the outer city.

The number of these markets increased for a simple reason: at the beginning of city construction, only the needs of the Emperors and nobles were considered; the needs of the masses were not taken into account. Therefore, when the city population increased (causing a natural increase in market transactions), the original market space became inadequate and had to expand around the city gates.

Another important factor is the design of the city walls and city gates. This was done mainly for security purposes and would be more of a hindrance and restriction to traffic and trade inside. Each city had only a few gates, even in Kaifeng, the Eastern Capital, there were only about twenty gates, including the water gates. Only very few goods could be transported through each gate, taking into consideration the size of the carriage carts or ships, not to mention that the gates would be closed at night. As a result, it was more convenient to trade outside the city and let its consumers come to the goods. Thus, the emergence of grass markets was a natural consequence.

1. Grass Markets in the Song Dynasty

The *Commentary on the Waterway Classics* in the Southern and Northern Dynasties (AD 386–589) provides the earliest known usage of the phrase "grass market." It is found in the section for Feishui. In addition, there is also the following story in the book, *History of Southern Qi · Biography of Xiao Baoyin, Duke of Poyang*:

> It became dark after Baoyin arrived at the Dulao residence and the city gate was closed. The guards shot arrows, and Baoyin was abandoned by the others who ran away. Baoyin hid for three days and asked an officer of the grass market to send a message to Emperor Qi, who welcomed him to the palace.

This story occurred in AD 501, when Zhang Xintai, the Regional Inspector of Yongzhou, held Xiao Baoyin as a hostage and tried to dethrone Donghunhou. When the group with the hostage arrived at Dulao's residence, they were discovered by the soldiers guarding the city, so they chose to flee. Xiao Baoyin regained his freedom after Emperor Qi welcomed him to the palace. Dulao's residence, outside the Nanye Gate of the city of Tai, was the residence of Ms. Pei, mother of Empress Du (Du is Emperor Jin Chengdi's wife.).

This incident occurred at night: Xiao Baoyin hid for three days before he dared to see the grass market officer, who he asked to send a message to the Emperor. This story revealed that a grass market outside the city of Jiankang existed, and more importantly there were officers who managed these markets. *The Peaceful World Records* also documented grass markets during AD 326–334 (the Xianhe era).

What is a grass market? There are three views. One is that they were places to store grass or grass heaps, which later evolved into markets. Another view takes the second meaning of grass in Chinese, i.e., something temporary and unfinished, or something informal. In this case, it was used to refer to the suburban temporary trade place, rather than the strict management system that markets in the city were subject to; hence, the name—grass market.[1] The third view is that trading was transacted in grass fabricated sheds.[2]

Grass markets appeared in the Jiangnan region (south of the lower reaches of the Yangtze River) as it was developing at an unprecedented speed, with many immigrants arriving from the Central Plains. These immigrants brought advanced agricultural technology. For the first time, South China was considered the land of riches, better than the Guanzhong Economic Region (a historical region of China corresponding to the lower valley of the Wei River). With this background of economic space transformation, rural sideline productions developed naturally and fruits, fabrics, terracotta, fish, livestock, and other goods were regularly exchanged. The grass markets, based on labor divisions, began to expand in scale.

Simultaneously, the social economy of the Yellow River Basin, plagued by lengthy wars, resumed its development after the unification of the Northern Wei. The small-scale peasant economy was greatly promoted, especially by the implementation of the equal land distribution system. Although the so-called slogan,

---

1. See Zhao Gang, *On the History of Urban Development of China* (Beijing: New Star Publishing House, 2006), 171–172.
2. See Fu Zongyi, *Studies on the Grass Markets in the Song Dynasty* (Fuzhou: Fujian People's Publishing House, 1991), 6.

"all the people got rich and harvested with pleasure"[3] may be the hyperbole of language, undoubtedly the economy recovered. At this time, a prominent phenomenon was the emergence of several small commodity markets that carried the name "*Dian*" (店, stores or shops).[4]

The grass market began to appear in the Southern and Northern Dynasties but was very limited in number until the early Tang—mainly because the Tang regime controlled the local economy strictly with various permits required for markets."[5] This means even markets in the capital and other important places would depend on the government for their existence. Thus, grass markets only developed slowly in the earlier Tang, though this laid the foundation for later.

Implementation of an equal land distribution or tenancy system gathered labor to agricultural production and promoted rapid recovery and development of this industry. Simultaneously, because of the vast territory of the Tang Empire, the government attached great importance to the transportation of supplies. Altogether 1,639 *Yizhan*s (communication stations established by the government to pass on government messages and military information) were established. Horses allocated by the government were available in remote, strategic locations for the convenience of information communication. *Shuiyi* (water communication stations) were also set up along waterways and ships were provided for government travelers.

The development of agricultural production led to the prosperity of the handcraft industry and commerce. Easy transportation provided convenience for the circulation of commodities. Therefore, economic prosperity and social stability shown in the mid-Tang was the result of early development.

Among them, one of the characteristics of economic prosperity was the many city stores formed on land and along water transportation lines. A passage by Du You, a historian of the time, was often quoted as testimony to the social stability and economic prosperity. He said, during the reign of Emperor Xuanzong, the stores were open along both sides of the roads, and there was abundant wine and food. Each store had a donkey to rent to visitors that could travel dozens of *li* in a very short time. These donkeys were called "traveling donkeys."[6] This

3. Yang Xuanzhi, *A Record of Buddhist Monasteries in Luoyang*.
4. "Dian," introduction to *Assets Section* (No. 8), in *Imperial Readings of the Taiping Era*, vol. 828.
5. "Markets," in *A Concise History of the Tang Dynasty*, vol. 86.
6. "Food and Commodity," in *The Tongdian* (*The Comprehensive Institutions*), vol. 7.

passage illustrates the busy, flourishing scene of city shops. Water transportation was dominant in the Jiangnan region.

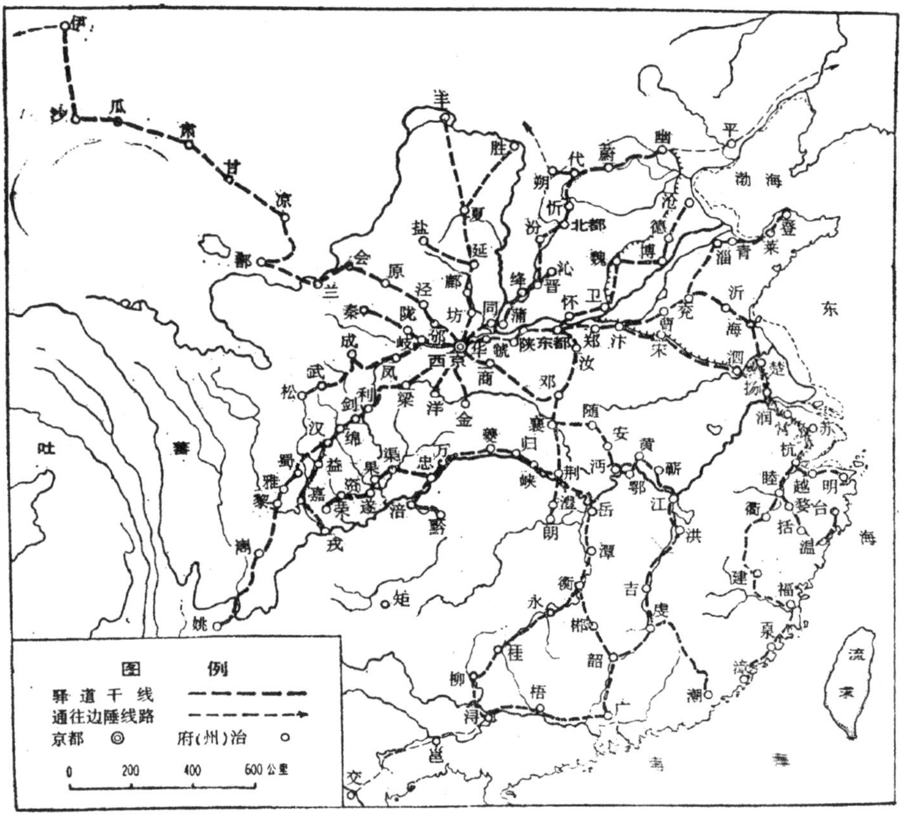

Fig. 7-1: Transport route map in the Tang Dynasty[7]

Consequently, many grass markets came into being along the waterway. As the famous poet Du Mu described, "The grass market in the Jianghuai area covered both sides of the waterway." We could read poetries from the five generations of the Tang Dynasty, that they often wrote about sand markets, boat markets, bridge markets, street markets, lake markets, river markets, and coastal markets. We could observe the close relationship between the waterway and markets. Poems in this aspect were too numerous to list.

7. Wang Yumin, *An introduction to Chinese Historical Geography* (Beijing: People's Publishing House, 1987), 407.

Fig. 7-2: A grass market close to the city in "Along the River during the Qingming Festival"[8]

Around the age of the Five Dynasties, a new feature emerged in the development of grass markets. That is, several grass markets grew around city centers. For instance, there was a grass market in the East Gate of Chengdu. There were grass markets close to the river outside Huacheng, Henan, as well as near Fenzhou, Shanxi. Among these, Kaifeng, the largest commercial city of the time, had the largest number of grass markets. There were so many grass markets outside Kaifeng that the government had to designate specific areas for them.

The Northern Song reestablished centralized national unity and its vast territory after the reunification process. It also promoted the prosperity of the grass markets. The farming mobilization system and water conservancy measures at the beginning of the Song enabled the restoration of the national economy.

Economic policies during this period were explained in the following way: "During the Jingde and Xiangfu eras, people became prosperous. Everyone was enjoying life. In the places where they lived, drums and musical instruments were often heard near and far. How could we not know the grace of His Majesty?"[9] It is self-evident that the favorable political and economic situation catalyzed the development of grass markets. However, they were effectively divided into the outer city grass markets and the rural grass markets, or bazaars, as they were called.

The development of the former, as previously mentioned, is a by-product of city development. After the Tang, the continuous expansion of the city made it

8. Yang Kuan, *Studies on Ancient Chinese Capital System History*, illustrations (Shanghai: Shanghai People's Press, 2003).
9. Chao Yuezhi, "Emperor's Orders in the Third Year of Yuanfu Era," in *Songshan Collected Works*, vol. 1.

impossible to fully accommodate urban households within the original walled space. As a result, many regular urban residents lived outside the walls. For example, in Chengdu during this time, "over a thousand households moved out of the outer city and settled down outside the walls."[10] Such a situation also appeared even in some smaller local cities.

Since the Northern Song, *Chengxiang* districts were set up in places outside the densely-populated city districts, with an administrative system consistent with those inside the city walls. But *Chengxiang* districts were not restricted by walls and had sufficient space to accommodate more people and urban activities. At first, Emperor Zhenzong established eight districts in suburban Bianjing for the management of residents outside the city.

This situation was more prominent in Lin'an, the capital of the Southern Song. In AD 1141, the Governor of Lin'an, Yu Si, offered suggestions to the Emperor: "The densely populated areas outside the capital were as long as 30 *lis*. It was like a small city, each to the south and north. I suggest establishing *Xiang*s in Jiangzhang Bridge and Zhejiang."[11] Jiangzhang Bridge and Zhejiang were originally two towns close in the outer city of Lin'an which became part of the city districts. Lower level cities also adopted such a system. For instance, there were the southern *Xiang* along the south gate of Jiankang City and six *Xiang*s in the suburbs of Fuzhou.

This *Chengxiang* system allowed urban space to break through the limitations of city walls. At the same time, retail services for these *Chengxiang* areas also formed. For instance, twelve markets surrounded Bianjing because of the large number of residents outside the city gates. Mingzhou, or today's Ningbo, also had markets surrounding the outer city.[12] The many consumers in big cities and their vast consumption provided the conditions for specialized market development, especially in agricultural products for daily use. From very early on, specialized markets emerged in the Eastern Capital of the Northern Song and Lin'an, with peasants gathering at specialized markets to sell their products. With a stable, reliable market, many suburban peasants gradually embarked on specialized production. The outskirts of Bianjing (refers to Kaifeng) and Lin'an had many peasants specializing in planting vegetables, flowers, and fruits.

---

10. Fu Zengxiang, *Works by Authors of Shu in the Song Dynasty*, vol. 17.
11. Gan Dao, *A Record of Lin'an*, vol. 2.
12. Shu Dan, *A Poetry Collection of Shu's*, vol. 1.

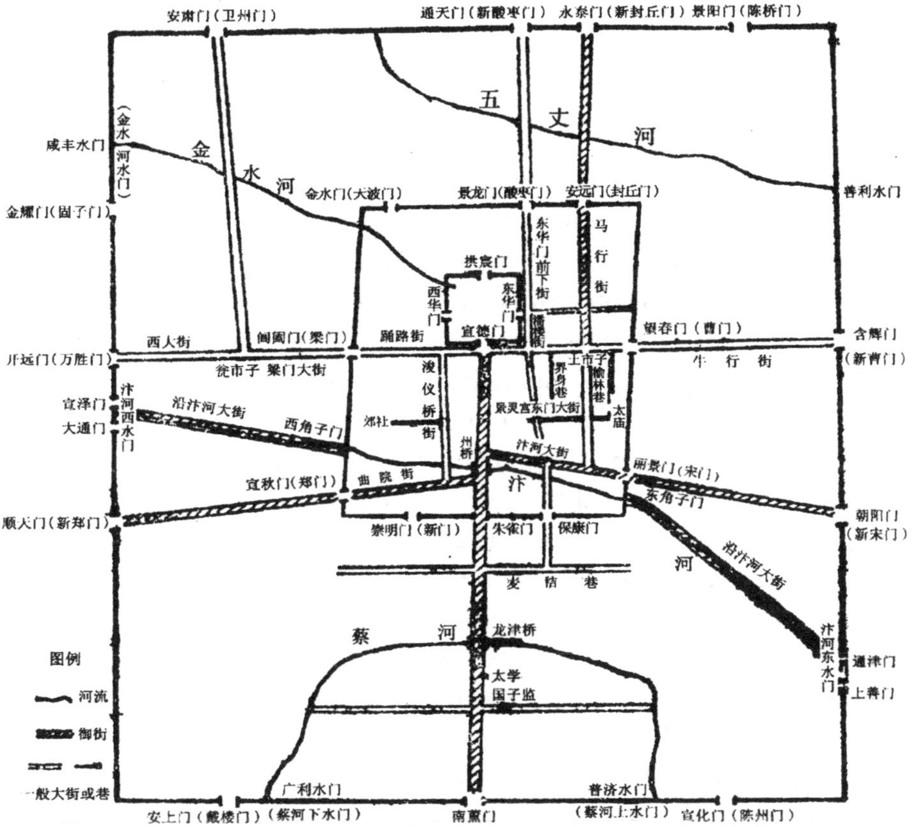

Fig. 7-3: Chengxiangs *of Kaifeng, the Eastern Capital of the Northern Song*[13]

The early rural fairs were quite similar, mainly providing exchange services for the peasants who were not self-sufficient. First, peasants should sell their products. Then, they should buy their daily necessities and non-staple foods with their money. A poem from the Song era vividly described the rural markets:

> When I walked into the valley's mouth, a small village revealed itself ahead. The peasants struggled for space along the roads, talking noisily with bustling sounds everywhere. Several hours passed like a second, and the shops were as many as endless clouds. Some carried mulberry branches; some drove

13. Yang Kuan, *Studies on Ancient Chinese Capital System History* (Shanghai: Shanghai People's Press, 2003), 322.

> their chickens and pigs. There were so many products in the markets that it is difficult to mention them.[14]

Since it was very difficult for peasants in the same area to produce varied products, it was almost impossible for them to acquire what they needed from other peasants. Hence, small businessmen would naturally appear in rural markets. Some purchased grain and other agricultural products to sell in the city. Others sold handcrafts, oil, salt, or other daily goods they acquired from city markets. Since both sides were sporadic with small transactions, there was no need to deal with intermediaries. Because sales volume in the rural markets for each commodity was limited, small traders could not derive much profit and survive if the market opened daily in the same place.

Consequently, early rural fairs were held and opened often but not always, and care was taken when scheduling such events. At the same time, to help the diligent street merchants, the government arranged shifts for them to operate their business according to the timetable and therefore obtain fixed income. In comparison, the markets in South China's rural areas, which lack regulations, are crowded during peak hours and empty for the rest of the day.

The booming grass markets inevitably became the target of the central government, who would look to leverage hefty taxes on them. Around AD 1020 in the Northern Song, a business tax was levied on grass markets. By the time of Emperor Renzong, not only were taxes levied, but also special regulatory tax agents were appointed. According to incomplete statistics, in AD 1076, a total of 27,607 collection points were established in the surrounding area of the capital as well as the crossroads, *fang*s and fields, river passes, etc., with total revenue of 4,203,189 units.

The large grass markets became an important component of the local economy. For instance, the Sand Head Market in Jingzhou, Hubei, became a hub where merchants and ships gathered.[15] Besides, some grass markets became specialized towns due to their locations as agricultural and sideline producers of minerals. For instance, Yongjiang in Sichuan grew into a salt town because salt was produced there.

---

14. *Canliaozi Anthology of Poems*, vol. 1.

15. *Yudi Jisheng (A Geographic Records of the Southern Song Dynasty)*, vol. 64.

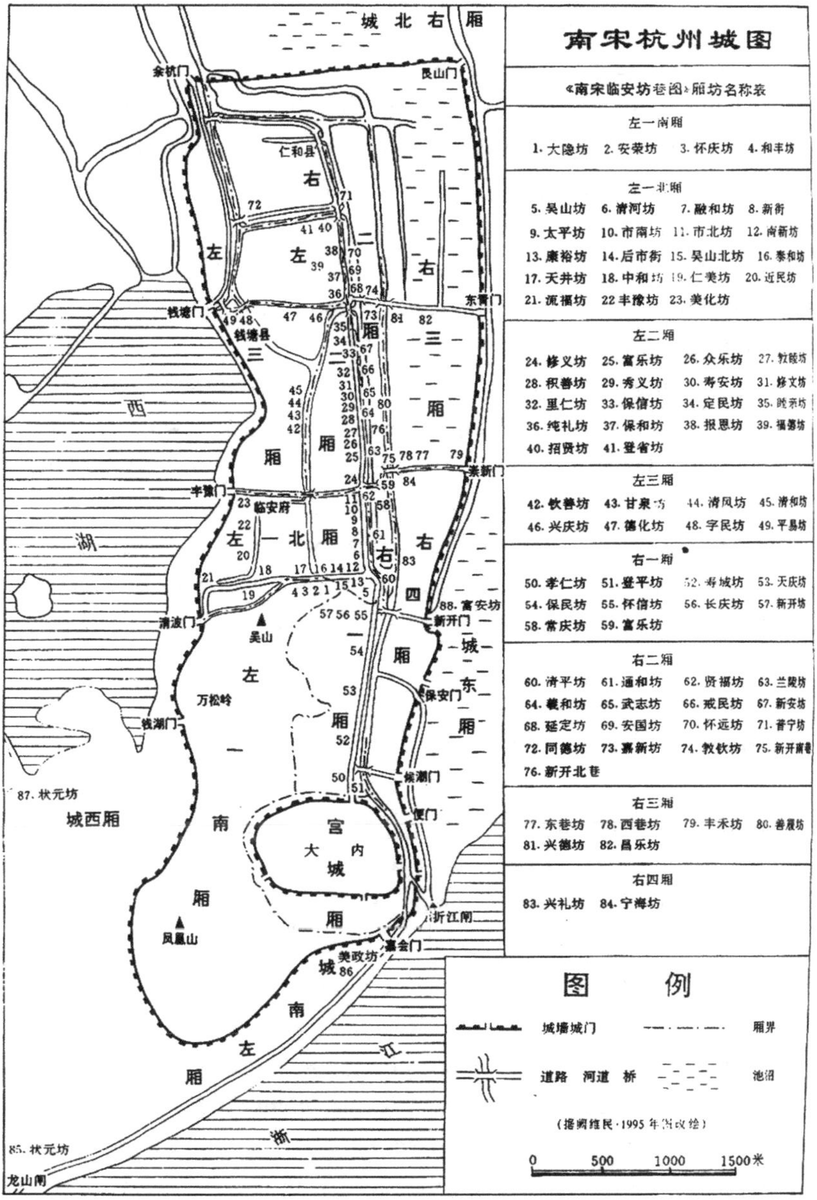

Fig. 7-4: Map of Ling'an in the Southern Song[16]

---

16. Que Weimin, *An Illustrated History of the Hangzhou City and the West Lake* (Hangzhou: Zhejiang People's Publishing House, 2000), 145.

With taxes collected and tax supervision officials appointed, the status of grass markets naturally grew, and they were treated like towns. Generally, the designation of tax supervision officials signaled the upgrading of grass markets into towns. Starting from AD 1023–1031, this policy was implemented across the country, becoming standard procedure. With the interaction of political and economic factors, the feudal economy and financial commercialization were strengthened significantly at the beginning of Emperor Renzong's reign. During Emperor Shenzong's reign, the implementation of the New Policies (a reform) further promoted this.

According to scholars' statistics, 137 towns were established during the reign of these two Emperors, accounting for 60% of the 226 townships during the Northern Song.[17] Because of this, towns and grass markets were paired in official documents, and sometimes these two terms were integrated—known as the grass market town. It was possible that town markets had become the main body of the local economy by this time and continued to impact the formation and establishment of the economic regions in the Ming and Qing dynasties.

2. Towns in the Ming and Qing Dynasties

With the emergence of outer city grass markets, military towns began to gain economic functions. The name, *Zhen* (镇, town), first appeared officially in the Northern Wei Period and was a military stronghold established by the state on the northern border; hence it was called the "military town." After the An-Shi Rebellion in the mid-Tang era, towns were developed to safeguard territories from separationists.

According to their military importance, military towns in the Tang were classified into the higher, middle, and lower towns, independent from local administration. Military towns were also in charge of their peoples' household registration, taxes, and other civil obligations within their jurisdiction. Among them, the higher towns held the position of *cangcao* (warehouse head), where job

17. See Fu Zongwen, *Studies on the Grass Market Towns in the Song Dynasty* (Fuzhou: Fujian People's Publishing House, 1989), 91.

responsibilities included market administration. In the middle towns, the *bingcao* (head of the soldiers) would concurrently take charge.

Garrisons were mostly located near strategic land or water, with the main purpose being troop facilitation for easy attack and retreat, which also provided trade convenience. With the convergence of population and development of business, military towns became business centers. Especially after the mid-Tang, military lords occupied territories, put restrictions on rivers, and levied taxes, all in conflict with the central government's interests. These activities objectively accelerated the process of town transformation from military strongholds to commercial centers. By the Five Dynasties Period, the military town had completed this transformation into a business town.

The reunification of the centralized state in the Northern Song marked the end of the two-century feudal warlord regime. Soldiers in garrisons were removed, towns were transformed into regional commercial centers, and civil service was established for management. Many regular rural fairs had grown into large-scale permanent markets. The Song government normalized these markets, set up taxes, and sent special personnel to levy these commercial taxes. Therefore, the Song era was a turning point in the history of China's town development: it marked the start of smaller towns being formed instead of larger cities. However, the towns wouldn't change significantly again until the Ming and Qing eras.

During these dynasties, due to the reduction of cultivable land and full utilization of traditional agricultural resources, it became common for a small piece of land to be shared by a large number of people. In other words, population pressure was increasing. Therefore, more attention was paid to the areas of commodity production and circulation, which had not yet been fully developed. After the establishment of the Ming, a series of positive political and economic measures were completed. Peasant subordination to others was weakened; this and the *tuntian* system (a system where garrison soldiers or peasants developed the wasteland and cultivated it), spurred the development of industry and commerce.

This greatly improved social productivity, especially in the fields of handcraft production, textiles, porcelain, mining and metallurgy, and shipbuilding, significantly surpassing the Song and Yuan dynasties. In addition, after the mid-Ming era, the northern border of the empire was harassed, and the demand for military items rose across the country. It also stimulated the development of handcrafts and commercial towns. This situation lasted almost until Emperor Qianlong's reign in the mid-Qing period.

Compared with the Song and Yuan dynasties, the functions of towns during the Ming and Qing were already further divided. This function differentiation of the town originated from the Song. As mentioned earlier, market towns emerged because peasants who could not be self-sufficient had to sell their remaining agricultural products in exchange for daily necessities, so the rural market came into being. This kind of town with the purpose of agricultural sideline products and handcraft retailing was called the traditional market town, which mainly functioned as stations for the purchase of grains and a small number of other agricultural products to supply nearby cities. At the same time, towns were also the venue for handcraft goods retailing to supply the surrounding villages. The peak for traditional towns occurred during the Song Dynasty without any doubt, but another category of towns also began to emerge during this period.

With the further popularization of cotton, mulberry, tea, and other economic crops, towns started to flourish as agricultural product trading and distribution centers. Many specialized towns emerged, which mainly focused on a particular industry or the exchange of handcraft products, such as textiles, printing, dyeing, and tea making. In these towns, peasants were mainly engaged in economic crop production or produced secondary items by relying on economic crops. This type of town was non-traditional, since they were principally areas to purchase agricultural side products, which would be sold in other places. Simultaneously, they were also retail outlets for merchants, who sold grain shipped from afar to the peasants nearby.

Traditional towns and new towns showed distinct differences both in terms of function and space distribution because of differences in their formation. The basic function of the traditional town was to facilitate peasants in selling surplus agricultural products in exchange for other commodities, with the transaction initiated by peasants. The function of a new town was to sell farm produce and side products in exchange for food. The transaction was greatly influenced by the market and often merchants were in control.

During the Ming and Qing dynasties, traditional towns still retained their original features and their main function to serve rural consumers. This situation was abundantly recorded in the local chronicles of the Ming and Qing dynasties.

For example, in Tongguan County, Shaanxi Province, which was now Tongchuan City, "There were no special things besides cloth millet and vegetables." Song County in Henan was similar, "The town was not a city, only stores the agricultural products, salt, and rice, which were for civilian use." Those who participated in the markets were mainly peasants in nearby villages. Rich, important merchants would never consider attending these traditional markets because the small volume of commodities was insufficient to attract them. Although Fuping County of Shaanxi was the homeland of rich merchants active in China during the Ming and Qing dynasties, the local town was very bleak. The town was recorded as: "There were lands for commercial use, trading period, and the commodities were daily necessities, not enough to attract important merchants." To meet rural consumer needs, traditional markets had to consider the specific circumstances of peasants. This determined the typical distribution of traditional markets. In the choice of location, convenient transportation is obviously important, however of more significance was whether locals could come and go within a day, i.e., commute. Therefore, traditional towns were evenly distributed in the countryside. This feature is unsurprising and not unique to China.

A German scholar, Walter Christaller, reached the same conclusion—the towns were evenly distributed in the country after utilizing a strict, complex calculation of the towns in southern Germany where agriculture was advanced. However, China's vast territory and differences in economic development and geographical environment determined the variances of distribution across the country. According to American scholar, Professor G. William Skinner, the average distance for peasants living in the Chengdu Plains was about 4 kilometers to attend a market. On the other hand, the rural market density in Hebei was one market within every 100 square kilometers during the Ming era, 1.5 markets in the Qing era, and 2.5 markets during the Republic of China, according to the study of the Japanese scholar, Jun Ishihara.

Since the Southern Song, traditional towns have developed slowly, far behind the development of new towns. This is mainly because low peasant income made it hard to raise purchasing power, which, in turn, led to stagnant market transactions in rural areas. Not only did fewer new towns emerge, but even existing bazaars were difficult to convert from regular to standing daily markets. It can be argued that the stagnation of traditional towns is a microcosm of rural development in the Ming and Qing dynasties.

A new type of town began to emerge after the Song and accelerated its development during the Ming and Qing dynasties. These new towns were more concentrated in the Taihu Lake Basin of the Jiangnan region. Therefore, they were also called "Southern Towns" in order to distinguish them from traditional towns.

The appearance of the new town seems to be a consequence of overpopulation and scarcity of arable land, when, in fact, it had a cause-and-effect relationship with China's urban management. From the Song to the Qing, due to the various factors, the absolute number of urban residents remained largely unchanged. Most population growth stayed in the countryside, which led to tension between people and land in rural areas.

In areas with serious population pressure, like the Taihu River Basin, peasants could not support their large families by relying solely on grain production. Hence, they turned to side agricultural products for extra income. Since the Ming era, peasants in the river basin mainly planted cash crops or produced handcrafted products to sell at the markets. From a variety of products, silk and cotton were considered the most suitable for household production. Therefore, these two industries became the most developed in the Jiangnan region, which became the basis for the formation of new towns in the region.

Almost every household in Jiangnan was engaged in the textile industry. These products were sold locally, and the surplus relied on distant and even foreign markets. Because of the need for long distance transport, the new town relied more heavily on transportation than traditional towns. Thus, most towns were located at transport junctions, and closely tied to big and medium cities in their area. Still, peasant producers could not sell their products that far due to transportation restraints. The Songjiang area, a production area for cotton cloth nicknamed "the clothing world," had to depend on merchants to sell cloth throughout the country. Also, because of the many textile products and the long distances involved, only very wealthy merchants qualified for the job.

Therefore, the economy of a new town had three characteristics: (1) it must rely on distant markets, (2) it requires long-distance transport, and (3) the participants are merchants with large funds. This is clearly different from the traditional town. These characteristics brought another distinction—the intermediary broker.

Intermediary broker agencies and agents emerged, since there were a few business buyers, while there were many peasant sellers. This phenomenon was rare in traditional towns. However, peasants in rural areas were still the service targets of the new town, whose travel was constrained equally by conditions and the inability to travel long distances. Consequently, the distribution of new and traditional towns was not essentially different, with only one exception. When handcrafted products or raw materials increased in yields, the size of the market turnover also increased, which led to population growth in the number of towns functioning as purchase locations. For this reason, towns in the Jiangnan region increased rapidly during the Ming and Qing dynasties.

Naturally, the most concentrated and most developed new towns were located around the Taihu area. Among them, the most prominent included Su (Suzhou), Song (Songjiang), Hang (Hangzhou), Jia (Jiaxing), and Hu (Huzhou). They were also the most important cotton planting and silkworm breeding areas in China. Local town industry revolved around the production and exchange of cotton and silk. Four towns became especially prominent—Linghu, the Huzhou Silk trade center; Shimen of Jiaxing, another silk trade center; Shengze, known for its different kinds of silk; and Shanghai, which exported its silk products to the world.

Puyuan of Jiaxing is also a typical example of new town formation. During the Song and Yuan dynasties, it was merely a market town, but during the Longqing and Wanli era (AD 1567–1619), when the cotton cloth was often replaced by silk cloth, Puyuan became well-known both near and far because of its superb manufacturing quality.

"Everyday thousands of pieces of silk cloth were made and wealthy merchants from afar rushed here in large numbers."[18] The town turned to handcrafts as its main industry. By the early Qing, Puyuan had been further developed into a handcraft industry center with tens of thousands of households. During Emperor Qianlong's reign (AD 1734–1795), Puyuan could produce tens of thousands of silk pieces. These silk products were exported across the mainland to regions like Shandong, Shanxi, Huguang, Shaanxi, Jiangxi, Fujian, Taiwan, the Ryukyu islands, and even Japan. Pu silk became well-known[19] and the city was known as the "silk city."

In fact, this new type of town was not confined to cotton or silk textiles in Jiangnan. There were many other new towns in the country, such as Jingdezhen,

18. Ming Xiaopei, "Stele in Xiangyun Temple," in *A Travelogue in Puchuan*, vol. 4.

19. "Customs," introduction to *A Record of Town Pu*.

which sold ceramic products all over; Quanzhou and Zhangzhou, which sold sugar products by vendors everywhere; Shunchang of Fujian that sold bamboo paper throughout China; and Huoshan of Anhui, which specialized in the tea industry. They all became commercial towns due to the development of the handcraft industry. There were also new towns, which became regional trade centers not rising from handcraft products, but from their superior transport conditions, such as Qingjiangpu of Jiangsu Province and Zhangqiu of Jining in Shandong Province. Among them, there was a canal excavated in Qingjiangpu along the Shahe River during the Ming Dynasty, both ships from north and south needed to pass through the Qingjiang canal. It was recorded as "a transport center for thousands of boats; traders and shops were active on both side of river embankment, tens of thousands of residents along the river, prosperous area for both land and water, a region with high commercial value."

During the Ming and Qing period, some of these towns surpassed county centers or even higher-level cities, serving as traditional political centers in population and economic functions. A few towns even developed into national business centers. There were different versions of the "Big Four Towns,"—Zhuxian of Henan, Hankou of Huguang, Jingdezhen of Jiangxi, and Foshan of Guangdong. Among these, Zhuxian and Hankou developed into business towns because of their advantageous positions. Jingdezhen and Foshan started with ceramics and iron cast respectively, and eventually became famous handcraft towns.

Besides, there are also similar descriptions in *Guangyang Zaji* (a book recording miscellaneous things by Liu Xianting during the Qing): "there are four centers in China: Beijing in the north, Foshan in the south, Suzhou in the east, and Hankou in the west." While this description cannot be verified, comparing Foshan and Hankou with the economic and cultural centers—Beijing in the north and Suzhou in the south—implies the scale of these two towns. For instance, according to historical records, Qingjiangpu had a population of more than 540,000 in AD 1775, during the Qing era. This would be a city of considerable scale today.

Under the centralization rule in ancient China, the special layout of towns grown naturally was obviously different from those chosen as administrative centers under the strict control of the central government. These commercial and trade-based towns were also formed naturally on the main axis of transportation, unlike the planned cities.

Since ancient times, the Jiangnan region was covered with waterway networks. Transportation was convenient thanks to boating. Rural and urban transport was mostly water based, supplemented by land. Under these circumstances, towns were established along the river. The dependence between the towns and the river network of the Jiangnan region also determined the layout of the town. The expansion would rely on the direction and even flow of the river. Although in some relatively low-level areas around Taihu Lake, because the rural farmland from the Song Dynasty has constantly been using dikes—bank ditch development form, the river course was tortuous, so the layout of the towns here was also different. In general, we can conclude there were four types of these towns: dash-pattern, cross-pattern, T-shaped, and ring-shaped.

A dash-pattern means the river flowing through the town is relatively straight, and a single market town has formed along the two sides of the river. This type was said to be most common south of the Yangtze. Regardless of the scale, it is always possible to form such a shape. There were also other towns with winding rivers in a variety of forms. For example, the town of Wangjiangjing in Jiaxing County was huge in scale. It was called "Five-*li* Long Street" in the late Ming Dynasty. However, most of them are small towns. For instance, Tudian Town in Tongxiang County was built along the river course, although temples like Jizhao, and Shijing were established in the middle of the town so that the town could be slightly expanded to the north and south. But it had nothing to do with commercial activities. There were two *Li* (厘) Bureaus at the east and west ends of the Shihe River, which could be regarded as a sign of the beginning and end of a linear city street, which was a very classical design. Although the rivers around other towns were not in straight line form, the distribution of the town's commercial activities centered along the linear city river, such as Shengze town of Wujiang and Xincheng Town of Jiaxing. In such a case, these towns would be considered as "dash" towns.

A cross-pattern town developed along two rivers across the city, forming a cross. For example, Nanxun of Wuxing County formed a cross with the north-south city river and the Tiaoxi stream, which flowed west-east. Commercial streets were formed along the banks of both rivers—a typical cross town. Keqiao of Shaoxing in eastern Zhejiang was similar in shape, with the urban area extending from the north-south river crossing with the Zhedong Canal going west-east.

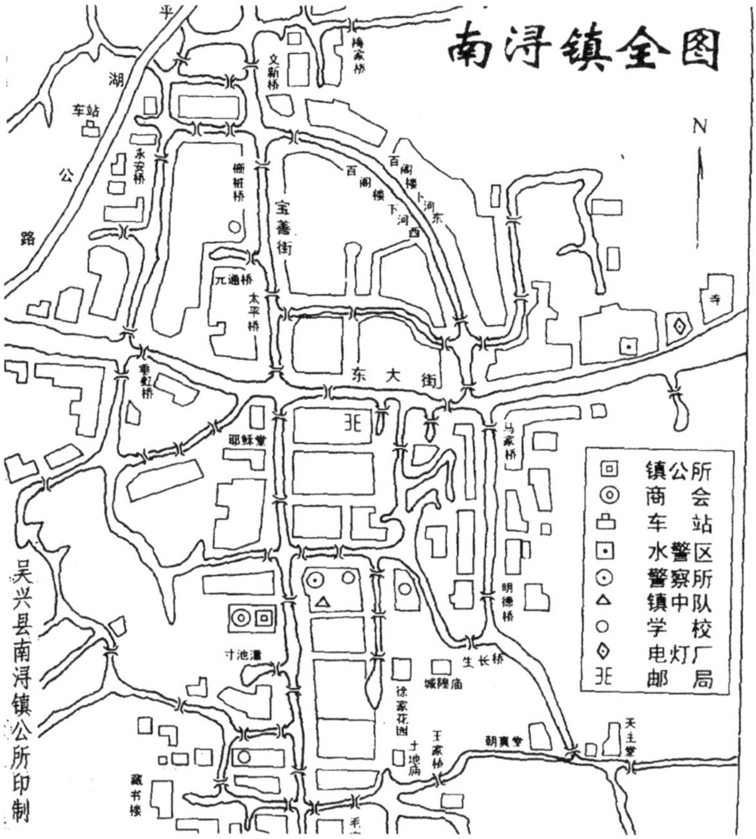

Fig. 7-5: Plan of a cross-pattern town[20]

Wuqing was a special cross-pattern town, located at the junction of Tongxiang County and Wuxing County. As a whole, Wuqing was a typical cross town that had the Beijing–Hangzhou Grand-Canal running north-south and slightly west-east and the other river running west-east slightly north-south crossing each other. However, the Grand Canal was so broad and only one bridge was set for crossing plus the fact that Wu and Qing towns traditionally belonged to Wucheng and Tongxiang respectively in terms of administration districts, the town districts on the two banks of the Grand Canal could also be considered as two separate T-shaped towns.

20. Bao Weimin, *Towns in the Jiangnan Region and Their Modern Destiny* (Beijing: Intellectual Press, 1998), 95.

The so-called T-shaped town, as the name suggests, is characterized by two rivers shaped like the letter T, with the town growing along the two rivers. Except that Wuqing Town mentioned above was actually composed of two separate T-shaped towns, Wuzhen and Qingzhen, which were located on the east and west banks of the canal, Wangdian Town in Jiaxing was a typical example. Wangdian of Jiaxiang was a typical example of a T-shaped town. One side of Wangdian was Long Water Pond, a branch of the north-south Grand Canal, and the other side was the west-east Plum Stream, which was also the city river for Wangdian. With Plum Stream joining the Long Water Pond forming a T shape, a certain scale of markets formed along these water areas to become the main parts of the Wangdian Market.

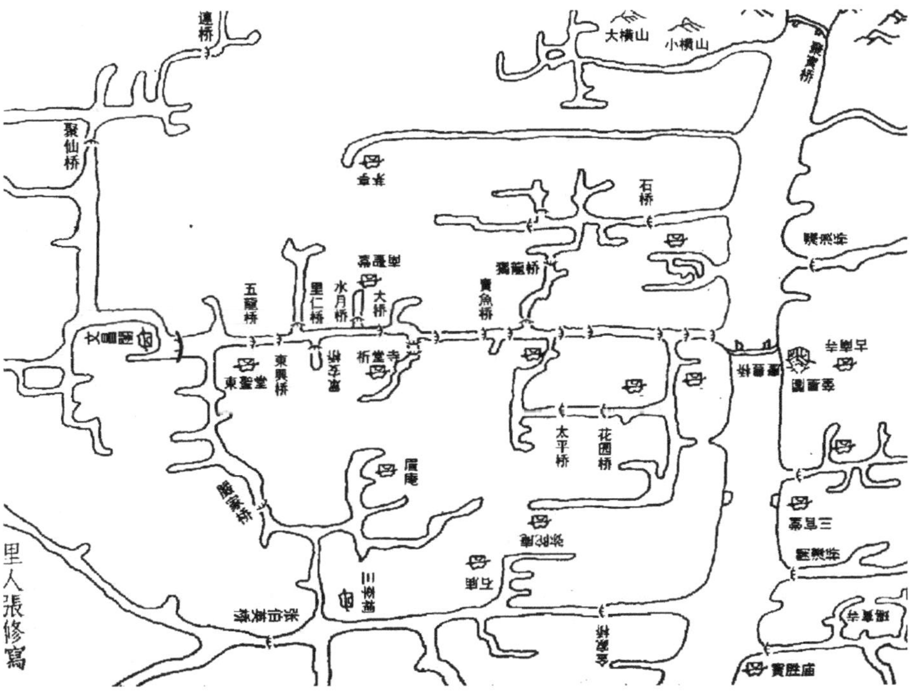

Fig. 7-6: Plan of a T-shaped town[21]

21. Bao Weimin, *Towns in the Jiangnan Region and Their Modern Destiny* (Beijing: Intellectual Press, 1998), 96.

Another example is Zhouzhuang, a popular tourist destination now. There is South Lake in the south of Zhouzhuang connected with Dianshan Lake. The South Lake extends to the north and becomes the north–south city river that runs through the town. In addition, there is an east–west river named Zhongshi River, which leads to the inner-city area. The two rivers meet near Fu'an Bridge, forming a T-shaped channel. The street market is formed along the river on the north side of the east–west river. Another street market is formed by the north–south river course, which together forms the main body of a T-shaped market.

Fig. 7-7: A town located in the Jiangnan region

Along the Taihu-Grand Canal Basin, many ring rivers formed as a result of the drainage ditches constructed for polder development. Although the markets for these towns were incomplete rings, the circular layout features of these town plans were very obvious. For instance, Zhouqian of Jiaxing County received its name because it was surrounded by water and shaped like coins.[22] In addition, Tongli of Wujiang, Fengjing of Jinshan, Xietang of Jiashan, Xinshi of Deqing, and Yuxi of Tongxiang had similar features.

22. "Towns," in *Jiaxing Garrison Annals*, during Emperor Guangxu's Reign, vol. 4.

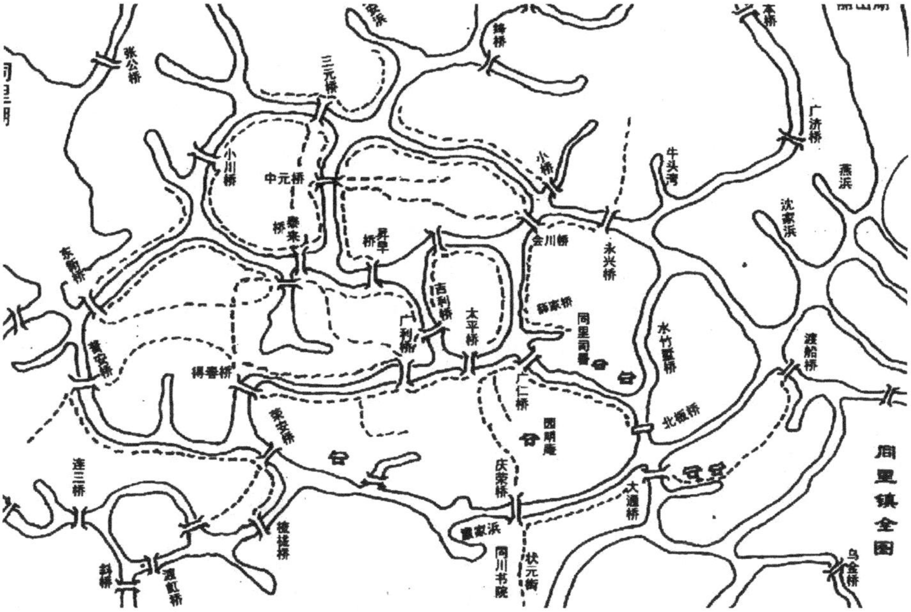

Fig. 7-8: Plan of a ring-shaped town[23]

The towns were classified in this way because, despite the differences in scales and shapes, they developed based on the river system. The features for market growth along the riverbanks remain the same. What changed was the relationship between river courses. Another common feature of the Jiangnan towns was that they were mainly part of a singular block system. More specifically, this means the buildings of towns—either shops or residential houses—would be established along the rivers in parallel structures. Streets were constructed between the rivers and houses, which extended along the rivers for miles. However, towns usually had only one block along the river, which means few secondary business streets could be found behind these riverfront buildings.

A reason for this basic feature lies in transport needs. Of course, people could solve this problem by using human or animal labor. However, it would be a better to have both the streets and houses facing the river directly. Thus, water transport needed by the town's economy restricted the growth of the

23. Bao Weimin, *Towns in the Jiangnan Region and Their Modern Destiny* (Beijing: Intellectual Press, 1998), 96.

second row of blocks not close to the rivers; thereby, hindering the formation of multi-block neighborhoods. In addition, from the view of the development of urban construction, a single block is the most suitable form for the preliminary urbanization development level for Jiangnan towns. In this form, the town street construction occupies the least proportion of land, with the lowest construction cost, particularly suitable for cities with expensive housing prices and high population density like Jiangnan. At the same time, a single block has lower requirements for sewage discharge: in addition to a simple ditch leading to the river, each unit building generally does not require more complex sewer systems.

Fig. 7-9: The town street river in the Jiangnan region

Fig. 7-10: Drainage facilities of a town in the Jiangnan region

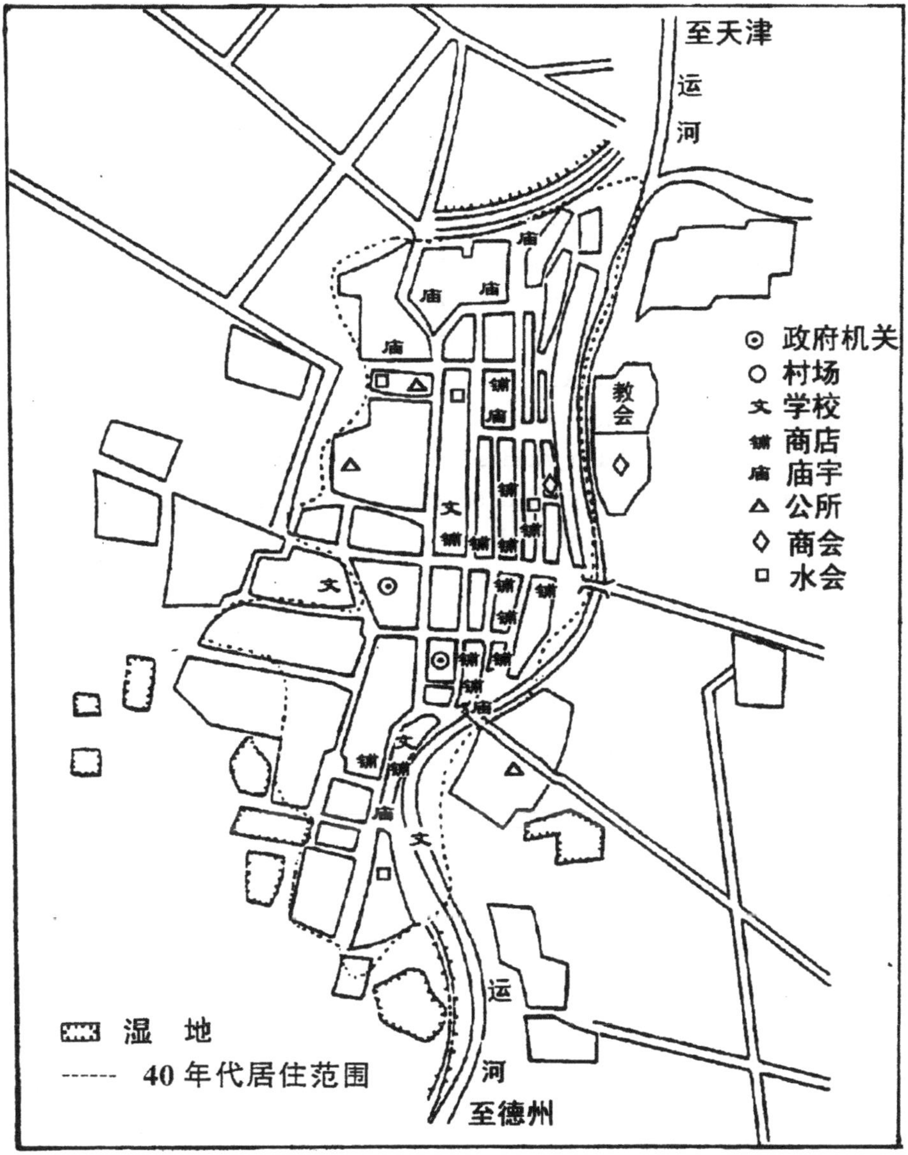

Fig. 7-11: Plan of Duliu, Tianjin[24]

24. Bao Weimin, *Towns in the Jiangnan Region and Their Modern Destiny* (Beijing: Intellectual Press, 1998), 100.

Transport in the northern towns of China mainly depended upon animal power, not shipping. Thus, multi-block neighborhoods formed more easily and the streets were generally grander than those in Jiangnan. For instance, Duliu of Tianjin was a typical example of a multi-block town. In addition, some towns formed from other factors developed into multiple-block neighborhoods. For example, Guancheng of Cixi County was in the harbor and originated from the Sea Watch Guard Station during the Ming. The town was established because of political and military factors. Hence, it was an organized city with planning. Even today, the entire town is still very organized with 57 horizontal and vertical streets, like a microcosm of a city.

Naturally, with the continuous development of a town's economy, those in the Jiangnan region gradually changed from a single block to a multiple-block structure. In conclusion, it is difficult to generalize about the variety of towns and how they came about across all of ancient China.

CHAPTER EIGHT

WATERWAYS AND CITIES: CITIES AND TRANSPORTATION

A very strong and comprehensive set of transport networks ensures that cities, as administrative centers, can pass government policy to the people, collect taxes, mobilize troops, etc. More importantly, transport routes guarantee city residents their daily supplies and transfer commodities for the entire area. It is no exaggeration to say that transport routes are the lifeline of urban development.

1. Ground and Water Transport

There is a long history in China of long-distance commercial transport. The *Book of Documents · Ban on Alcohol* documented, "A person named Zhao drove his ox-driven cart and served a merchant far from his home so he could support his family and show his fidelity." While, *Biography for Merchants* in *Records of the Grand Historian* wrote, "Exceedingly wealthy traders go all over the country and there is nothing that cannot be traded and people can get what they desire." Since the Warring States Period, well-known handcraft products were labelled with where they were produced and the name of the manufacturer. Words like "Cheng-Shi-Bao" were inscribed on some of the lacquerware unearthed in the Mawang Tomb, Hunan Province. According to textual research, these words meant "made in Chengdu." This shows long-distance transport was relatively common during this time.

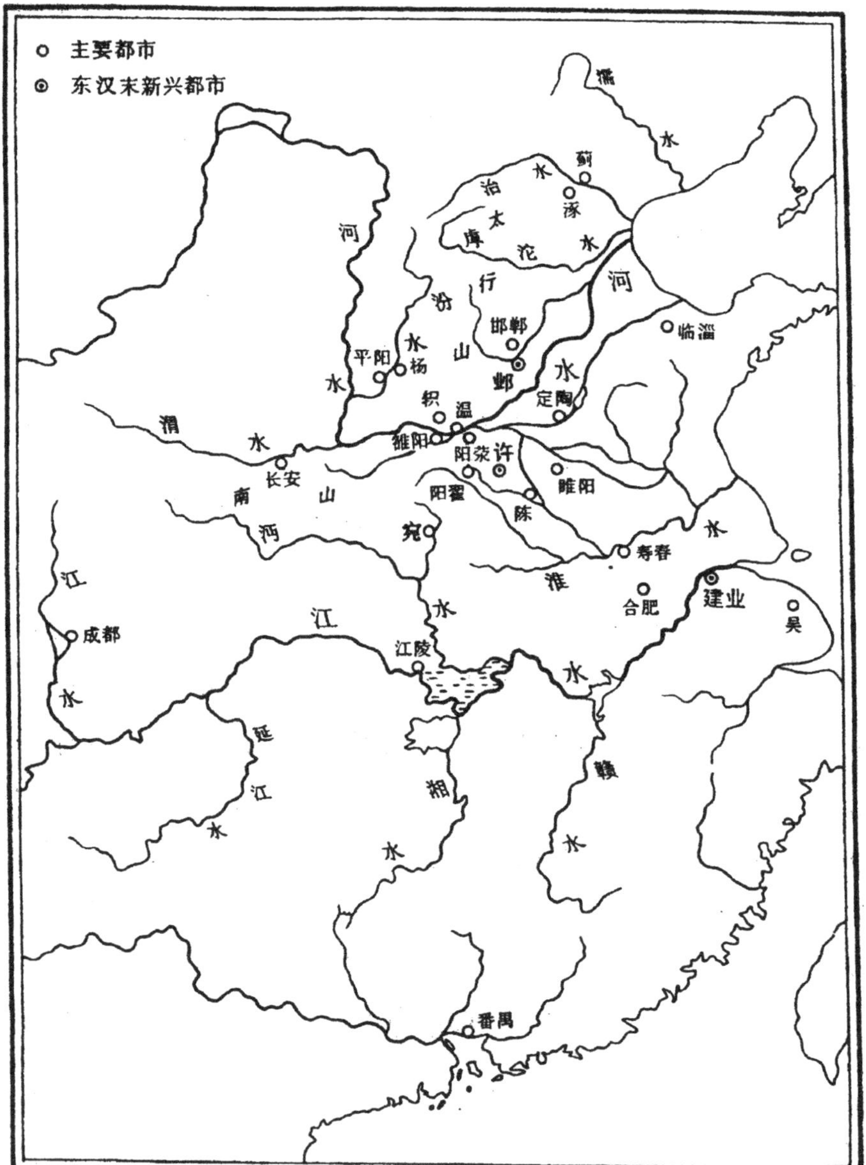

Fig. 8-1: Distribution of main cities from the Warring States to Western Han[1]

1. Zou Yilin, *An Outline of Chinese Historical Geography* (Shanghai: Shanghai Education Press, 2005), 332.

In addition to merchants, governments in Chinese history also devoted national financial resources to maintaining transport networks centered in the capital city, ensuring public affairs were handled in a timely fashion and people's opinions were heard by the rulers. The *Ground Officials* of *Rites of Zhou* documented:

> On any road of the country, there would be shelters with food provided every ten *li*. There would be lodging provided with facilities every thirty *li*. There would be cities with official welcome residences every fifty *li*.

This refers to the postal system in the Spring and Autumn Period, when stations and shelters were established for travelers, and sometimes even warehouses were provided for the temporary storage of goods for merchants.

The modes of transportation in pre-industrial China could be broadly divided into three categories: land, water, and sea. China's ancient transportation was said to depend on ships in the south and horses in the north. In fact, the ancient Chinese took advantage of waterways as much as possible, even digging artificial canals to ensure the smooth transport of goods, considering the limitations of land travel for large, bulky supplies.

Scholars believe a road system with the capital at the center may have formed during the late Shang Dynasty.[2] The *Book of Songs* also indicated there were long, sturdy land roads built during the Zhou Dynasty. Despite this documentation, the transport network system between cities, and between cities and other places, did not come into being until the Spring and Autumn and Warring States periods. During this time, the national transport network was established with frequent exchange between the states and a gradual development of industry and commerce. At this time, various links between states led to numerous, crisscross road networks.

Chenggao Road, an important major transport route, began east from Chenggao and extended west along the Yellow River until it reached the Hangu Pass connecting the eastern states and the Qin State in the west. In the north-south direction, there was East Avenue of the Taihang Mountain Range, the most

2. Zou Yilin, *An Outline of Chinese Historical Geography* (Shanghai: Shanghai Education Press, 2005), 326–327.

important road in ancient northern China and the main channel for the Yan and Zhao states to connect with the Central Plains. The Chu State in the south of China connected with the Central Plains through the Funiu Mountain Pass, which veered north after its exit from the east of the Nanyang Basin—also known as the Xia Road. In addition, there were some secondary interregional roads, such as the Jinniu Road excavated by the Qin State to reach the Sichuan Basin and the road along the Fen River Valley in the Shanxi plateau to reach the Guanzhong or Heluo region, all of which were essential channels that connect various areas.

Long distance transportation by inland waterways was even more important. In 647 BC, Duke Mu shipped large amounts of grain from Yong, the capital of Qin (present-day Fengxiang of Shaanxi) along the Wei, the Yellow, and then back to the Fen River to Jiang, then-capital of the Jin state, to assist the Jin people in the famine. This event is well-known in Chinese history—the Rafting Battle.

More economical than human labor, waterways became the key mode of transport in this era. After King Weihui moved his capital to Daliang (Kaifeng), the first thing he did was to connect the two major water networks of the Yellow and Huai rivers by digging the Great Ditch. This endeavor connected the Jishui, Ru, Ying, Guo, Sui, and Si Rivers, forming a water transportation system centered on this ditch. It made moving products across the Central Plains and southern China more convenient and faster.

Transportation development undoubtedly promoted the rise of the city. Some important cities were formed, especially along main traffic routes. Furthermore, the relationship between the city and transport routes goes far beyond our imagination. It can be said that all important cities in the Spring and Autumn Period were along key transport routes. For instance, Xianyang, the capital of State Qin located on the northern shore of the Weihe River, was one of the most convenient channels to the Central Plains region. After the chasm was excavated, the Great Girder of Wei became a transportation hub connecting north, south, east, and west.

Ji of Yan State (today's Beijing) and Handan of Zhao State were also located along the East Avenue of the Taihang Mountain Range. Luoyang, which had been the center since the Zhou, was a transport hub between states, such as Qin, Qi, Chu, and Zhao. In fact, during the Spring and Autumn and the Warring States periods, there was also a city considered as the center of the country—Tao—an intersection of the Ji and Si Rivers, the two main water transportation routes for the Central Plains. Tao is today's Dingtao County in Shandong, which used to be the national cargo trading center and could access Heluo in the west and the Yangtze and Huai Rivers in the south.[3] It is worth noting that most of these cities still survive and have functioned as stages of many important events in Chinese history.

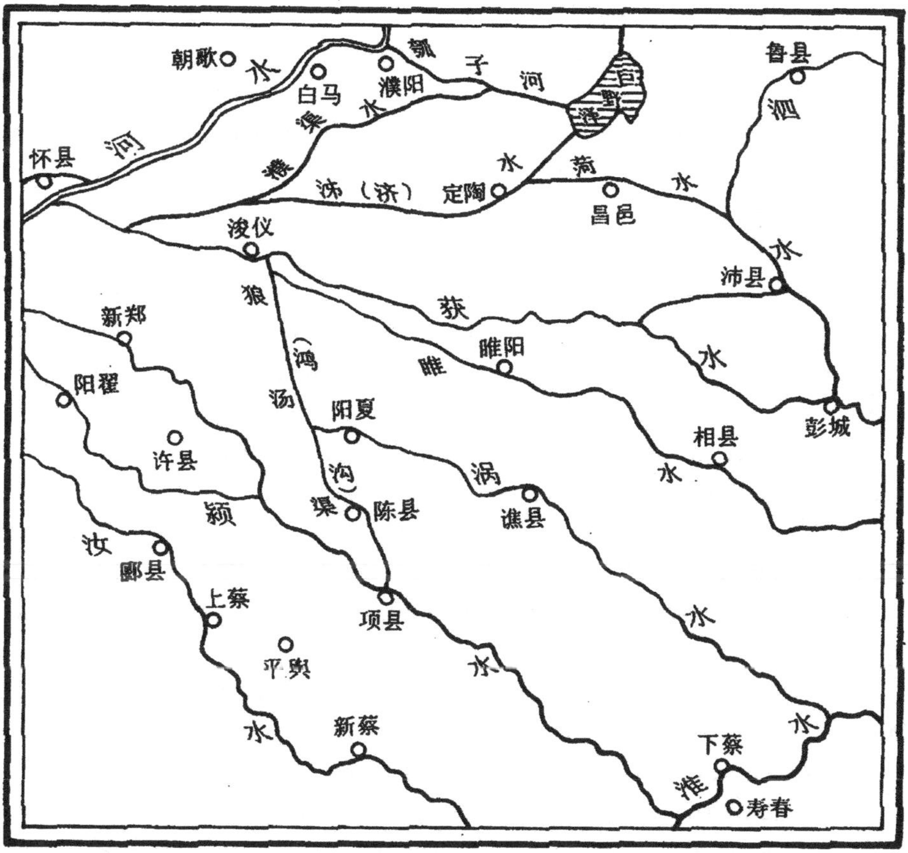

Fig. 8-2: Great ditch in the Warring States[4]

After the unification of the Qin and Han dynasties, a national transportation network was formed, as well as a city system based on the administrative center

3. "Merchant Biographies," in *Records of the Grand Historian*, vol. 129.
4. Zou Yilin, *An Outline of Chinese Historical Geography* (Shanghai: Shanghai Education Press, 2005), 328.

of the county. However, the relationship between the urban layout and transport routes did not change. This can be illustrated by the description in *Salt and Iron Monopoly Discussions · Agriculture*: "if we look around all over the country, from the east to the west, from the south to the north, the wealthy capitals of all states would be located along the transport intersections without exception. These places attracted many merchants and developed quickly."

However, after the fall of Eastern Han, the productivity of the Central Plains was heavily devastated, especially after the Disaster of Yongjia. Commerce stagnated and the natural economy dominated completely. The commercial cities also declined with the loss of their economic foundation. Transport routes and urban distribution took on new features because of the changes in warfare and political patterns.

During the Jian'an era (AD 196–219) at the end of Eastern Han, Cao Cao (who established the Wei regime during the Three Kingdoms Period) presided over a vast territory that included Baigou, Licao, Pinglu, and Quanzhou. After these endeavors, a water route from south to north was formed, beginning from Qimen of Henan and ending in today's Tianjin in northeast China.

Yecheng was already a transport hub, however, the construction of this water route improved its prosperity further, and it became the main city of the Hebei Plains. Later, many other regimes during the Sixteen States and the Northern Dynasties periods, such as the Later Zhao and the Eastern Wei, established their capital here. This had a very close relationship with the advanced water route system of the Yecheng area.

However, the Chang'an–Luoyang axis—the foundation for many generations—was greatly damaged during the Southern and Northern Dynasties period (AD 386–589). This was only reversed after Emperor Wen of Sui reunited the country, ending two centuries of turmoil. This axis was then restored as the core framework of the national-city system. The presence of a unified empire, and the construction of the south-north Grand Canal, laid the foundation for the national transport network. At the same time, the Yangtze River Basin was gradually restored to its previous economic prosperity. This contributed greatly to the formation and development of the national urban system. "To support the capital and its army, a canal was used to transport grain and food from the southeast." Although it was the situation after the mid-Tang Dynasty, the formation of this situation certainly could not be achieved overnight. As an important channel connecting the two economic zones, the Yellow River, the Huai River, the Yangtze River, and the Grand Canal contributed significantly to the formation and development of the national urban system. The book of the *Old Tang Dynasty · Biography of Cui Rong* recorded the busy and prosperous waterway transportation in the Tang Dynasty: On the canal, ships were gathering and docking from everywhere in the world. With vast fleets of ships, often carrying thousands of goods, there was no difference between morning and evening, and it was always as lively as day. This showed the prosperity of inland waterway shipping in the Tang Dynasty.

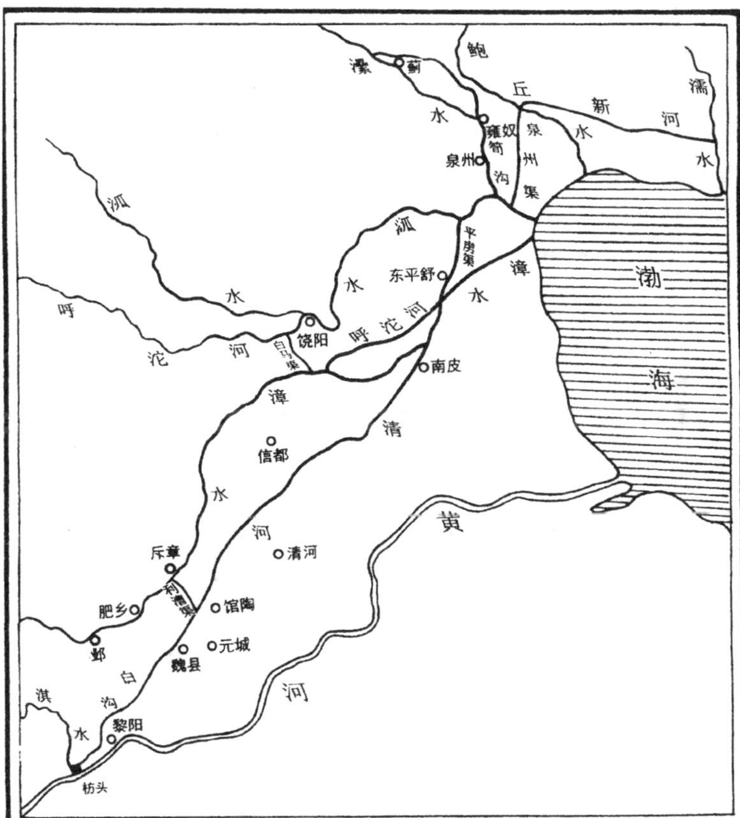

Fig. 8-3: Canal system in Hebei area during the Cao-Wei period[5]

5. Zou Yilin, *An Outline of Chinese Historical Geography* (Shanghai: Shanghai Education Press, 2005), 333.

Several port cities were developed into trade centers along the banks of main waterways based on inland shipping. In the Yellow River Basin, Chang'an and Luoyang have already been mentioned. Other important cities, such as, Bianzhou (now Kaifeng), Songzhou (now Shangqiu), Chuzhou (now Huai'an), Wujun (Suzhou today), and Yuhang (now Hangzhou) prospered due to the canal network.

Chengdu, Jingzhou (now Jiangling), Ezhou (now Xiangyang, Hubei), and so on were also established along the Yangtze River and its major tributaries. For instance, the city of Jiangling "connected with Bashu on the right, Wuyue on the left, Wuling in the south, and Shangdu in the north."[6] These connections were achieved through waterways and made Jiangling the largest city in the middle reaches of the Yangtze River. What needs to be mentioned was that the most developed industrial and commercial cities in China had moved southward to the Yangtze River Basin, namely Chengdu and Yangzhou, at the beginning and the end of the Yangtze River, respectively. They were also called "扬一益二" at that time. Yangzhou was located at the intersection of the Jiangnan Canal and the Yangtze River. Because it was called "the intersected area for north-south goods," it later became the transport center of grain, salt, and iron in the Tang Dynasty. The passage in *Tang Yu Lin* can also serve as circumstantial evidence for the change in the distribution of such vital cities: "All counties and towns in the southeast had access to the waterway, so the large proportion of goods was transported by boats."

Exports were also very important during the Sui and Tang dynasties. In line with bustling trade along the Silk Road, maritime foreign trade also flourished, which led to the development of port cities. Nationally, important port cities in the north of Yangzhou included Chuzhou, Dengzhou (Penglai), Laizhou (Ye County), and Duli Town (Lüshun) south of the Liaodong Peninsula. Cities south of Yangzhou included Guangzhou, Chaozhou, Quanzhou, and Fuzhou. Quanzhou was arguably the key city. As a sugar and tea production center, Quanzhou frequently traded with Southeast Asia, Japan, and South Asia and became the most important trading port city in the southeastern coastal areas of China. Therefore, many foreign businesspeople became residents in Quanzhou to engage in local business activities.

---

6. Yan Zhenqing, "Acknowledgement of the Military Commissioner of Jingnan Region," in *The Entire Works of the Tang and Five Dynasties*, vol. 336.

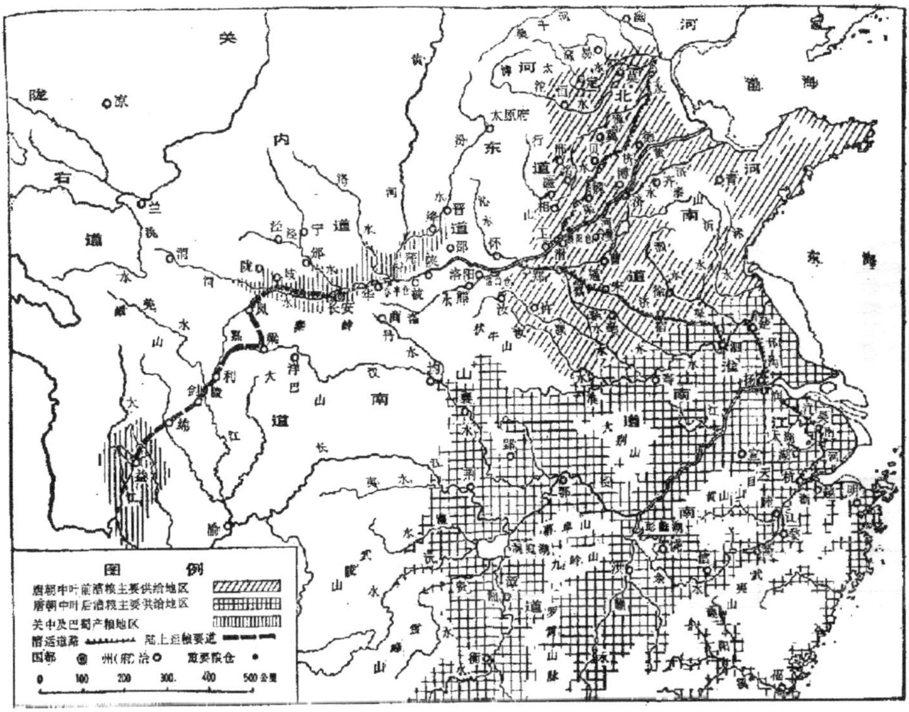

Fig. 8-4: The shift of the economic center during the mid-Tang[7]

7. Wang Yumin, *Chinese Historical Geography: An Introduction* (Beijing: People's Publishing House, 1987), 363.

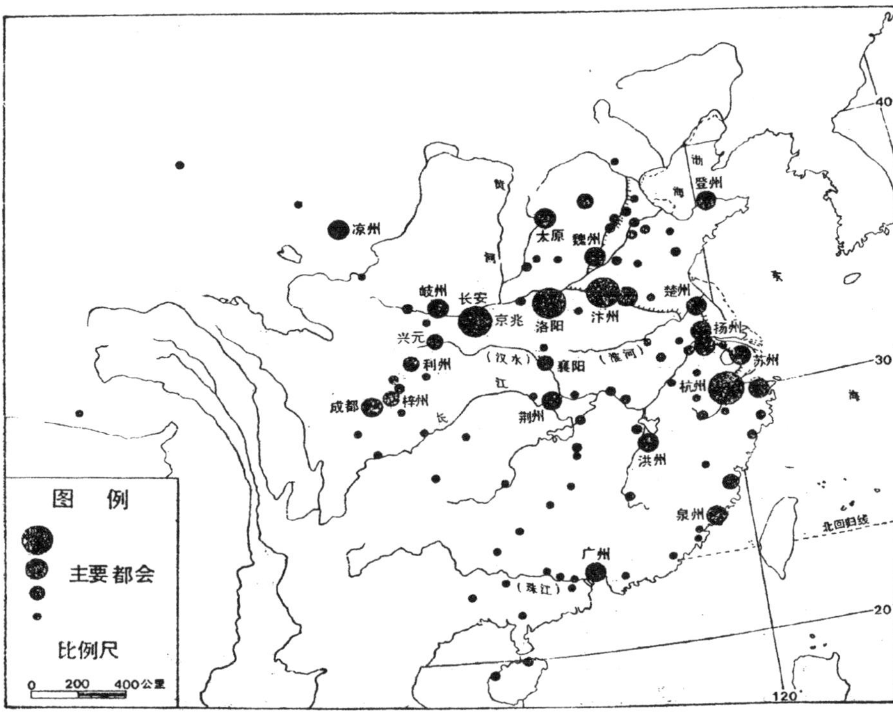

Fig. 8-5: Distribution of southeastern cities during the Tang and Song[8]

Along with rivers and ports, land transportation also improved greatly during the Sui and Tang dynasties. In Emperor Yang of Sui's reign, the "Taihang Mountains was tunneled through to connect with Bingzhou for road expansion."[9] A three-hundred-step wide Imperial Road was also built, which "reached Ji in the east approximately 3,000 *li* away."[10] During Emperor Xuanzong's reign in the Tang Dynasty, Dayu Ridge was excavated again, enabling communications between Guangdong and the mainland. During Emperor Xianzong's reign, more than 400 *li* of land routes were dug in Fujian; the trade routes were more convenient.

Not only were road conditions improved, but a road network centered on Chang'an and well stocked with government stations, was constructed. Among these, four roads were of particular significance:

8. Ma Zhenglin, *A Brief Introduction of Chinese Historical Geography* (Xi'an: Shaanxi people's press, 1987), 404.
9. *Book of the Sui Dynasty · The Economic History.*
10. *Book of the Sui Dynasty · Emperor Suiyang.*

(1) From Chang'an to the West Regions (referred to as west of China, including the eastern part of Central Asia);
(2) Running southwest of Chang'an through the mouth of the Baoxin Mountains to Hanzhong, and reaching Jiannan and Xichuan;
(3) Running southeast of Chang'an through Ezhou, Nanchang, and reaching the Lingnan region;
(4) Running east of Chang'an through Luoyang, then south through Su, Hang, Fu, and Quan in the southeast of China. Along this radial road system, many cities emerged, such as Chuzhou (now Huai'an), Hongzhou (now Nanchang), Liangzhou (now Zhangye, Gansu), Dunhuang, and Fanyang (Beijing).

After the Song and Yuan dynasties, the economic center stabilized in the middle and lower reaches of the Yangtze, the Chang'an–Luoyang axis also shifted to the Beijing–Nanjing axis, crossing Kaifeng in between. Simultaneously, the large-scale emergence of handcrafts and commerce was significant in China's urban development. Besides, transport played an important role in this. The most typical example was the establishment of Bianzhou (Kaifeng today) as the capital of the Northern Song.

The Tongji Canal, or the Bian River, excavated by the Sui Dynasty, was neglected and gradually abandoned during the late Tang. In AD 961, Zhao Kuangyin, founder of the Northern Song, began dredging and increased water flow to the Bian as soon as he came to the throne. Three rivers—Huimin, Wuzhang, and Jinshui—were dredged by the government. Together with the Bian Canal, they were called the Four Canals of transport.

The connection between these four canals and the Yellow River made Kaifeng the largest water transportation hub of the time. The status of Bianliang (Kaifeng) was described in the *History of the Song Dynasty · Rivers and Canals*. "These four canals—Huimin, Jinshui, Wuzhang, and Bian River—enable water transport. There will be no want in the country with the easy transport of goods." Among these four canals, Bian River was the most important because "it runs across the country and connects with the Yellow River. It connects with all the canals for water transport. Half of the country's tax and a multitude of commodities arrive through this canal." Urban life in Kaifeng during the Northern Song Dynasty was colorful because several major rivers flowed through the city.

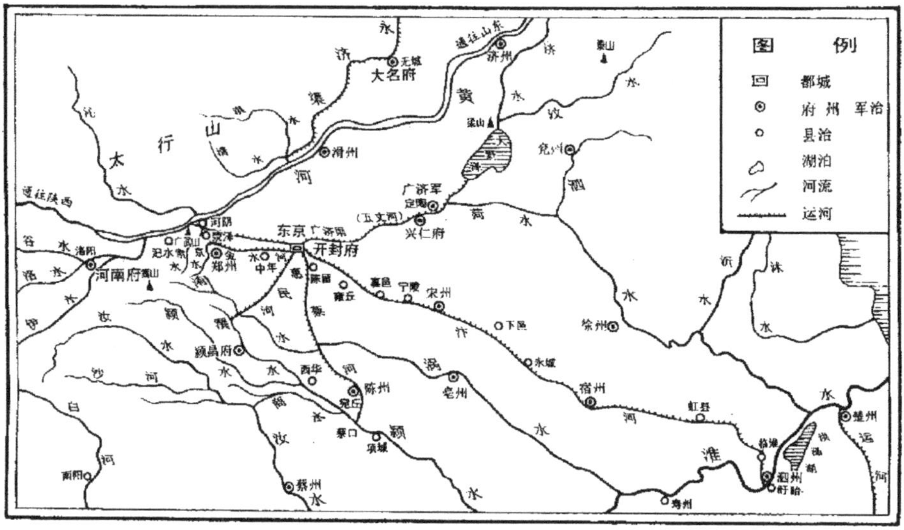

Fig. 8-6: Water transport with Kaifeng at the center[11]

Fig. 8-7: Land transport during the Yuan Dynasty[12]

---

11. Zou Yilin, *An Outline of Chinese Historical Geography* (Shanghai: Shanghai Education Press, 2005), 340.
12. Ibid., 344.

By the later Yuan, Ming, and Qing dynasties, it was clear urban development in southern China exceeded that of the north, especially in the Yangtze regions. The southeast coastal areas grew. For example, Suzhou along the Grand Canal became a prominent commercial hub during the Ming and became a cultural center in the south.

Nanjing, a city beside the Yangtze, became the capital in AD 1378. By AD 1391, it was so prosperous "there was almost no open space remaining."[13] When Emperor Yongle moved the capital to Beijing, Nanjing still served as the alternative capital, and because of its central position along the river, it became an important industrial and commercial city: "a popular destination for merchants all over the country because of its convenient transport and openness."[14] Most of the fastest growing cities during this period were located on the Yangtze River–Grand Canal axis.

2. The Canal Cities

The distribution of political and economic centers in Chinese history is often inconsistent. To handle the separation, governments often used a variety of measures. The most important was connecting political centers to commerce hubs (i.e., highly taxable areas). Canal construction was a result of this desire. The Grand Canal was largely a product of economic gravity shifting south, but political gravity shifting north. Emperor Wen of Sui ended hundreds of years of separatist unrest and the formation of a unified empire allowed for the construction of large-scale water conservancy projects with coordinated effort. During this time, the Grand Canal came into being. From this point of view, the Grand Canal is not only the product of this political and economic pattern but also the result of the political center gradually moving to the north and the economic center already moving to the south after the mid-Tang Dynasty.

In fact, China has a long history of canal construction, but the original purpose was for farmland irrigation and soil improvement, rather than transport. The most famous water conservancy projects in the pre-Qin period include the

13. "Households," in *A Chronicle of Shangyuan County*, vol. 2, during the Wanli era.

14. "Merchants," in *Songchuang Mengyu*, vol. 4.

Twelve Ditches to connect Zhang, the Dujiang Dam of Central Shu, and Zhengguo Canal of Guanzhong. In 247 BC, a powerful state in western China, Qin, became a threat to the eastern states. State Han sent a water engineer, Mr. Zheng, to convince the King of the State Qin to work on water conservancy projects with the purpose of exhausting State Qin. This means, consuming Qin's resources and preventing them from conquering the east. Unexpectedly, Qin completed the canal within ten years and it became more powerful. There is a commentary on the Zhengguo Canal in *Records of the Grand Historian · Book of Canal*: "After the canal was completed, the water from the canal was used to irrigate more than 40,000 hectares of saline-alkali land, yielding one hour per mu. As a result, the land in Guanzhong became fertile and there was no disaster in a year." The Zhengguo Canal utilized the sediment in the Jing River to dilute the saline-alkali components of the saline-alkali land in the low-lying areas downstream, making it fertile soil suitable for planting crops. Therefore, the main function of the Zhengguo Canal was to improve the soil in the irrigation area, and the second was to irrigate crops, but it had little significance for shipping.

In the pre-Qin period, there were also artificial canals constructed for shipping. The most famous is the Grand Ditch dug during the Warring States Period by State Wei. The opening of the chasm connects the Ji, Ru, Ying, Wu, Sui, Si, and other rivers. Formed a water system network with the chasm as the main channel and connecting the two major water systems of the Yellow River and the Huai River, which promoted navigation in this area and led to the prosperity of riverside cities such as Tao and Daliang. There was also the Hangou Canal built by State Wu connected the Yangtze and Huai Rivers' water systems for sending the Navy of Wu to the north and transporting supplies for the military. State Qi also built the Jizi Canal, which connected the Ji River with the Zi River. However, these canals were short and could not in any sense compare with the Grand Canal built during the Sui and the Beijing–Hangzhou Grand Canal during the Yuan.

Later, when the Sui Dynasty came about, they established their capital in Guanzhong; to meet the demands of the capital, surplus grain from the Guandong region was required. It was imperative for the new empire to connect the Wei and Yellow Rivers. In AD 584, a canal was dug northwest of Daxing (today's Xi'an) to achieve this—Guangtong Canal. Then, in AD 587, the Hangou Canal between the Yangtze and Huai Rivers was re-excavated for the purpose of conquering Chen, which was renamed the Shangyang Ditch.

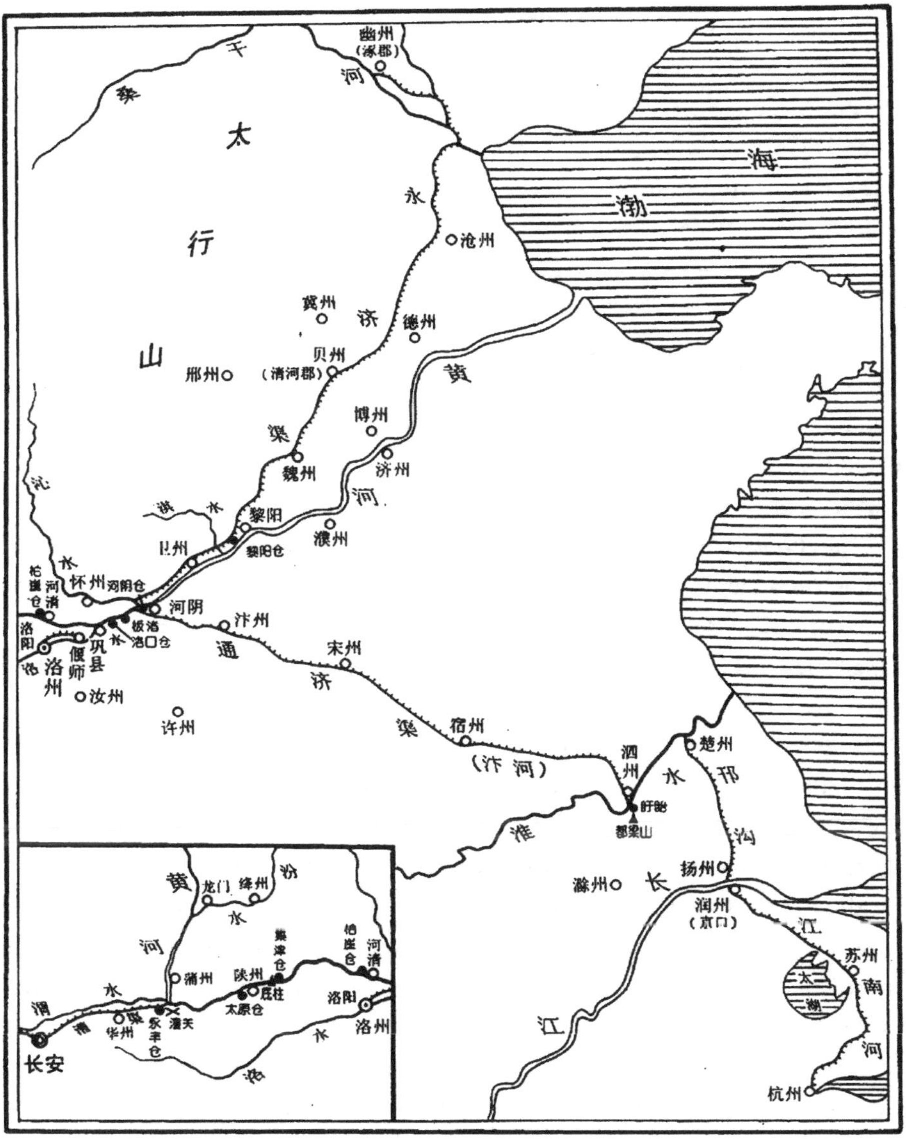

Fig. 8-8: The Grand Canal during the Sui and Tang dynasties[15]

15. Zou Yilin, *An Outline of Chinese Historical Geography* (Shanghai: Shanghai Education Press, 2005), 336.

After Emperor Yang ascended the throne and made Luoyang his capital, the Tongji Canal was channeled through Goushui and Luoshi from the west and Yanshi in the east. From here, the canal was channeled east; it flowed passed several places, including Kaifeng, and joined the Huai River in Xuyi, Jiangsu. This was the most important part of the Grand Canal built by Emperor Yang. In AD 608, the Yongji Canal was channeled to connect the Qin River with the Qing River and the Qi River as part of the preparation for an expedition to Beijing. The canal followed the original river course of Baigou. In the sixth year of Daye (AD 610), the Jingkou (now Zhenjiang) to Yuhang (now Hangzhou) canal was rebuilt. So far, several sections of the canal have been completed, connecting the five major water systems of the He, Hai, Jiang, Huai, and Qiantang Rivers, forming a fan-shaped canal. With Chang'an and Luoyang as political centers, it extended to the northeast and southeast, with a total length of more than 2,000 kilometers.

The Tang Dynasty also established its capital in Guanzhong. Its transport routes were almost the same as the Sui. However, the influence of the Grand Canal on urban development began to emerge in this era. Many cities along the canal, such as Hangzhou, Suzhou, Runzhou, and Yangzhou grew into important cities. In particular, Yangzhou became a water transport hub in southeast China. With its political and economic status greatly improved, it became the number one industrial and commercial city of the Tang. The convenience of water transportation also helped the development of the cities north of the Jianghuai River, which included Weizhou (now east Hebei Daiming) along the Yongji Canal; Beizhou (now Qinghe), Bianzhou (now Kaifeng) along the Tongji canal; Song Zhou (now Shangqiu), Xuzhou which Bian River and Si River intersected; Sizhou (now Hongze Lake near Xuyi, Jiangsu Province) which Bian River and Huai River intersected.

The Northern Song, however, abandoned its plan to make Guanzhong the capital, and instead chose Bianzhou, the water transportation hub. This was effective for alleviating pressure on food supply to the capital, in contrast to the Tang, who was constantly under threat of food shortages, in spite of the Grand Canal. In Emperor Dezong's reign, the situation became so severe that the imperial grain-houses were depleted to their final ten days' worth of supplies.

In fact, the Northern Song chose Bianjing (Kaifeng) as its capital mainly because of the water transport system. Among these, the most important was the Bianqu Canal, which directly connected the city with grain producing areas by the rivers. We can use the following data as an illustration: In AD 981, the total volume of water transport in the four canals of Kaifeng reached 5.5 million *dan*, of which the Bianqu Canal took on 4 million *dan*, accounting for more than 72%. The role of the Bianqu Canal in Kaifeng, the capital, was evaluated by Emperor Taizong of the Song Dynasty: "Kaifeng raises hundreds of thousands of soldiers, millions of residents, and all the grains transferred from the whole country depend on the Bianqu Canal." Zhang Bo's statement quoted in *Song History · On Rivers* is more comprehensive:

> Today more than 100,000 soldiers and 100,000 horses are gathered in the capital. We have gathered soldiers and civilians from all seven kingdoms in our army, ten times more than in the Han and Tang dynasties. To deal with floods and droughts in the suburbs, the water from the four channels was diverted to the capital so that the rivers in the capital were bustling with boats. Water resources could be used for public and private use, so there was no shortage of water resources. Of the four channels, only the Bian River stretches across the capital and can be called a river. The water channel leads to various rivers and lakes, and goods can be transported to the South China Sea. Half of the world's money and taxes, and all the exchanges of goods from various mountains and rivers, are carried out through this river.

Because of its location between the intersection of the Yellow and the Bian Rivers, this canal could connect with other water systems. The urban economy of Kaifeng formed a spectacular scene of "ships shouldering with each other and extended tens of miles: there were crew members from Yue and Wu cities. The ships of the government mixed with private ships of the merchants; different accents were heard everywhere. All kinds of goods were shipped back and forth. This provided high tax income."[16]

Later, the people of Jin in northern China expanded their territory south and the Song Dynasty was forced to move its capital to Lin'an (Hangzhou). Already an important industrial and commercial city during the Northern Song, Lin'an continued as an important port of foreign trade with a prosperous economy and dense population. After the Jianyan Incident, when the Song regime had to

16. Hong Mai, *Essays of Rongzhai*, vol. 4.

retreat south; it sojourned in Jiangning (Nanjing) and Yuezhou (Shaoxing) but eventually decided to settle in Lin'an (Hangzhou), considering water transport a major benefit of the city. In this regard, *The History of the Song Dynasty · Rivers and Canals* made it very explicit:

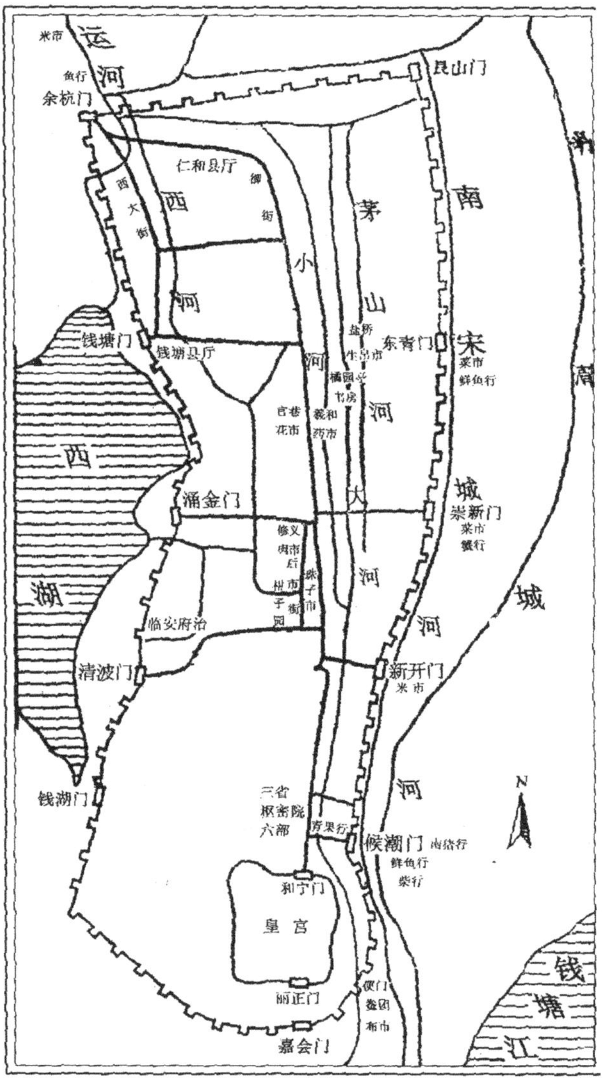

Fig. 8-9: Urban commerce of the Southern Song (Ling'an)[17]

17. Yang Kuan, *Studies on Ancient Chinese Capital System History* (Shanghai: Shanghai Education Press, 2005), 397.

> The country decided to settle in Qiantang (where Hangzhou is located) because of the vital importance of grain transport. The passage of water transport would flow down the Yangtze into Zhenjiang and into the Grand Canal, and the rest would be easy. Giant ships could arrive in the capital directly. It was so convenient.

Because of this, the situation was recorded as "Since Lin'an became its political center, the people from Kaifeng and other places, such as scholars, merchants, officers, all gathered together here."

After conquering the Southern Song, the Mongolians moved their ruling center from the northern Prairies to the Central Plains and changed Zhongdu of the Jin to Dadu (Beijing today). Because Dadu was far from the economic center, it relied on long-distance transport from southern China to meet its needs. At the beginning of the Yuan, three transport routes, heading from south to north, were employed: (1) The sea; (2) A joint network of seas and rivers; (3) A mixed land-river route, which took advantage of several sections of the Grand Canal, but was inconvenient, nonetheless.

In AD 1293, the Yuan government conducted a thorough renovation of the Tonghui and Huitong Rivers. The Beijing–Hangzhou Grand Canal, with a total length of more than 1,700 kilometers, was open to navigation, and the north-south grain transportation route was roughly formed. During the entire Yuan reign, the Grand Canal was not always used because of maintenance reasons. Still, it made striking contributions to the economies along the route, particularly the urban development of China.

The Ming Dynasty established its capital in Nanjing initially, which was advantageous for food supplies. However, Emperor Yongle soon moved the capital to Beijing; thus, it was necessary to restore the north-south water transport route fully. During the early stage of the Yongle era, grain was mostly transported by sea, but after the Huitong and Tonghui rivers were dredged and widened, the Grand Canal became prominent once again. Most Qing Dynasty areas inherited the old Ming Dynasty system without significant changes, and the Grand Canal still played an essential role in north-south traffic.

At the same time, during the Ming and Qing dynasties, handcrafts and commerce advanced considerably around the Yangtze region. The river basin was an important production area for commodity grains and cotton, jute, tea, mulberry, and other economic crops, and thus promoted urban development along the Grand Canal. Most important cities were along the canal, such as Tongzhou, Tianjin, Dezhou, Liaocheng, Jining, Huaiyin, Yangzhou, Zhenjiang, Changzhou, Wuxi, Suzhou, Hangzhou, etc., all famous for their economic prosperity. Among those cities, Yangzhou was the most prosperous.

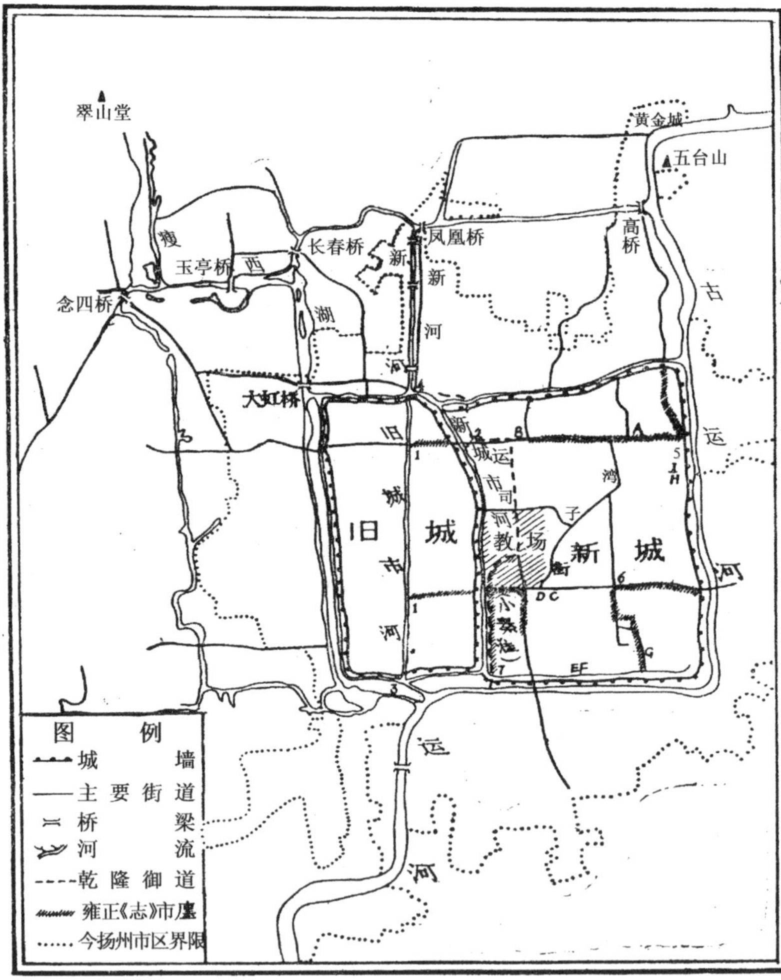

Fig. 8-10: Yangzhou in the Ming and Qing dynasties[18]

18. Wang Zhenzhong, "The Regional Structure of Yangzhou and Salt Merchants during the Ming and Qing Dynasties," in *History and Geography*, vol. 10 (Shanghai: Shanghai People's Publishing House, 1992).

During this period, Yangzhou's economy boomed. Salt was an especially important product here, where it was administered for the region. The city's main transport lines were interlinked with the canal. The densely distributed river courses not only facilitated goods to be delivered anywhere in the city, but also were the lifelines of the crisscross streets and lanes within Yangzhou. Because the canal was in the east, a business center gradually formed between the old city and the canal. The business was particularly prosperous and wealth accumulated along the canal bank outside the old city. Thus, during the Wanli era (AD 1573–1619), the expansion included this area.

According to local chronicles during this time, many of those who lived in the new city were wealthy merchants, while many who lived in the old city were gentry families.[19] With Emperor Kangxi and Emperor Qianglong's reigns during the Qing, new business districts expanded rapidly, particularly along the route inspected by Emperor Qianlong. "From the Tianningmen, enter the east of Caiyi Street, turn left at Yunsi Street, pass Jiaochang, Yuanmen Bridge, Duozi Street, Gengzishang, then exit through Tax office, turn right at Huajue Street, and enter Jiufeng." It became the most bustling business street of Yangzhou. The area around the Small East Gate and the Little Qinhuai River (the city river) were lined with famous brands and shops. "The shops were very densely packed, and any exotic or rare commodity could be found. These two areas were particularly prosperous. The land was as expensive as gold."[20] Yangzhou in this era was a city of luxury by virtue of its connection with the Grand Canal.

As the main north-south transport line, the Grand Canal played its most important role during the Yongle era of the Ming to the mid-Qing. After this, many parts of the Grand Canal were seriously blocked. Thus, it could not be dredged. Consequently, at the beginning of Emperor Daoguang's reign, top officials debated on whether marine transport should be considered. In AD 1826, the imperial court of Qing eventually established a Marine Administration Bureau and hired merchant ships to transport grain from the sea to Beijing. Since then, canal transport was abandoned. As the Grand Canal lost its status, most of the canal cities gradually declined and were replaced by seaports.

---

19. *A Chronicle of Jiangdu County,* during the Wanli era.

20. Jiao Xun, *Collective Writings of Yangzhou.*

3. Rivers and Maritime Transport

Although China boasts a long coastline with many harbors, marine trade was not developed in its early stage. The first record of marine transport in China was found in the Western Han. The Sino-foreign marine trade grew during the Western and Eastern Han dynasties. However, port cities were not fully developed.

During this time, Korea and Japan were the main destinations of marine transport in the north, but mainly for cultural communication purposes. In the south, Rinanzhang (today's Shunhua of Vietnam), Xuwen, and Hepu would be the departure ports, destined for Southeast Asian countries. Gold and silk were the main exports; glass, agate, amber, herbs, and spices were the main imports. During the Wei, Jin, and Southern and Northern Dynasties, marine trade become more frequent. Large foreign trade ports, such as Guangzhou, emerged in southern China. Meanwhile, marine communications in northern China were mainly concentrated in the Jiaodong Peninsula in Shandong.

With the unification of the Sui and Tang dynasties, maritime transport was taken more seriously. The promotion of trade abetted the rise of several coastal port cities, including Dengzhou (now Penglai, Shandong) and Laizhou in the north, Chuzhou (now Huaian), Yangzhou, Huating County (now Songjiang, Shanghai), Wenzhou, Fuzhou, Mingzhou (now Ningbo), Quanzhou, Chaozhou, Guangzhou, Jiaozhou (now Hanoi, Vietnam) and other cities in the south. Among them, Guangzhou was developed into China's largest foreign trade port. More than ten foreign ships would arrive there daily, and a large number of Chinese silk and Arabic spice ships passed through this port. *The New History of Tang · Biography of Liu Ze* documented how the Foreign Trade Administration had been established in Guangzhou during the Kaiyuan era (AD 713–741).

In addition to Chinese records, visiting foreign merchants were also deeply impressed by Guangzhou. At the beginning of the tenth century, an Arabian, Abu Said, recorded in his *China and India Travelogue* that in the late ninth century in Guangzhou, there were about 120,000 foreigners living in the city, including Islamic, Jewish, Christian, and Zoroastrian people. Of course, the data need further verification. Yet, there were certainly many long-term foreign residents in Guangdong who engaged in trade activities during the Tang judging from the foreign living quarters in Guangzhou.

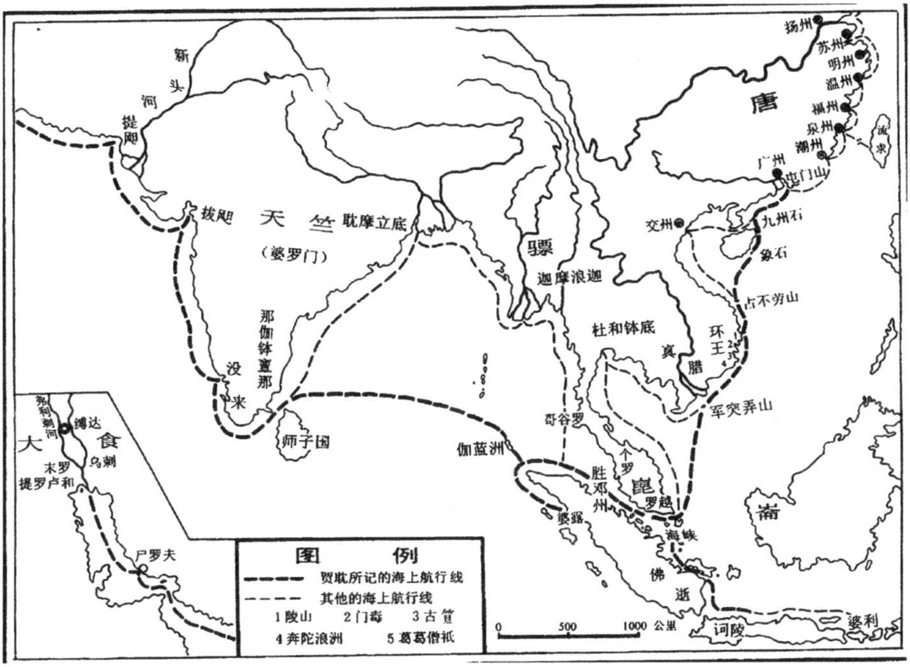

Fig. 8-11: Maritime transport route to India and the west during the Tang Dynasty[21]

During the Song and Yuan dynasties, maritime transport developed further. Chinese merchants also expanded their pan-sea trade. Records show they reached the Persian Gulf Coast and the Arabian Peninsula. With the rise of port cities, more seaports appeared. At this time, the Song government established foreign administration agencies (customs) on three levels: *Si*, *Wu*, and *Chang* to manage foreign trade across the country. The establishment of these in cities would be an indicator of foreign trade. Six cities held the foreign trade administration agency *Si* during the Northern Song: Guangzhou, Hangzhou, Mingzhou, Quanzhou, Banqiao town of Mizhou (Jiaozhou of Shandong), and Huating County of Xiuzhou (Songjiang, Shanghai).

During the Southern Song, Wenzhou Foreign Trade *Wu*, Jiangyin Military Foreign Trade *Wu* and Haiyan Ganpu Foreign Trade *Chang* of Xiuzhou were added. In AD 1277, when the Mongols acquired Fujian and Zhejiang, they

21. Zou Yilin, *An Outline of Chinese Historical Geography* (Shanghai: Shanghai Education Press, 2005), 355.

followed the Song system and established *Si* in Quanzhou, Qingyuan (Ningbo), Shanghai, and Ganpu and further added Guangzhou, Wenzhou, and Hangzhou later. In AD 1293 (the thirtieth year of the Zhiyuan era), the Wenzhou *Si* merged with the Qingyuan *Si*. Hangzhou *Si* was integrated into the local tax bureau. Later in AD 1297 (the first year of Dade era), the Ganbu and Shanghai *Si* merged into the Qingyuan *Si*. With this, there were only three *Si*: Qingyuan, Quanzhou, and Guangzhou left during the Yuan Dynasty.

The establishment of foreign trade administrations was indirect evidence of the high foreign trade volume in these cities. This led to the prosperity of their ports. The following are several examples: first, Guangzhou topped the list among foreign trade ports. The tax income was several times that of other cities.[22] In addition, "many foreign merchants flocked to Guangzhou, crossing oceans from the Champa kingdom, Kmir, Samboja, and Duo Po. There were many rare and valuable foreign items, such as rhinoceros and elephant products, as well as unnamed pearls and uncountable spices."[23] Besides Guangzhou, Quanzhou's foreign trade flourished, because it was at the intersection of the East China Sea and South China Sea routes. After becoming part of the Southern Song, it developed by leaps and bounds. Many sea ships were moored here and many foreign merchants resided in Quanzhou. Like Guangzhou, it also had special living quarters for foreigners.

By the Yuan Dynasty, Quanzhou had even replaced Guangzhou as the largest foreign trade port. Back then, merchant ships from more than 100 countries and regions, such as Southeast Asia, India, Persia, and Arabia gathered in Quanzhou. It was filled with all kinds of merchandise, and "the city was second to none in terms of rare valuables as well as the residences of rich merchants."[24] Therefore, Quanzhou was also considered the capital of the Seven Min Counties (Fujian Province).

In addition, the overseas trades in Mingzhou, Ganpu of Xiuzhou, Qinglong Town of Huating, and Shanghai Town were also flourishing. In fact, besides the mentioned cities above that setup bureau of foreign shipping, other towns along the seaport cities, such as Tongzhou (now Nantong), Chuzhou, Haizhou (now

---

22. *Historical Data in the Song Dynasty · Official Posts.*
23. Hong Shi, "Notes of Shiwu Hall," in *Panzhou Essays*, vol. 30.
24. Wu Cheng, *Preface to Jiang Manqing's Assumption of Duty to the Quanzhou Circuit*, See *Wu Wenzheng's Collections*, vol. 16.

Donghai County), Yuezhou (Shaoxing), Taizhou (now Linhai), Fuzhou, Zhangzhou, Chaozhou, Leizhou (now Haikang, Guangdong), Qiongzhou (now Haikou City), etc., had also achieved specific development due to maritime trade.

At the start of the Ming era, China's maritime transport continued to develop on past foundations. Especially during the Yongle and Xuande eras (AD 1403–1435), the seven voyages of Zheng He (a Chinese explorer, diplomat, and fleet admiral who commanded expeditionary voyages to much of Asia and Africa) not only promoted economic and cultural exchange with Southeast Asia, but also showed advanced Chinese navigation technologies of the time.

During Emperor Hongwu's reign in the early Ming period, foreign trade administrations—*Si*—were established in Ningbo, Quanzhou, and Guangzhou with a clear division of labor. Ningbo would administrate trade with Japan, Quanzhou with Okinawa, and Guangzhou with Champa, Siam, and the Western countries.[25] However, since the mid-Ming period, corruption, lax borders, and harassment by Japanese pirates have deteriorated the coastal areas. A ban on foreign trade was enforced: in AD 1522, Quanzhou and Mingzhou (Ningbo) were the first ports to shut down, leaving only Guangzhou for foreign trade. Subsequently, this policy shrank the nation's foreign trade and its major coastal and middle seaport cities fell into stagnation and decline. Although in AD 1567 (the first year of the Longqing era), the ban was lifted, the famous harbor of Quanzhou had silted, making port transport difficult. The city completely lost its advantageous position in international trade.

The Qing Dynasty followed the trade system of the late Ming Dynasty at first. However, to fight against the southern Ming forces, an anti-Qing regime occupied the southeast coast of China. In AD 1655, 1656, 1662, 1665, and 1675, the Qing government issued bans on marine trade five times, and no ships were allowed to sail. Likewise, in AD 1660, 1662, and 1678, the Qing government issued the Great Clearance three times. Residents within 20 *li* of the coast were all moved away; the Qing government implemented stringent maritime prohibition policies. Under this blow, the prosperous port cities were naturally unsustainable and declined one after another.

However, the first two bans were lifted in AD 1684, following the unification of Taiwan a year earlier in the twenty-second year of Kangxi. Foreign merchants

25. *The Economy History (Part V) · Customs* in *The History of the Ming Dynasty*, vol. 81.

traded in designated ports, such as Guangzhou, Zhangzhou, Ningbo, and the Yuntai Mountains (now Lianyungang) and customs were again established for administration. At that time, "The eastern sea area of Guangdong starts from Chaozhou in the east, south of Lianzhou in the west, and Hainan in the south. There are three directions, all of which have good seaports." The coastal areas of Fujian, Zhejiang, and Jiangsu were also blessed with clear sea breezes and crowded sea lanes. Never have they been so prosperous. In the northern coastal areas, ports in Shandong, Hebei, and Liaoning were also busy with lighter ship traffic. The coastal port cities in China entered a new phase of development, with 127 ports open to foreign merchants for trade purposes. An axis of port cities along the coast was formed from north to south, including Niuzhuang, Tianjin, Shanghai, Ningbo, Fuzhou, Xiamen, Chenghai, and Guangzhou.

However, this did not last long. After the mid-eighteenth century, British merchants "repeatedly violated the ban and completed secret trading in Ningbo." To strengthen customs before it was too late, many ports, including Ningbo, were closed again in AD 1757, and foreign merchants were only allowed to trade in Guangzhou.

The commercial production of agriculture and handcraft production developed rapidly in China in this period, especially in the Jiangnan region, which largely depended on external markets. Thus, private foreign trade rose once the official ban was implemented, even exceeding official government-led foreign trade. Internationally, a new global market was forming, as Western colonial empires like Portugal, Spain, and the Netherlands, began extending further east with bases in Malacca, the Philippines, and south China. This stimulated foreign trade with China, leading to the formation of various trade-oriented towns in the coastal areas. For example, Yuegang in Zhangzhou, Meiling in Zhao'an, Anping in Quanzhou, Fuqing in Fuzhou on the coast of Fujian; Nan'ao and Meiluxu on the coast of Guangdong, etc., were all foreign trade towns that emerged after the middle of the Ming Dynasty.

Yuegang of Zhangzhou, originally a small fishing village at the beginning of the Ming Dynasty, rose to be a prominent town in southern Fujian with tens of thousands of households because of the popularity of private trade since the Jiajing era. This town was even honored with the title of "petit Su-Hang" of Fujian (Su-Hang refers to Suzhou and Hangzhou, which have traditionally been regarded as lands of abundance).

This example indicated the conflict between the port-closing policies by the Ming and Qing governments and the formation of global markets, which led to fluctuations in the development of port cities in China. A direct consequence of this conflict was the decline of the big- and medium-sized port cities, which depended on government operations, and the rise of a large number of small ports prospering with private operations.

CHAPTER NINE

CHINA AND THE WORLD: CITIES AND CROSS-BORDER COMMUNICATION

Located at the eastern end of the Eurasian continent and the west bank of the Pacific Ocean, China's material and cultural exchange with other parts of the world are almost as long as its history. Along the trade routes of the high mountains, wide deserts, and vast oceans, many cities rose. Foreign trade had a far-reaching influence on this, which is most represented by the Silk Road during the Han and Tang reigns, and the coastal cities of the late Qing period.

1. Cities along the Silk Road

In ancient times, the Silk Road was undoubtedly a big artery connecting China and the West in terms of economy, politics, culture, and thoughts. In fact, before the Age of Discovery and the opening of new navigation routes, the Silk Road started from China and passed through the West Regions, ancient India, Arabia, and Persia, all the way to Greece and Rome. This road was the main connection between East and West, transporting silk and many other goods, as well as information and ideas.

Looking at a map, the so-called Silk Road is actually a network running through numerous cities. It starts in the east from Chang'an (Xi'an), the largest Chinese city of the time, goes through the Hexi Corridor, crosses the Gobi

Desert and reaches the oases. Eventually, the Silk Road arrives in Rome after passing through countless cities. On this busy road, there were soldiers and sailors, caravans and monks, pilgrims and tourists, scholars and artists, servants and envoys, victorious troops, and defeated generals; streams of people busily coming and going from all walks of life. Three major religions of the world—Buddhism, Islam, Franciscan, and Nestorian Christianity—as well as some popular local religions, such as Zoroastrianism, Manichaeism, and Judaism, were spread to China through this road. China's early experience of sericulture, paper making, printing, theories of governance, ethics, and natural science, also spread globally through this route.

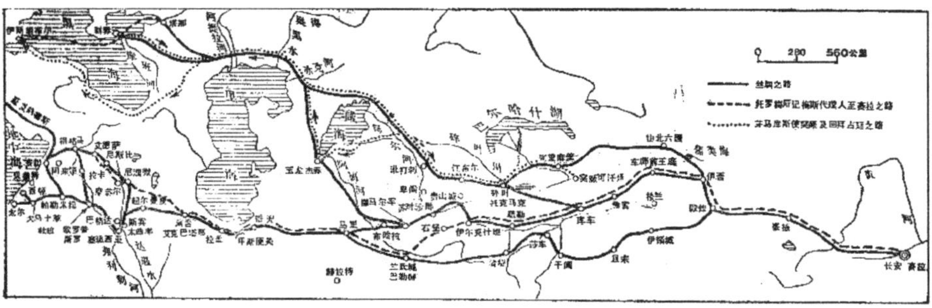

Fig. 9-1: The Silk Road from the Western Han to the Yuan[1]

However, the Silk Road was initially formed with no relationship to silk. Since its establishment in 206 BC, the Han Empire reached unprecedented prosperity in less than 100 years due to its policy of restraining commerce and emphasizing agriculture. During Emperor Wu's reign, it began to expand its territory further. Despite the repression, business and industry flourished during the Han Empire, especially the silk industry. At this time, the western frontier was often threatened due to the rise of the Xiongnu (a minority ethnic group). Therefore, in 139 BC, Emperor Wu sent Zhang Qian to the Western Regions to attack the Xiongnu with help from the Darouzhi government. Although Zhang Qian made no military progress, this voyage unexpectedly opened the door for East and West communications.

1. Ma Zhenglin, *A Brief Introduction of Chinese Historical Geography* (Xi'an: Shaanxi People's Press, 1987), 434.

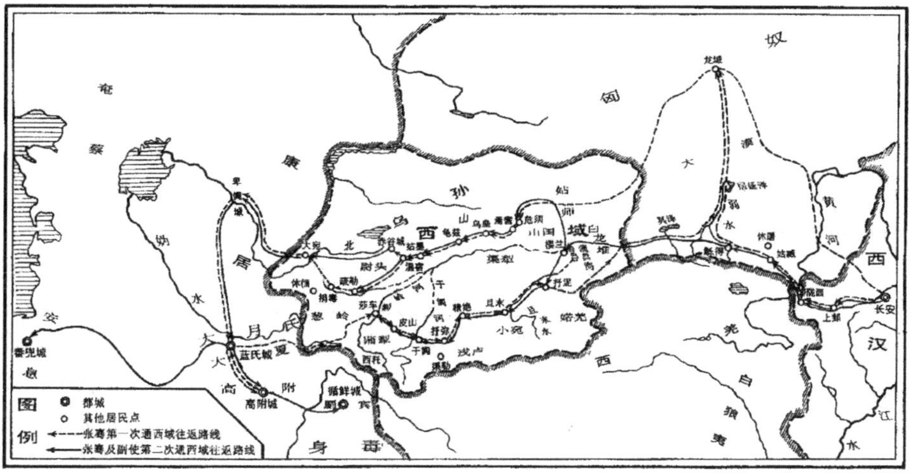

Fig. 9-2: Zhang Qian's route to the West Regions[2]

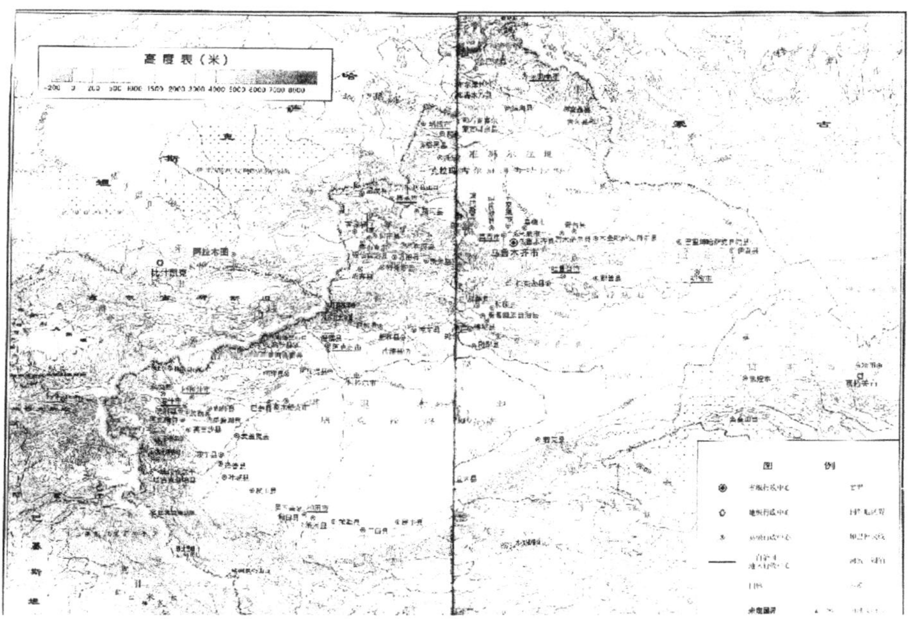

Fig. 9-3: Geography of the West Regions[3]

2. Zou Yilin, *An Outline of Chinese Historical Geography* (Shanghai: Shanghai Education Press, 2005), 349.
3. *Atlas of Xinjiang Uygur Autonomous Region* (Beijing: SinoMaps Press, 2003), 5–6.

Subsequently, the Han continued to win military victories to the west, and the border gradually expanded westward. Since 115 BC, four counties—Hexi, Jiuquan, Zhangye, and Dunhuang—were established in Longxi. Later, the Western Regions were brought under the administration of the Han, which designated officials to govern the 36 countries within the area. These were changed to Protector-general during Emperor Xuan's reign. These vast desert zones grew into well used paths for merchants and envoys, following the consolidation of Han territory. Trade with the Western Regions thrived. *Records of the Grand Historian · Dawan* documented: "At the beginning of Han, the fortification was built in Lingju (northwest of Yongdeng, Gansu today) and Jiuquan County was built to communicate with countries in the northwest. Gradually, envoys reached Anxi, Ancai, Lixuan, Tiaozhi, Shendu, etc."

As described in the *Book of Han · The West Regions,* this is a "region that has mountain ranges to the south and north with rivers in the middle. It is more than 6000 *li* from east to west and more than 1000 *li* from south to north. It is adjacent to Han eastwards at the Yumen and Yangguan passes, and its boundary in the west ends at the Cong Mountains."[4] Later in the *Book of Han,* other territories near the Ili River and Tianshan Mountains, as well as places near the Syr and Amu rivers, were included. Deep inland and far from the sea, the climate of this area is arid. The vast expanse of the Gobi Desert is divided by steep mountains, though tiny streams formed by the perennial snow converged into rivers, bringing precious water to rivers and the arid inland. The routes that cross this area depend on the oases that rely on these inland rivers.

For the inland east-west transportation routes of the Han Empire, a very detailed description was given in the *Book of Han · The West Regions* concerning two routes, one in the south and one in the north:

> There were two routes to the West Regions, starting from Yumen Pass and Yangguan Pass. One could go westbound to Shanshan along the Southern Mountain Range and the North Bo River until Shache. This was the southern route, and one could arrive at Darouzhi and Anxi beyond the Cong Mountains. One could continue westbound to the former capital of Cheshi along the Northern Mountain Range and the Bo River until Shule. This is the north-

4. "The Western Regions," in *Book of Han*, vol. 36.

ern route, and there would be Dayuan, Kangju, and Yancai beyond the Cong Mountains.

Specifically, both routes to the West Regions started from Dunhuang and passed the borders of the Yumen and Yangguan passes. At Lop Nor, the route forked. The southern route went through Shanshan to Shache, across the Cong Mountain Range, and then arrived at Darouzhi and Anxi. The northern route went through Yiwu (Hami), then west to Gaochang (Turpan), crossed the southern foot of the Tianshan Mountains, to Qiuci, Kucha, and finally Shule (in Kashgar). From here, one could cross the Cong Mountains to reach Dawan (Fergana). Turning southwest, one would reach Kasmira (today's Kashmir). This was also called the Southern Tianshan route.

The southern route was a key path to India. There was a shortcut which turned southwest from Pishan, just before reaching Shache, "via Wucha, Xuandu, and Kasmira. Within 60 days, one could arrive at Wugeshanli ... turn southwest and travel about 100 days on horse, one could arrive at Tiaozhi."[5] Tiaozhi is Syria today. This route from the Wugeshanli Country to Syria was explored by Gan Ying. He was sent as an envoy to the Roman Empire by the Eastern Han. This shortcut to India is the "Kasmira-Wugeshanli Road," well-known by geographical history scholars of Central Asia. The itinerary of this road is:

> Kasmira (Kashmir) – Lituo (Chitral, Southern Pakistan) – Xuandu Mountain – Nandou (Gilgit, west of Kashmir) – Jiecha (Taxkorgan County, Xinjiang) Shache – Pishan – Yutian (Hotan) – Qiemo – Kroraina – Dunhuang – Suzhou (Zhangye) – Ganzhou (Wuwei) – Chang'an.

When Zhang Qian visited the Western Regions, Kasmira was still unknown to the world. It did not appear in records until the end of Emperor Wu's reign during the Han Dynasty.

Interactions between Kasmira and China continued until Wang Mang's era. Not only during the Han Dynasty, but also in later generations, monks who traveled to India for Buddhism would mostly follow this route. During this period, the transport network, including Afghanistan, Kazakhstan, and China's

5. "The Western Regions," in *Book of the Later Han Dynasty*, vol. 88.

Xinjiang, parts of Central Asia stretched from east to west and formed a colossal international market. In this, China's silk was the most widely traded commodity and was well received in the West.

Roman aristocrats of the time were known as major silk consumers, but the silk worn by Romans was monopolized by the Anxi people (Persians). To pursue a lucrative business, the Anxi merchants would first travel to Kasmira, northwest of India, over the high Cong Mountains, crossing the Gobi Desert, and finally arrive in China. Silk is the common thread here, connecting the cities of the region and forming a long, multi-route silk road.

This inland road connected China with Central Asia. Even India and the Mediterranean, via the Western Regions, had become communication thoroughfares since the Han Dynasty. Besides the commodity trade, the cultural exchange also took place. Xuan Zang, a well-known monk during the Tang era, returned home with Buddhist scripts acquired from India by this southern route. Other monks, including Faxian, Tanwujie (Fayong), Song Yun, and Huisheng, took pilgrimages to India on this path. Besides Chinese monks, foreign monks also came to China this way. For instance, during the mid-sixth century, committed to the cause of Buddhist script translation, Jnanagupta came to China along this route from Gandhara.

During the prosperous Tang era, national strength and efficient government helped the Tang expand their territory to the Hezhong area between the Yaoshashui (Syr Darya) and Wuhushui (Amu Darya) rivers. More importantly, the Tang administered the Western Regions effectively, guaranteeing the Silk Road's smooth flow and increased local development.

The Gaochang City Site in Karakhoja is about 50 kilometers southeast of Turpan in today's Xinjiang, China. The city, founded in the Han and called Gaochangbi during the Wei and Jin dynasties, was the official residence of local officials. It became the capital of the Gaochang Kingdom during Northern Wei. In the Tang Dynasty, it was the seat of the Anxi Protectorate. Gaochangbi served as the capital of the Gaochang Uighur Dynasty for more than 500 years before it was abandoned at the end of the Yuan. Extant ancient ruins were modified and added to the foundation by the Gaochang Uighur regime in the Tang era.

As the central city of the ancient Turpan Basin, Gaochang is of high importance due to its strategic position on the route heading from Dunhuang through the Hexi Corridor and then the Yumen Pass. This route was called the Northern

Road during the Han Dynasty and the New Route since the Wei and Jin dynasties. *Three Kingdoms · Book of Wei*, volume 30 stated:

> The New Route started from the northwest of Yumen Pass, passed Hengkeng, Sanlongsha, and Longdui, then to the north of Wuchuan, and finally reached Gaochang, the official residences along the Cheshi border. The route turned west and merged with the road to Kucina.

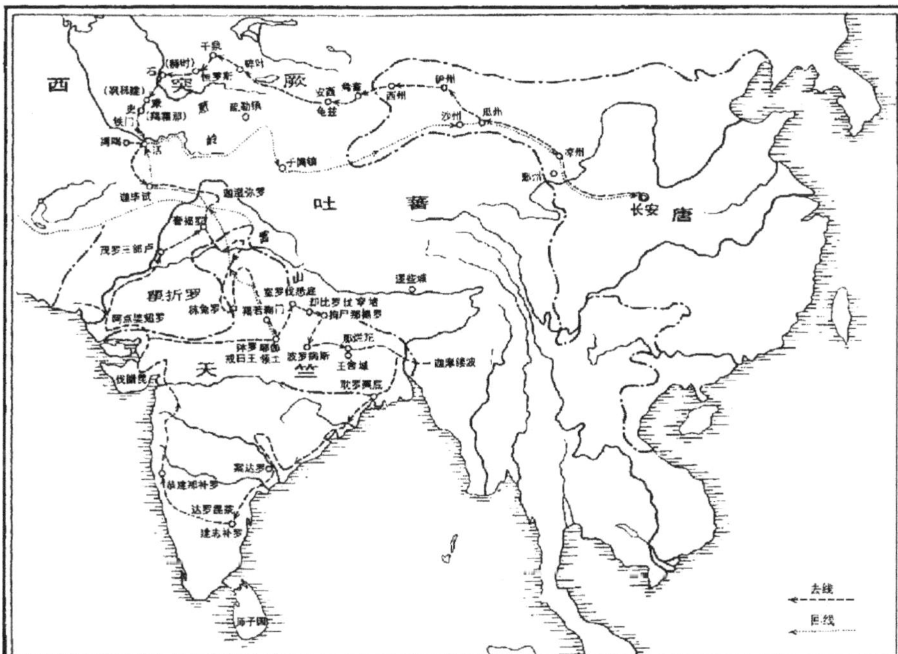

Fig. 9-4: Xuan Zang's route to India[6]

Today, the Ancient City of Gaochang consists of an outer and the central city. The outer city is a slightly irregular square with a circumference of about 5,000 meters and walls still intact. The residual walls are about 5–11 meters, and the base is about 12 meters thick. There is also a thin layer of 8–12 cm ramming

6. Zou Yilin, *An Outline of Chinese Historical Geography* (Shanghai: Shanghai Education Press, 2005), 351.

earth. The walls have an arc and concave structures. Dense, protruding defense towers were built in the well-preserved walls on the east, west, and south sides. Judging from the outer wall gaps and the unearthed documents in Turpan, there should be nine gates in the outer city of Gaochang. There are two gates on the north side, namely the North Gate and the Lu Gate, which are called Wucheng Gate and Xuande Gate in the literature. There are two gates on the east side, East Gate and the New East Gate, recorded as Qingyang Gate and Jianyang Gate; two gates in the west, Xinfu Gate and Jinzhang Gate; three gates in the south, New South Gate, Old South Gate, and the Front Gate. The nine gates system and their naming were influenced by the Central Plains culture. Gaochang also houses a temple and the remaining ruins of commoners' residences.

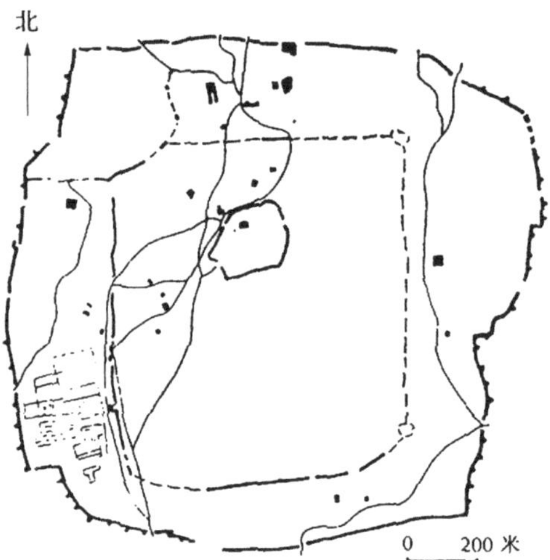

Fig. 9-5: Plan of the Gaochang City Site[7]

The central city is located in the middle of the outer city and is slightly rectangular. Most of the walls on the west and south sides are well-preserved with rammed earth and are as tall as the outer city. There is no trace of gates, and only some palaces and temple buildings remain. In addition, there is a castle type of building in the center towards the northern part of the central city—the inner city, known locally as "Khan Fort," probably the palaces of the Gaochang Kingdom. The inner city's plan is a slightly irregular, oval shape, about 700 meters

7. Qu Yingjie, *Ancient Cities* (Beijing: Cultural Relics Press, 2003), 186.

in circumference. The *Book of Sui · The West Regions* recorded that the capital of Gaochang Kingdom had a circumference of about 1,830 steps, or 3,415 meters. Compared with the actual archaeological site, the central city is very likely the capital of Gaochang, while the outer city could be Xizhou City during the Tang era.

After the Song and Yuan dynasties, with the Central Plains regime unable to maintain control of Central Asia, the Silk Road was often blocked by political unrest. Simultaneously, with the growing prosperity of maritime trade between the East and West, the trade center shifted from the lands of Central Asia to the seas. No longer being the only east–west transport network, the Silk Road was still used for regional transport and the cities along its way also continued as the political, economic, and cultural centers of their respective regions.

2. Commercial Port Cities

In AD 1840, when the Opium War broke out, the Qing government was forced, by powerful gunboats, to open its borders along the coastal and Yangtze River regions—forming a series of trading port cities (treat ports). By the end of the Qing Dynasty, two urban axes with a total of more than one hundred ports were formed: the coast route, which ran north-south and was centered in Shanghai, and the river route running east-west along the Yangtze. Unequal treaties, concessions, and the introduction of foreign capital had a profound impact on the economy and landscape of the port cities.

There were 20 port cities, including Andong (today's Dandong), Dalian, Yingkou, Qinhuangdao, Tianjin, Longkou, Yantai, Weihai, Qingdao, Haizhou (Lianyungang), Shanghai, Hangzhou, Ningbo, Wenzhou, Fuzhou, Xiamen, Shantou, Guangzhou, Chikan, and Danshui. Obviously, these cities are in the eastern coastal area. There were also thirteen cities on the river axis from east to west, including Shanghai, Suzhou, Zhenjiang, Nanjing, Wuhu, Anqing, Jiujiang, Yueyang, Hankou, Shashi, Yichang, Wanxian, and Chongqing. Among them, Shanghai has the characteristics of both a coastal city and a riverside city. Because the port economy was integrated into the world economic system, which is largely export-oriented, these port cities were required to have easy access and contact with overseas countries, particularly in the West.

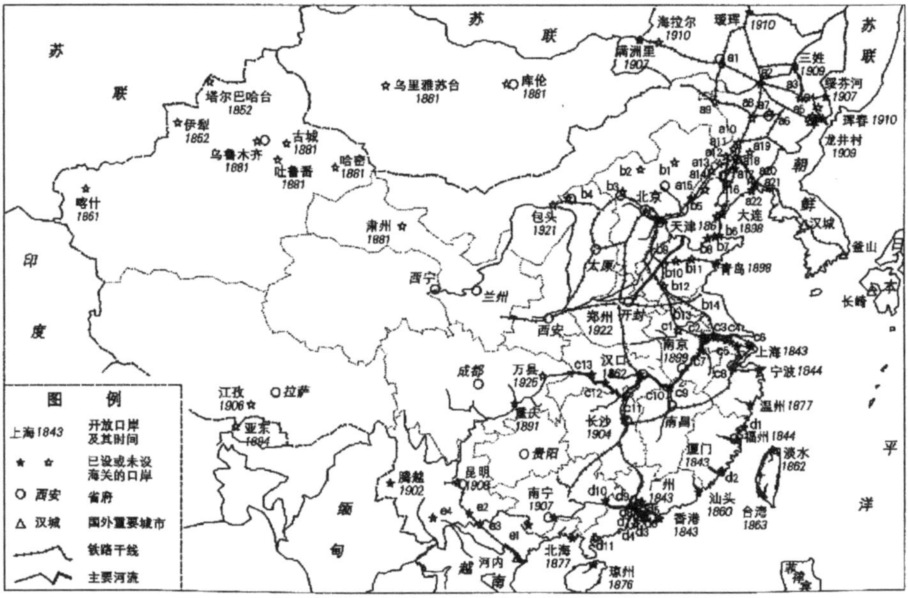

Fig. 9-6: Commercial port cities in modern China[8]

In the eighteenth and nineteenth centuries, sea transportation was the principal method of global trade and even communication. Because maritime transport can shift large volumes at a low cost, port cities gained unprecedented opportunities for development in this period. On the other hand, the foreign powers forcibly opened the door of China; of course, their purpose was to grab enormous wealth from ancient China. Therefore, they also must rely on China's original economic and spatial pattern to penetrate deep into the Chinese mainland and obtain more benefits.

According to the Nanjing Treaty, the earliest five opening trading cities were Guangzhou, Fuzhou, Xiamen, Ningbo, and Shanghai. Among them, Guangzhou, Fuzhou, and Ningbo were the provincial capitals or the political and economic centers of their regions. Only Xiamen and Shanghai were average county towns but these two cities occupied important positions in foreign and internal trade as early as the Ming and Qing dynasties. They became typical, regional economic centers developed by trade.

---

8. Wu Songdi, *A Jigsaw of Chinese Economy in a Hundred Years: Port Cities, Their Vicinity, and Modernization of China* (Jinan: Shandong Pictorial Press, 2006), 5.

Therefore, foreign powers still attached great importance to the use of China's traditional economic and geographical resources. In this way, we can understand why many important cities along the Yangtze were also included in the treaty ports besides the coastal cities, which turned into trading ports. Obviously, since the Ming and Qing dynasties, areas along the Yangtze had been highly developed and densely populated, not only providing a huge hinterland for the coastal cities, but also serving as a dumping ground for foreign merchandise. Cities along the river were favored by the Imperial powers.

The rise of treaty port cities changed China's urban system where domestic demand dominated—demand represented by the distribution of cities within the Grand Canal–Yangtze River axis. The distribution pattern of modern cities subsequently emerged, altering the traditional Chinese layout.

- ***Single Shore versus Double Shores***

Traditional Chinese settlements along rivers were almost invariably single shore cities. More precisely, although Chinese cities developed along rivers, they would normally only develop on one side of the riverbank. With the continuous growth of cities, urban areas gradually inched closer to the bank. The business districts, especially, tended to congregate here. Still, these cities would be always located on one side of the river and did not develop symmetrically on the other side—for instance, Shanghai, Ningbo, and Nanjing before the opening of the city ports.

Shanghai only developed on the left bank of the Huangpu River. Although it also took advantage of the water transport of the Huangpu River and was located near the Dadongmen (now Shiliupu area) on the bank of the Huangpu River, it was very lively and bustling. Still, it had never intended to cross the river for development. At the same time, before opening to the outside world and becoming a trading port, Shanghai County was far away from the Suzhou River, the later development axis called the Wusong River. Therefore, it was always a city on the west bank of the Huangpu River before it opened; Ningbo was the same. It was connected to the inland by the Yongjiang River but was only located on one side of the Yongjiang River. Nanjing was even more so. The Yangtze River, regarded as a natural moat at that time, naturally restricted Nanjing's development to the opposite bank. Not only that, but the Yangtze River also became an effective defense line for Nanjing. Thus, the topography of Nanjing was like a coiling dragon and crouching tiger. However, after opening the ports, city layouts changed as the urban economy continued to develop. Not only did dual-shore cities appear, but they gradually increased in number.

On November 17, AD 1843, Shanghai opened for trading according to treaties with Britain. As a trading port, Shanghai's status was subsequently strengthened because of its location at the Yangtze River estuary. In AD 1845, the area between Pidgin (Yan'an East Road) and Lijia Village was designated as the British Concession. From Henan Middle Road, a series of shops and foreign warehouses were built along the west bank of the Huangpu River to the north—the formation of the Bund.

The Huangpu was too wide to build bridges for the technology of the time, thus it was difficult to cross the river. Consequently, Shanghai developed north along the Suzhou River (called the Wusong at the time). This river was arguable of equal importance to the Huangpu since it connected Shanghai with China's interior and the Jiangnan region. It can even be said that the British listed Shanghai as a trading port mainly because of the Jiangnan Region on which Shanghai relies.

Fig. 9-7: The view of Shiliupu, Shanghai County[9]

9. Wu Jiang, *A Hundred Years History of Architecture in Shanghai* (Shanghai: Tongji University Press, 1997), 5.

The development of the other side, the northern bank of the Suzhou, was marked by the construction of the American Concession. At this time, the Episcopal bishop of America, William Jones Boone, started to lease land and build houses without permission when he saw the vast expanse of cheap land along the northern riverbank. In AD 1848, Boone made a claim to the Shanghai Circuit for this to be considered an American settlement; surprisingly, he received permission. Back then, officials in Shanghai considered it a barren area far from the city. Permission was granted without due deliberation. Unexpectedly, this became a turning point for the development of the northern bank of the Suzhou River. More surprisingly, Shanghai had become a double shore city.

It should be noted the importance of the Suzhou River to Shanghai started earlier than the opening of the port. During the Ming and Qing eras, it was already a key gateway between Shanghai and Taihu. At this time, the busy Suzhou River (then called Wusongjiang) with ships coming and going, led to the rise of some markets along the river. According to the *Shanghai County Chronicle*, during Emperor Jiaqing's reign, prosperous markets formed around the ferries of the Old Gate (today's Fujian Road Bridge) and the New Gate (today's New Gate Road Bridge), etc. Particularly, the New Gate market, as the main harbor to the Wusong River downstream shipping, was very prosperous with its shipping works, iron shops, and business areas. But no more than that. The northern bank of the Wusong River was sparse with few villages or markets. Only farmlands common to southern China were present with rivers and branches crisscrossing each other.

However, the American Concession completely changed the landscape along the Suzhou. Here, urban areas expanded rapidly and were soon joined with the British Concession of the southern bank. In AD 1863, Anglo-American settlements were incorporated, and the Shanghai International Settlement was established. It covered the area that reached Hongkou in the north, Yangshupu in the east, and Zhoujing (now Xizang Road) in the west. Shanghai became a city of development on both banks of the Suzhou.

Fig. 9-8: Building distribution of Shanghai during the Republic of China

Simultaneously, with the development of its economy and increasing dependence on external markets, Shanghai became increasingly reliant on the Huangpu. Foreign merchants gradually extended their forces to the other side, utilizing the coastline in the Pudong District to build docks and warehouses and setting up factories and enterprises. As early as AD 1866, eleven pier warehouses had been established along the Yangtze (the Yangtze feeds into the Huangpu River) in Pudong, including Lidecheng Wharf, Guanglong Wharf, Libaili Pier, and Duanxiang Pier. By 1921, the number of piers in Pudong surpassed that of Puxi.

More importantly, factories and companies kept appearing in Pudong. Out of trade and shipping needs, foreign merchants first established ship repair factories on the Huangpu River. In AD 1859, there were more than four or five shipyards in Pudong operated by William Muirhead. In addition, some light industry enterprise also appeared along the Yangtze, such as the Mitsui Plant, the Hongyuan Cotton Mill, the Pudong factory for British-American Tobacco, the Xiechang Match Company, the Longzhang Paper Mill, and the Changyu Soap Company. With the construction of ports, warehouses, and factories along the Pudong River, the roads leading to the river, such as Dongchang Road, Lujiadu Road, and Yangjiadu Road, were developed. Despite this, the original scenery was mostly retained along the east coast of the Pu River in the twentieth century.

After the reform and opening up in the 1990s, the Shanghai government made great efforts to develop the Pudong District. In less than ten years, a financial trade zone and an export processing zone were established. Presently, Shanghai is a typical double-shore city developing along both sides of the Huangpu.

The same is true for Ningbo. From city maps of the Song, Yuan, and Ming dynasties, Ningbo (Ming Zhou) was a city built on the west bank of the Yao and Fenghua rivers. Although it extended towards the riverbank with urban expansion, it was restricted to the west banks of the two rivers. In AD 1842, Ningbo was designated as one of the five trading cities in the Sino-British Nanjing Treaty. Customs of Zhejiang was established here and opened to foreign investors. Since then, foreign merchants poured into the city and built commercial and residential areas to complete business activities adjacent to Fenghua, later known as the famous Jiangxia District. Ningbo gradually developed into a cross-river dual-shore city.

- ***Function Divisions and Partitions***

Due to convenient transportation, the port cities in China soon developed into commercial and trade centers in their own regions, with their functions quite different from those of traditional cities. The port cities centered on commerce and trade activities, while the administrative function was relegated to second place and even became the most neglected part of urban space. Functional zoning gradually developed and became increasingly prominent. Of these cities, Shanghai was the most eminent example.

After opening as a commercial port city, along with the development of the urban economy, Shanghai formed foreign communities first because of the foreign settlements. At the juncture of these settlements, industrial and commercial areas formed due to frequent population mobility and commercial development. During the period of the Taiping Heavenly Kingdom and afterward, with the acceptance of large numbers of Chinese refugees from the war, the downtown became overcrowded and rich foreigners began to flee to the western suburbs, forming new and luxurious residential districts. Now, the different styles of villas near Xujiahui, Jing'an District, and Changning District are the legacies of this.

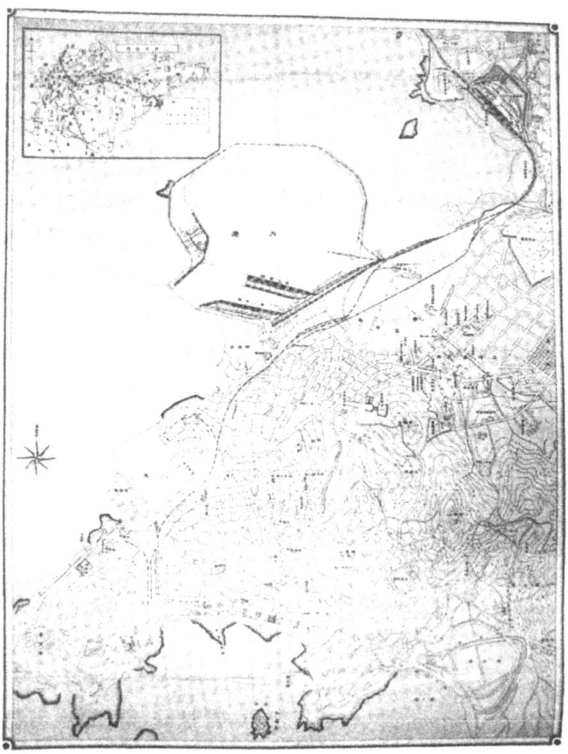

Fig. 9-9: Plan of Qingdao City[10]

With the operation of the Beijing–Shanghai Railway, land became scarce within the Concession area, and land prices soared. The Zhabei District, near the old train station, attracted many Chinese and foreign manufacturers because the land was cheap, and waterways were available as a new area. For instance, in AD 1904, the *Commercial Press*, a top publisher in China, moved to Baoshan Road in

10. Li Xiaocong, *Historical Urban Geography* (Jinan: Shandong Education Press, 2008), 427.

the Zhabei District and pioneered the East and West Baoxing area. By AD 1909, there were more than 600 workers in the Jiucheng Reeling Mill in New Zhabei and more than 800 workers in the Xiehe Reeling Mill.

Around the 1911 Revolution, a variety of companies, such as reeling and rice mills, weaving, printing, and leather factories, cigar factories, mineral refineries, music organ factories, and flour, soap, and match companies, were founded in Zhabei. Zhabei Hydropower Company was also established, providing water and electricity for part of the city: the Zhabei District became the most important industrial area in modern Shanghai. In the periphery, however, a large number of bankrupt and poor Chinese from other regions gathered here to make a living by selling labor. These people had a low standard of living and only relied on shacks for shelter, forming a large area of shanty towns.

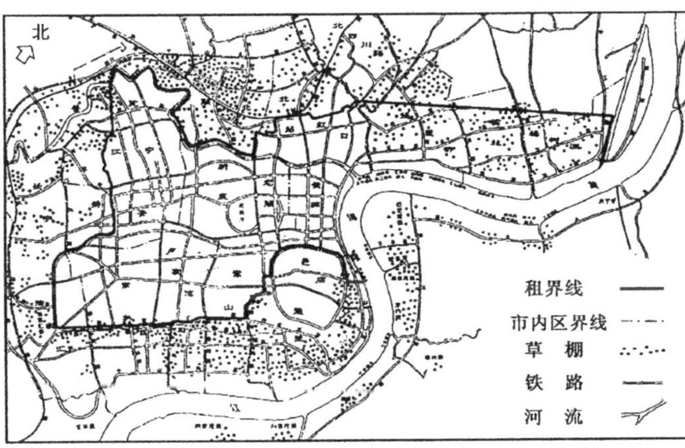

Fig. 9-10: Shanty towns' distribution in Shanghai[11]

As a matter of fact, such functional zoning was very common in modern port cities of China. For instance, after Tianjin, the largest city in northern China, opened as a commercial port in AD 1860, Britain, France, and the United States coerced the Qing government to designate the Purple Bamboo Forest area along the Haihe River in the south as the Concession district, quoting the Shanghai treaty port precedent.

11. (US) Han Qilan, *Northern Jiangsu People in Shanghai, 1850–1980* (Shanghai: Shanghai Ancient Books Press, 2004), 43.

Fig. 9-11: Plan of Tianjin City[12]

12. Li Xiaocong, *Historical Urban Geography* (Jinan: Shandong Education Press, 2008), 416.

Later, six other countries—Germany, Japan, Russia, Austria-Hungary, Italy, and Belgium—also established their respective concessions along the northern and southern banks of the Haihe River. The Bamboo Forest section of the Haihe was wide and deep, ideal for large ships and moorings. Therefore, countries and shipping companies competed to build warehouses and wharves along this section, laying the basic outline of a modern Tianjin port.[13]

In addition to the treaty ports, new industrial zones formed along railways or near railway stations because of convenient transport, or on the outskirts because of low land prices. Modern industry developed. For instance, modern railway stations, roads, factories, schools, and municipal administration institutes were built in the Hebei New District of Tianjin, taking advantage of the approval of the new Hebei Railway station in AD 1902. This new district quickly emerged as Tianjin's political and cultural center and became a modern industrial zone.

Fig. 9-12: The Bund, Shanghai in 1868[14]

13. Fan Rusen, *Tianjin and the Economic Modernization in Northern China (1860–1937)* (Shanghai: Oriental Publishing Center, 2007), 281–282.
14. Zhong Fulan, *China's Hundred Years of Change in Pictures: Social Life, Travel, and Trade* (Shanghai: Xuelin Press, 2001), 60.

- ***The Exotic Feel***

Because of historical reasons, most port cities in China had relatively centralized and independent living quarters for foreigners, where architecture had more of a homely style—often drastically different from traditional Chinese cities. This had a profound impact on the architectural landscape of the port cities.

The most typical is still Shanghai. Along the Bund of the Huangpu, a unique architectural style was formed, sometimes called the "the International Architecture Exhibition," because of the construction of Western-style buildings by several foreign banks. In downtown Dalian, Liaoning, Zhongshan Square is surrounded by Western architecture, forming a unique urban landscape.

Because of the different origins of overseas residents, the architectural styles of port cities differed greatly. For example, most foreigners in Harbin came from Russia. As a result, buildings are influenced by Russian architecture, and the city was even dubbed "petite Moscow." On the other hand, Dalian was influenced by both Russia and Japan, and its architecture is characteristic of both countries. Another city, Qingdao in Shandong, although later controlled by Japan, was more influenced by German culture. Many small European-styled villas were built near the Lao Mountains.

Fig. 9-13: Landscape of the French concession, Shanghai[15]

15. Wu Liang, *Old Shanghai: Shanghai Time* (Nanjing: Jiangsu Fine Arts Publishing House, 1998), 39.

Fig. 9-14: A foreign hospital in Qingdao[16]

In general, the colonial landscape of Chinese cities is closer to the style of the Suzerain states. This can be seen clearly in the zenith painting in Pudong Development Bank's business hall in the Shanghai Bund. In particular, the iconic buildings in these cities are more exotic. Cities like Shanghai have a number of national concessions—the characteristics of individual nations can also be clearly distinguished from their architectural styles. For example, the construction of the British Concession in Huangpu District is clearly different from the architectural style of the Japanese area in Hongkou.

Another manifestation of the city's foreign influence is road naming. In the port cities, the roads were frequently named after outstanding foreign nationals—a clear distinction from traditional Chinese cities. The naming of the roads in different Shanghai concession areas was inconsistent, but each had its own system. Since AD 1862, the British Concession tended to name the roads after Chinese provinces and city names. After a short time, the British authorities passed a motion in AD 1865, which was strictly followed. That is, in the British concession, N-S roads would be named after Chinese provinces while E-W roads would be named after important Chinese cities. For the sake of clarity, the concession authorities even took special pains to change some of the old road names. The naming system to the west of the Bund was the most obvious, such as the N-S Yunnan Road, Shandong Road, Sichuan Road, E-W Nanjing Road, Beijing Road, Tianjin Road, Ningbo Road, Hankou Road, etc.

16. Zhong Fulan, *China's Hundred Years of Change in Pictures: Social Life, Travel, and Trade* (Shanghai: Xuelin Press, 2001), 60.

Fig. 9-15: Landscape of the Hongkou District, Shanghai[17]

Although the American Concession was combined with the British Concession in AD 1863, its naming of roads was independent to a degree. The United States did not follow this rule. Even in the newly expanded areas of the Shanghai International Settlement in AD 1899, the British naming method was not fully implemented. Instead, the names of British and American nationals were used. For instance, the present Hanyang Road was named Hanbury Road. Hanbury was a British businessman, who prospered in Shanghai real estate. He funded the construction of some schools in Shanghai; therefore, Hanbury's name was used to name the road. Another road was named Boone Road or William Jones Road (Tanggu Road today). Both roads refer to William Jones Boone, a pastor who laid down the American Concession. In addition, there was the Gordon Road, now the Jiangning Road. Gordon was the victorious leader in the suppression of the Taiping Army. Moreover, Handan Road, where Fudan University is located,

17. Wu Liang, *Old Shanghai: Shanghai Time* (Nanjing: Jiangsu Fine Arts Publishing House, 1998), 160.

was not named that way at first but was named Wedemeyer Road in honor of American General Albert Coady Wedemeyer.

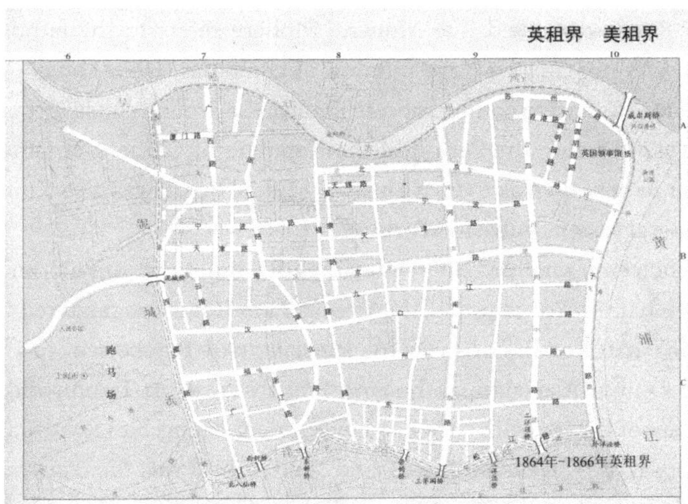

Fig. 9-16: Road system in the Huangpu District[18]

The French Concession in Shanghai used another road naming system. Within the initial concession, Chinese street name resources were used. For instance, Mansion Road (now Jinling Road) was adjacent to the town, so a similar conception of county street names was adopted to show respect to Chinese cultures, such as Yong'an Road and Pawn Street (now Gold Gate Road). This had been the traditional cultural policy of the French colonists. For its second expansion in 1900, west of Zhou Jing, the names of Chinese mountains and rivers were used to name the roads: N-S roads were named after mountains, and E-W roads were named after rivers. For example, there were Tianshan Road, Taishan Road, Huashan Road, Songshan Road, and Hengshan Road in the north-south direction, while there were Yangjingbang Road (now Middle Yan'an Road), Wusong River Road, Yellow River Road, Pearl River Road in the east-west direction. This naming principle was not implemented well, because the French later used the names of famous Frenchmen instead.

18. Zhou Zhenhe, *Historical Atlas of Shanghai* (Shanghai: Shanghai People's Press, 1999), 71.

For instance, today's East Lake Road was called Doumer Road to commemorate General Paul Doumer, the French Governor of Vietnam from AD 1896 to 1905. This man contributed by sending Annan (Vietnam) police to the French Concession in Shanghai. He served as President of France in 1931. Today's Xiangshan Road was called Rue Moliere. Moliere refers to the famous French playwright who produced a large number of comedies, while today's Julu Road was named Rue Ratard to commemorate Ratard, the French consul general during AD 1901–1909. During the Period of the Republic of China, the famous Xiafei Road, commonly known as today's Huaihai Middle Road, was also a memorial to French General Joseph Joffre in World War I.

The French later changed the road names of Chinese mountains and rivers to more French names. For example, the Yalong River Road was renamed Gros Road (today's Songshan Road); Gros was the special envoy France sent to China after the Second Opium War, signing the Sino-French Treaty of Tianjin and the Sino-French Treaty of Beijing with the Qing government. Hengshan Road was changed to Rue Chapsal (now Danshui Road), and Mr. Chapsal was the General Director of the Public Management Bureau at the French Concession.

The commercial port cities of China were rooted in traditional business intersections, but their design and urban planning were undoubtedly based on a Western model. Germany's urban design in Qingdao and the British design in Hong Kong, Shanghai, and Xiamen were remarkable examples. The urban landscape in these newly-emerged cities was quite different from their traditional counterparts. As R. H. Tawney pointed out: "This is the new lace embroidered to an old-fashioned robe."

A BRIEF CHRONOLOGY OF CHINESE HISTORY

Xia Dynasty		2070–1600 BC
Shang Dynasty		1600–1046 BC
Zhou Dynasty	Western Zhou Dynasty	1046–771 BC
	Eastern Zhou Dynasty	770–256 BC
Qin Dynasty		221–207 BC
Han Dynasty	Western Han Dynasty	206 BC–AD 25
	Eastern Han Dynasty	AD 25–220
Three Kingdoms	Kingdom of Wei	AD 220–265
	Kingdom of Shu	AD 221–263
	Kingdom of Wu	AD 222–280
Jin Dynasty	Western Jin Dynasty	AD 265–317
	Eastern Jin Dynasty	AD 317–420

<table>
<tr><td rowspan="9">Southern and Northern Dynasties</td><td rowspan="4">Southern Dynasties</td><td>Song Dynasty</td><td>AD 420–479</td></tr>
<tr><td>Qi Dynasty</td><td>AD 479–502</td></tr>
<tr><td>Liang Dynasty</td><td>AD 502–557</td></tr>
<tr><td>Chen Dynasty</td><td>AD 557–589</td></tr>
<tr><td rowspan="5">Northern Dynasties</td><td>Northern Wei Dynasty</td><td>AD 386–534</td></tr>
<tr><td>Eastern Wei Dynasty</td><td>AD 534–550</td></tr>
<tr><td>Northern Qi Dynasty</td><td>AD 550–577</td></tr>
<tr><td>Western Wei Dynasty</td><td>AD 535–556</td></tr>
<tr><td>Northern Zhou Dynasty</td><td>AD 557–581</td></tr>
<tr><td colspan="3">Sui Dynasty</td><td>AD 581–618</td></tr>
<tr><td colspan="3">Tang Dynasty</td><td>AD 618–907</td></tr>
<tr><td colspan="2" rowspan="5">Five Dynasties</td><td>Later Liang Dynasty</td><td>AD 907–923</td></tr>
<tr><td>Later Tang Dynasty</td><td>AD 923–936</td></tr>
<tr><td>Later Jin Dynasty</td><td>AD 936–947</td></tr>
<tr><td>Later Han Dynasty</td><td>AD 947–950</td></tr>
<tr><td>Later Zhou Dynasty</td><td>AD 951–960</td></tr>
<tr><td colspan="2" rowspan="2">Song Dynasty</td><td>Northern Song Dynasty</td><td>AD 960–1127</td></tr>
<tr><td>Southern Song Dynasty</td><td>AD 1127–1279</td></tr>
<tr><td colspan="3">Liao Dynasty</td><td>AD 907–1125</td></tr>
<tr><td colspan="3">Jin Dynasty</td><td>AD 1115–1234</td></tr>
<tr><td colspan="3">Yuan Dynasty</td><td>AD 1206–1368</td></tr>
<tr><td colspan="3">Ming Dynasty</td><td>AD 1368–1644</td></tr>
<tr><td colspan="3">Qing Dynasty</td><td>AD 1616–1912</td></tr>
<tr><td colspan="3">Republic of China</td><td>1912–1949</td></tr>
<tr><td colspan="3">People's Republic of China</td><td>Founded on October 1, 1949</td></tr>
</table>

INDEX

A Greek destroyer photographed near Crete in June 1963.

of the Shackleton, the RAF lost twelve aircraft with a cost of over 120 lives. The causes varied from hitting the sea following a low-level attack, poor weather conditions, flying at low level into a hill side and engine fires. Fortunately, operations in the Mediterranean were less hazardous from weather. In my two-and-a-half years on 38 Squadron, we were only diverted once because of obvious bad weather at RAF Luqa. However, on 24 January 1964, Crew 7 was tasked to fly to Gibraltar with a plan to carry out a navigation exercise heading west into the Atlantic (turning point a weather ship) and then turn south to reach the Canary Isles and head back to Gibraltar. We took off at 0200 hours and just over five hours later arrived over the airfield in Gibraltar. There are three interesting features to this airfield. At both ends, the runway runs into the sea; there is a road leading to the border with Spain across the single runway, which is heavily used, and is obviously closed once there is air traffic on finals or take-off. A less obvious feature is the very variable effect of air turbulence over the runway due to the proximity of the Rock, particularly in strong gusty wind conditions. On our first attempt to land, there was a strong crosswind, it was still dark, we overshot and went around again. During the second attempt, and when at around 800 feet on finals, the aircraft was suddenly caught by a strong down draft (there was a twenty-five-knot crosswind from the south), one wing dipped, and the aircraft lost 400 feet and the airspeed dropped dramatically despite the application of full power. To recover the aircraft, both pilots had to pull on the controls together maintaining full power to regain control and height to overshoot. In addition to the crew of ten, we had five of our ground crew on board who were sat on the floor of the aircraft with very rudimentary safety harnesses. After the sudden loss of height and violent recovery, the inside of the aircraft was

ABOUT THE CHIEF EDITOR

Ge Jianxiong, PhD, born in 1945, is a professor at the Center for Historical Geographical Studies of Fudan University in Shanghai, China. He is also a doctoral supervisor and Director of Fudan University Library. His research focuses on historical geography, population history, migration history, and cultural history.

Selected publications of Professor Ge include:

- *History of the Population in China*, editor-in-chief and author of Vol. I
- *History of Migrations in China*, editor-in-chief and author of Vol. I & II
- *History of the Development of Population in China*
- *A Perspective of Chinese History: Unification and Separation*
- *A Short History of Cartography in Ancient China*
- *The Changes of Boundaries and Administrative Divisions in China*
- *The Natural Environment for Human Being in the Future*
- *Biography of Tan Qixiang*, Vol. I & II

ABOUT THE AUTHOR

Zhang Xiaohong is a professor, doctoral supervisor, current director of the Center of Historical Geographical Studies of Fudan University, director of the Center of the Studies of Humanities and Social Sciences of the Ministry of Education, director of the Historical Geography Research Center of Fudan University, director of the Institute of Humanities and Communication, One-Belt-One-Road, and Global Governance of Fudan University. She is a Yanjing scholar of Harvard University, vice president of the Shanghai Geographical Society, member of the Professional Committees of Historical Geography and Cultural Geography of the Geographical Society of China, member of WorldMap Committee of Harvard University, and academic member of the China Biographical Databases (CBDB).

Zhang is mainly engaged in the study of historical geography and environmental evolution, including the study of environmental change in northern China, historical urban geography and cultural geography. She has presided over a number of key projects of the Ministry of Science and Technology, the Ministry of Education, the Ministry of Foreign Affairs, the National Natural Science Foundation, and the National Social Science Foundation. She has published many monographs and more than 50 academic papers in domestic and foreign academic journals (SCI, SSCI, CSSCI, etc.), and she has been invited to national and international academic conferences many times to make special theme reports.